Improving English and Maths in Further Education

Praise page

This is an interesting and engaging read from Jonny, who has produced a book that brings together contemporary educational literature, with a personal and honest take on leading and teaching English and Maths in FE. The book will appeal to experienced managers and teachers, who may wish to compare their own experiences and perspectives in FE, and for those new to teaching or managing, who will find some very useful hints, tips and approaches.

Steven Wallis, Executive Director Quality, NCG

How refreshing to read a book dedicated to delivery of post 16 English and maths. Teachers and leaders from curriculum areas across the sector will find scenarios and anecdotes that resonate in this book; timetabling, accountability, motivation, effective feedback to name a few. The handy tips for reflection at the end of each chapter and links to further reading on specific areas of interest throughout make this a must read.

Catherine Sezen, Senior Policy Manager – FE

English and maths are an important part of the further education landscape and Jonny Kay has been a leading practitioner in this field for a number of years. I had the great privilege of working with Jonny and watching him teach on a regular basis. Furthermore, we had endless chats about how to improve the College's English & maths provision. This superb book by Jonny will be an invaluable resource for all further education English and maths practitioners and Jonny has done a great job to distil the key considerations.

Darren Hankey, Principal and CEO of Hartlepool College of FE

This book caters for the many different voices, people and characters in FE - it does exactly what it says on the tin. With a mighty research base, it highlights the intricacies and addresses the commonality of issues for both English and Maths. The book covers a raft of situations, from leadership to student and staff motivation, and attendance to vocational relationships, and it is well-considered. It will give you all the tools for a great job with an evidence base to boot.

Julia Smith, @tessmaths

Improving English and Maths in Further Education

A Practical Guide

Jonathan Kay

Open University Press

Open University Press
McGraw-Hill Education
8th Floor, 338 Euston Road
London
England
NW1 3BH

email: enquiries@openup.co.uk
world wide web: www.openup.co.uk

and Two Penn Plaza, New York, NY 10121-2289, USA

First edition published 2021

A catalogue record of this book is available from the British Library

ISBN-13: 9780335250370
ISBN-10: 0335250378
eISBN: 99780335250387

Library of Congress Cataloging-in-Publication Data
CIP data applied for

Typeset by Transforma Pvt. Ltd., Chennai, India

Fictitious names of companies, products, people, characters and/or data that may be used herein (in case studies or in examples) are not intended to represent any real individual, company, product or event.

This book is dedicated to Steph, Nancy and Maggie – thanks for your patience, kindness and love

Contents

Acknowledgements

This book would not have been possible without the support of many friends, family and colleagues (past and present). Thanks to everyone at McGraw-Hill and your unending support. You have all been enormously supportive on the journey to completing this book and I have no doubt that it is due in large part to our shared North East heritage.

Thank you to Jan for being at the other end of the phone and listening to my endless rambling about what this book was and was not going to be, and thanks also to the many friends from Teesside University, Hartlepool and Verdansk who have supported the book – your input has helped more than you know.

Thanks to Suze, Pip, David and the English and maths teams at TCC, all at Newcastle College (especially Di Thurston – your support has been immense – and Lauren Middleton for her cover work) and everyone associated with the mE+ Conference for the generosity and kindness you've all shown. Thanks also to Mark Stewart for speaking so much sense – apologies this book is not what we discussed!

Thanks particularly to colleagues past and present at Hartlepool College of Further Education: the coaching and mentoring I have been lucky enough to receive has been more than I could have ever hoped for. Thanks to the English and maths team there, and thanks to Richard for the resources you kindly donated for this book. Thanks especially to Jo Mac, Sharon and Aunty Marie for your endless support; Shaun for your patience, feedback and constant availability; Darren, for your expert guidance and advice, and thanks particularly to Steve for the continuous encouragement and belief and imparting your considerable knowledge, experience and artisan skill set (if you do say so yourself).

Most of all, I would like to thank my wonderful wife Steph. Funny, intelligent and supportive, your feedback has been vital and you are the teacher and person whose level I aspire to. Your assurances that you could have completed a much better book in half the time have also helped no end. Thanks for being everything this book and I needed and thanks for being a great mam to Nancy and Maggie.

Love ya x

Introduction

'I don't want to do English or maths at college. I did it at school. I'm not doing it again …'
Many, many students (2014 – present)

With more than one third of 16-year-olds failing to achieve a grade C/4[1] in recent years, and resit achievement rates amongst 16- to 18-year-olds remaining depressingly low (and continuing to fall, as the number of students being entered for exams continues to rise[2]), many of us in further and post-16 education have heard the above words many, many times from students of all backgrounds and in all contexts.

Since the Wolf Report was published in 2011 (requiring all students who did not achieve a grade C/4 or above in English and maths to continue studying English and maths), more students than ever before are resitting these subjects. And with around half of all working-age adults sharing the same numeracy level expected of a primary school child[3], and over 7 million adults functionally illiterate[4,5], we also know that these challenges continue into adulthood.

The challenges don't stop there. Minimal increases in funding in the last ten years[6] (many would argue longer), mean significant cuts have been made to what Further Education can and does offer, and to its role in education.

I'll admit, I wasn't quite ready for how many times I would hear the words quoted at the start of this chapter when I first started in Further Education (FE). Having spent so long in secondary teaching before moving to FE, I did (and still do) understand where it comes from, and why some students felt and feel like this. With as many as 15 per cent of all schools in England graded less than 'Good'[7], we know the challenges our students face and that they don't always

1   https://assets.publishing.service.gov.uk/government/uploads/system/uploads/attachment_data/file/840032/2019_KS4_Provisional_statistical_release.pdf (accessed 11 January 2021).
2   www.aoc.co.uk/news/gcse-results-day-2019-aoc-comment (accessed 11 January 2021).
3   Department for Business, Innovation and Skills (2012) *The 2011 Skills for Life Survey: A Survey of Literacy, Numeracy and ICT Levels in England.* BIS Research paper number 81. London: BIS.
4   M. Kuczera, S. Field and H. Windisch (2016) *Building Skills for All: A Review of England: Policy Insights from the Survey of Adult Skills.* OECD Skills Studies. Paris: OECD.
5   https://neu.org.uk/press-releases/reformed-gcses-are-damaging-mental-health-young-people-and-failing-accurately (accessed 11 January 2021).
6   J. Britton, C. Farquharson and L. Sibieta (2019) *2019 Annual Report on Education Spending in England.* London: Institute for Fiscal Studies.
7   www.gov.uk/government/publications/state-funded-schools-inspections-and-outcomes-as-at-31-december-2018/state-funded-schools-inspections-and-outcomes-as-at-31-december-2018 (accessed 11 January 2021).

receive the support they need at school (or at home, in some cases). We know too about the impact exams have on students' mental health after roughly a decade of assessment in our schools[8], and that some students just don't *like* school[9].

Looking back, I'm not sure how ready I was for the many challenges in FE. From frantic enrolment and identifying a classroom to delving into Functional Skills and discovering that many English and maths teachers were in fact engineers, plasterers and hairdressers, it was a whirlwind. Hugely exciting, but a whirlwind.

Thankfully, FE has many saving graces. Innumerable, frankly. The outrageously talented professionals (from teachers to administrators to exams officers to leaders), the unique students, the enormously rewarding opportunities throughout the sector, and that indescribable feeling of seeing a student's face light up and their world alter forever on results day, having worked so hard to achieve their final grade.

Much has changed in FE English and maths since the Wolf Report was published (the Functional Skills reforms and the impact of Covid-19 in the last 18 months alone), but two things have remained consistent: the questions we ask, and the people who ask them.

The questions asked back in 2011 are the same as the questions being asked now: what are the challenges and how do we fix them? Most of you will have many answers to the 'what', and will (hopefully) be eagerly reading this book for answers to the 'how'.

Though this book contains plenty of answers for both, it is important to remember that there is no 'silver bullet' or 'quick fix'. (If there was, this book would have been written much sooner, by someone who would now be much richer!)

As we remember that the challenges our students face in classrooms (and in the outside world) are the result of a range of factors occurring over a span of years, we must also remember that not every solution will work immediately (or in some cases, at all). With this in mind, this book has been structured to make sure that there is always an alternative approach, method or suggestion and any resulting challenges are accounted for.

The Challenges we Face

With no defining structure for English and maths departments across the country, the biggest challenge we face is consistency. How can we be consistent with such a range of experience(s) and qualifications in our staff rooms (if we have them)? How can we be consistent with students of all backgrounds and abilities, and varying levels of engagement entering from across the spectrum of education? And all of this is before the teaching starts!

---

8   T. Roome and C.A. Soan (2019) GCSE exam stress: student perceptions of the effects on wellbeing and performance, *Pastoral Care in Education*, 37(4): 297–315.

9   D.T. Willingham (2009). *Why don't Students like School?: A Cognitive Scientist Answers Questions about How the Mind Works and What it Means for the Classroom.* San Francisco: Jossey-Bass.

The majority of these challenges will fall into one of these summarised categories:

- **Attendance**

  Though no official government data exists, I am yet to meet an English and maths leader who has attendance rates of higher than 85 per cent (and this is usually reported with the support of A level provision, with those colleges without A level provision reporting closer to 75–80 per cent). Students don't attend regularly enough, and this has a predictable impact on their knowledge and understanding.

- **Motivation**

  Those who do attend are often deflated and apathetic towards English and maths due to their own previous experience. They feel they have failed, and will fail again (and are more than prepared to share this), so what is the point of even trying? More problematic still, this mindset can spread like wildfire across a student body.

- **Engagement and behaviours**

  Similar to a lack of motivation, some students attend lessons but simply do not engage. Furthermore, there are a minority of students who actively disrupt and look to interrupt learning, for a variety of reasons which are generally linked to being unable to access the curriculum, underlying special educational needs, or perhaps more traumatic previous experiences in English and maths.

- **Vocational collaboration**

  With the majority of students receiving 4–5 hours of class time per week at key stage 4 (KS4) (as well as intervention, revision, homework and additional sessions), they then move to just 3 hours (or less) per week of class time for English and/ or maths in post-16 education. For colleges to be effective in delivering high-quality English and maths, collaboration with vocational staff is vital. However, with many staff lacking confidence in their own English and maths knowledge, this can be difficult to achieve, and vocational staff are not always able (or willing) to fully support English and maths as teachers would like.

- **Embedding college-wide literacy and numeracy**

  Further to collaborating with vocational peers, a whole-college approach is essential to help students regularly use and develop their skills in English and maths. 'Joining the dots' between what happens in English and maths and what happens in all other areas of the college is key in developing student motivation and embedding the importance of English and maths. However, with all other courses jostling for the same position throughout the college, this too can be difficult to achieve.

Tackling these Issues

This book will tackle each of these historical challenges head-on, providing practical solutions by drawing on research, evidence and a range of experience in FE to offer simply administered, effective and practical approaches. From strategies as simple as harnessing behavioural science methods by sending timetabled texts to boost attendance and achievement[10] to managing challenging students and classes using nothing more than a wireless presentation controller (the fabled PowerPoint 'clicker'), this book caters for the many different voices, people and characters in FE.

Also, in dealing with the challenges described above, it is not always possible to keep on top of existing workloads, let alone consistently innovate in English and maths teaching. With this in mind, there are also great sections of this book dedicated to identifying, developing and innovating current pedagogy in English and maths classrooms. There is room for guidance on this also within these pages, as classroom innovation and consistently good teaching will make the biggest difference to each of these challenges. Informed by evidence and research, all of these strategies are based around cutting workload and maximizing effectiveness.

All Different, All the Same

As mentioned, though they all have similarities, no two colleges are the same. Each has its own unique strengths, weaknesses, staff, students and quirks. This is why it is important to have a range of alternative strategies for each challenge.

This also reminds us that no two students are the same either. Though they share similarities, they each have different backgrounds, strengths, areas to develop, motivations and goals. And this is what makes college so unique.

From home-schooled students who have spent little time in a 'traditional' classroom to adult learners (who thought their opportunity to succeed in English and maths had long gone) and everyone in between, this book attempts to ensure there are approaches for all students, and for all contexts.

A Structured Approach

Firstly, each chapter will identify and detail a challenge faced in English and maths resit classrooms in colleges. As these challenges differ in different contexts, and with different student groups (i.e. 16- to 19-year-old students in comparison to adult groups, for example), each chapter will then identify a range of potential solutions to the challenge, detail possible issues with implementing these solutions, and then cover potential alternatives or remedies: best practice, what could go wrong, how to make sure it doesn't.

Each chapter will also include practical takeaways, key considerations and next steps.

---

10 R. Chande, M. Luca, M. Sanders et al. (2017) *Increasing Attendance and Attainment Among Adult Students in the UK: Evidence from a Field Experiment.* Working paper. London: Behavioural Insights Team.

Who is this Book For?

'Two things have remained consistent: the questions we ask, and the people who ask them.'

This book is for the people who ask the questions. As all colleges and students are different, so too are the many teachers who make up an English and maths team. From those teaching exclusively GCSE or Functional Skills, to those lucky enough to be blessed with English and/or maths hours on their otherwise vocational timetable, colleges (and college leaders) have continued to adapt staffing requirements to meet ever growing student resit numbers and specialist teacher shortages[11]. The technicolour personalities in English and maths teams reflect this.

Though primarily aimed at English and maths teachers, with vocational tutors tasked with embedding English and maths, vocational leaders attempting to do the same as well as continuing to support their staff, and senior leaders juggling both alongside their college-wide responsibilities, this book offers a range of practical approaches for everyone with a stake in English and maths.

There are also sections of this book (specifically motivating staff and English and maths department structure) which are aimed more at leaders. However, these sections are not only for current leaders, but also teachers with aspirations to lead and manage.

With obvious similarities in all Further Education classrooms, many of the strategies and approaches in this book can also be effectively transferred to vocational classrooms – the challenges seen in English and maths are often the same challenges seen throughout further and post-16 education.

The Names we Use

Having become accustomed to the idiosyncrasies of Further Education, my first 'culture shock' moment came when a student said my name. Not Mr Kay, my name for the best part of a decade in secondary schools, but my actual name. Shortly afterwards, I was quickly in hot water for referring to a colleague as a 'teacher'.

'Oh ... are you not a teacher?' I asked.

'No, I'm not a teacher; I'm a lecturer.'

Thinking on this, it made me reflect on the importance of the names we use and the way that we use them. It defines who and what we are.

With this in mind, I thought it was important to add a note about some of the names and titles that will be used in this book. 'Students' is an easy one. When I use this, hopefully all readers understand that I'm referring to any person in further or post-16 education (from 16 to 19 years old and 19+) enrolled on a

---

11 L. Sibieta (2020) *Teacher Shortages in England: Analysis and Pay Options*. London: Education Policy Institute.

course or study programme – basically, anyone in a classroom apart from the people who are either standing up when the teaching starts or being paid to be in the room.

Some may prefer a different title rather than 'teachers'. And I agree, we should each be allowed our preference: we are lecturers, practitioners, teachers, facilitators and everything in between. In the interests of consistency and simplicity, however, I will mostly use 'teachers' in this book, but I am referring to all of the above and do not see one as any more important or relevant than the others.

For English and maths leaders, this can be tricky too. We are Heads of Department, Curriculum Leads, Assistant Principals (with responsibility for English and maths), Directors of English and maths, Faculty Leads, Lead Practitioners in English and maths, and many other titles. For the purposes of this book, I will be using 'Head of Department'.

What Next?

This book has partly been written as a tool for sharing good practice: use what is written in the book; share if it works; share if it doesn't; take to social media; engage members of your department or college. The key to consistency and helping young people achieve is collaboration, and sharing the strategies in this book is intended to support that.

Thanks for reading, and I hope you find the strategies contained here useful.

1 Starting Points and Evaluation

'I have to do an English and maths test? Why do I have to do another test? I've just finished my GCSE exams.'

A travel and tourism student (2017)

I remember my first experience in an FE college very well. It involved presiding over enrolment sessions in late August or early September, with many emails flying back and forth referencing 'IA' or 'Initial Assessment'. At that time, I had little to no idea of what this was or what it meant, and I remember being confronted by a furious exams officer who was attempting to make sure it was completed properly. For the uninitiated, the initial assessment process, which all colleges complete on student enrolment, can be a confusing and stressful time.

But does it need to be this way? Why do we complete these initial assessments? What is their purpose? And, for that matter, what is the difference between initial assessment and diagnostic assessment?

Well, firstly, this term can mean different things to different people. Most will see this as a reference to the (mainly) computer-based assessments which are completed at enrolment to determine a student's current knowledge and understanding of areas of English and maths. Once captured, this information is then used to help place students on the correct course (i.e. Functional Skills or GCSE) and the correct level (Entry, Level 1, etc.).

Once this has been completed, students then complete a diagnostic assessment – having found the right course and level, this identifies their strengths and areas for development (with a computer-based assessment giving detailed feedback on next steps).

Though they can be difficult to complete at times, for a range of reasons (staffing, engagement, attendance, available computer rooms – among others), these initial assessments provide vital starting points for students and for staff. For English and maths especially, this is an enormously important time.

For vocational areas, this marks an opportunity to identify potential weaknesses in the months to come. However, for English and maths, this assessment is two-fold. Firstly, we identify areas of strength and for development, which will need to be catered for in the following academic year. Next, we are also able to identify what gaps have opened up since the end of the last academic year, and the key terminology and practices we need to plug these gaps[1].

---

1   A. Quigley (2018) *Closing the Vocabulary Gap*. Abingdon and New York: Routledge.

However, we must remember the importance of completing this process **with** students, and not **to** them[2]. Is it best practice to complete these assessment as soon as possible? In many ways, yes, but what about the lasting impact? If first impressions are everything, for students entering from school, this can be perceived as representing an experience too similar to the one they have left in KS4; students can become fearful there will be a range of over-testing[3]. The negative impact of this can be quickly felt by both student and teacher[4].

So, what are the alternatives?

Unfortunately, avoiding initial and diagnostic testing is nearly impossible. Firstly, when administered properly (more on that later), the majority of computer- and paper-based initial and diagnostic assessments give accurate results which help teachers and leaders to effectively place students on the right course, at the right level. Secondly, and much less importantly, it provides evidence and justification for student placement on particular courses and at particular levels.

All assessment is important in some way, but only when completed in the most effective way possible. For initial and diagnostic assessment, this means setting, support and standards:

1 Setting

Often neglected in collecting accurate and reliable data, the physical environment (i.e. the 'where' of assessment) in which assessments are completed is a vital component in the assessment process. As a result of this environment, too often students can rush through assessments, as previously mentioned, giving poor measures of their ability, strengths, weaknesses and knowledge. To obtain accuracy in assessments, the environment is vital.

Small group environments should be encouraged. Cramming as many students as possible into a computer room creates an uncomfortable setting, and students may well be anxious or nervous about what is to come and display challenging behaviour[5]. Yes, it can be logistically challenging (particularly at this point in the year) to find the space and resources to complete assessments in this way, but what is the alternative?

Staggering assessment times, using laptops and libraries, and asking adult learners to complete assessments remotely are all ways to utilise the available resources and ensure high-quality initial and diagnostic assessment. To achieve this, work with senior leaders and clarify that initial and diagnostic assessments,

2   L. Clough and A. Foster (2001) *Initial Assessment of Learning and Support Needs and Planning Learning to Meet Needs.* Sheffield: DfEE.

3   S. Strickland (2020) *Education Exposed: Leading a School in a Time of Uncertainty.* Melton, Woodbridge: John Catt Educational Ltd.

4   D. Koretz (2017) *The Testing Charade: Pretending to Make Schools Better.* Chicago: University of Chicago Press.

5   Cowley (2006) *Getting the Buggers to Behave.* London: A&C Black.

vital in identifying starting points, are not only key to achievement, but are also auditable.

2 Support

But how much support? Well, more than 'It's a test. I can't help you.' This is likely to alienate students and deepen feelings of anxiety and discomfort, which can again lead to challenging behaviour. We have all been in this situation before – whether initial assessments of our own, exams, driving tests, dental check-ups etc. If we understand what they are going through, the best course of action can be to simply show empathy[6].

This isn't to say that we should saunter around the room giving students the answers to create some sort of anxiety-free assessment nirvana, but we don't have to be overly strict or menacing either. If a student doesn't understand a question, or can't access some of the content, quickly and quietly explain what is being asked and let the relevant teacher, team or leader know that the student had difficulty in accessing the content. Everything that happens in a college is an assessment opportunity – and not just to collect and analyse data, but to effectively support students.

Additionally, give sentence stems or starters, reasonably break a question down or ask the student what method they would use to answer a question – the importance of discussion and questioning[7] should not be underestimated in these environments.

3 Standards

The physical environment is very important, but not without the establishment of continuous high standards[8]. A teacher occasionally giving a cursory glance to the 35 students who are completing an initial assessment over a mobile phone screen, with a quick comment about 'trying your best', is likely to provide a raft of worthless data – these are not the standards we expect of students, so we can't exhibit them ourselves.

This isn't to say that we should patrol the classroom, giving pep talks or re-enacting inspirational speeches, but there is a middle ground and we must inhabit it. These assessments are an important part of the college journey, and

---

6   T. Bennett (2010) *The Behaviour Guru: Behaviour Management Solutions for Teachers*. London: Continuum.

7   V. Brooks (2002) *Assessment in Secondary Schools: The New Teacher's Guide to Monitoring, Assessment, Recording, Reporting, and Accountability*. Buckingham: McGraw-Hill Education.

8   C. Rubie-Davies (2014) *Becoming a High Expectation Teacher: Raising the Bar*. Abingdon and New York: Routledge.

Figure 1.1

will help shape a student's next steps – remind them of this, and give them the support in an environment they deserve by setting and maintaining high standards. If challenging behaviour is exhibited, deal with this as it would be dealt with in a classroom.

It is also important that English and maths are a priority when completing enrolment paperwork, and be aware that there is the possibility that this may not happen if enrolment stations are staffed only by administrative or vocational staff. This is not to say that these staff do not recognise the importance of English and maths, but they may not have the subject-specific knowledge to identify potential pathways for learners based only on the documents they bring to enrolment. As a result, it is vital that English and maths staff are available throughout enrolment to ensure students are given high-quality, detailed advice on their next steps in English and maths and their journey is plotted.

However, this shouldn't be our only assessment[9]. The reality should be that initial and diagnostic assessment are just the starting point on a comprehensive assessment journey, not the only stops. Yes, it is true that we do not want to over-assess students, and this is why many of the following steps are bespoke, inclusive and even covert.

So, what are the next steps?

Free Writing

Sometimes, the issue with evaluating student need and strengths is that students simply do not produce enough material for us to evaluate[10]. At times,

9   H. Torrance and J. Pryor (1998) *Investigating Formative Assessment: Teaching, Learning and Assessment in the Classroom.* Buckingham: McGraw-Hill Education.

10 K.L. Greenberg (1986) *Writing Assessment: Issues and Strategies.* Longman Series in College Composition and Communication. New York: Longman.

students can attempt to complete initial and diagnostic assessments as quickly as possible, meaning we do not gather an effective measurement of their capabilities and skills.

Many of us have experienced the wonder and mystery of a student with a GCSE grade 3 achieving a pre-entry-level score on their initial assessment, only to find on further investigation that the student had spent all of 2 minutes and 36 seconds completing the hour-long assessment.

With this in mind, free writing can be an enormously beneficial task when properly applied. Though computer-based assessments give us lots to analyse, watching students in the actual process of writing, witnessing thought processes and evaluating spelling, punctuation, grammar and a range of other skills, can be invaluable.

The key here is to provide a suitable environment, a suitable task and suitable support. Without these elements, students will quickly perceive that this is an assessment, feel that speed is more important than quality and finish it as soon as possible. Identify and ask students to write about topics they are invested in, and they will likely give proper time and effort to the process[11]. If properly invested, teachers and leaders will have a greater body of work to evaluate, and a greater likelihood of placing students onto the correct qualifications and levels, and giving relevant feedback.

If students should write about what they know[12], they must also write about the topics they are invested in. So, what do all students know a lot about and invest in? Easy – themselves. With this in mind, ask students to complete free writing around their topics of interest, past experiences, hopes for the future and their initial thoughts on the college. However, this doesn't mean that topics should be limited to these choices. Identifying random and seemingly bizarre topics through questioning can also illicit a range of extended writing responses with minimal scaffolding.

Using resources such as Ian Gilbert's *The Little Book of Thunks: 260 Questions to Make your Brain go Ouch!*[13] can spark all kinds of debate which can then be turned into extended writing. Asking students to create and write about their own season, a historical event they would change and why, what items they would take to a desert island (for survival or comfort) or even the qualities they admire in their friends can all be good starting points for free writing.

As mentioned above, a suitable environment is key here. Students are unlikely to produce extended writing in a room with 25–30 peers. Try as we might, there still remains a stigma amongst (particularly male[14]) peer groups around extended writing. Split into smaller groups, and given time to adequately

---

11 E. Gruwell (2007) *The Freedom Writers Diary: How a Teacher and 150 Teens Used Writing to Change Themselves and the World Around Them.* New York: Broadway Books.

12 A. Cowan (2013) *The Art of Writing Fiction.* Abingdon: Routledge.

13 I. Gilbert (2007) *The Little Book of Thunks: 260 Questions to Make your Brain go Ouch!* Carmarthen: Crown House Publishing.

14 M. Pinkett and M. Roberts (2019) *Boys Don't Try? Rethinking Masculinity in Schools.* Abingdon and New York: Routledge.

Table 1.1

GCSE grade	Initial assessment result	Placement
3	N/A	GCSE
2	>50% at Level 1 IA	GCSE improver group
2	<50% at Level 1 IA	Level 1 Functional Skills
1	>50% at Entry Level IA	Level 1 Functional Skills
1	<50% at Entry Level IA	Entry Level Functional Skills

plan a response[15], students will produce a piece of work which can be used in the next step of their English and maths journey: the placement forum.

A Placement Forum

All of the steps detailed so far are excellent – and necessary – but how else can we monitor that we are effectively placing students onto the right qualifications, at the right levels? The benefits of initial and diagnostic assessment have already been discussed, and free writing certainly helps to build a more complete picture, but what other information can we use? The answer? Placement forums.

If quality is defined as 'something good and worth having'[16], a college should have a framework or flow chart to adequately place students on the correct qualification and level. An example can be seen in Table 1.1.

There are of course exceptions, but this is why we hold a placement forum. Placement of the majority of students will probably take very little time, with most grade 3 students being placed on GCSE programmes (and some moving to Level 2 Functional Skills – for example apprentices or those requiring only a Level 2 qualification as entry requirements to higher education (HE)). The majority of the remainder will be placed on either Entry Level or Level 1 Functional Skills qualifications after all of their available data has been evaluated – which is where the placement forum comes in.

Held during enrolment, when the majority of initial and diagnostic assessments have been completed, this forum takes the form of a one-off meeting involving all relevant staff and leaders looking at all of the information and data which has been collected during enrolment. An ideal attendance list will include the head of English and maths (or similar), the exams officer, manager

---

15 J.C. Hochman and N. Wexler (2017) *The Writing Revolution: A Guide to Advancing Thinking through Writing in all Subjects and Grades.* San Francisco: John Wiley & Sons.

16 G.A. Cole (2004) *Management Theory and Practice.* Andover: Cengage Learning EMEA.

of data and/or exams, the special educational needs co-ordinator and an English and/or maths teacher. Ideally, one forum should be held for each subject. This collaborative approach ensures that all aspects of an assessment are evaluated – we must remember that there are many types of assessment, and each performs a different role[17].

The information to hand should include initial and diagnostic assessment results, any free writing which has been completed, any relevant special educational needs and disability (SEND) paperwork (including transition paperwork and educational and healthcare plan documentation), exam concessions or adjustments or additional support needs. The use and analysis of these documents is as vital to a student's success as anything we teach in the classroom, because it informs how and what we teach.

As mentioned, an English or maths specialist will also be on hand to provide a summary of the skills shown in the free writing or initial/diagnostic assessment, and can provide information about the level of students already placed on qualifications, levels and groups.

Though this approach can take time (depending on the number of students, it can take a number of hours), it very much places the work at the beginning of the year – as opposed to identifying that students are on the wrong level or qualification throughout the year and missing precious teaching time. There may be resistance from senior leaders (due to time or workload constraints), but try and communicate the amount of time that will be saved in the long run, and the impact this will have on individual students and their achievement. A student spending two to three weeks studying at one level/qualification and then being moved is two to three weeks of missed teaching – what impact could this have on their final achievement?

Of course, there are exceptions to this rule: if the entire provision is GCSE, it can be argued that there is no need for a placement forum. However, it is still an excellent opportunity for practitioners and leaders to come together and discuss the additional support some learners may need, or best practice approaches for learners. Placing students on relevant qualifications and at relevant levels can also be a delicate balancing act: placing a majority of students on GCSE is generally good for progress data, but overall achievement results (i.e. grade 4+ rates) can be damaged (some students will improve their overall result, but still not achieve a grade 4+). However, placing students onto a Level 2 Functional Skills programme can boost overall achievement (students can sit multiple exams, potentially increasing the likelihood of passing), but if they do not pass, this can limit progress data.

With this in mind, it is vital that students are placed correctly, and the placement forum is an important step in this process. It is also vital that placement is in line with the best options for students, and not based on achievement/progress data alone.

---

17 W. Harlen, C. Gipps, P. Broadfoot and D. Nuttall (1992) Assessment and the improvement of education, *The Curriculum Journal*, 3(3): 215–30.

In-class Assessment

For many, this is where the real initial and diagnostic assessment takes place. As important as the steps before in-class assessment are, many teachers can tell more from the opening 15–20 minutes of a lesson than can be gleaned from a raft of data and spreadsheets. Retrieval quizzes, reading comprehension, an analysis of working methods or even just engaging in a group discussion on a range of topics can tell us an enormous amount about the strengths and gaps our students have. This is also completed without an over-reliance on the memorization of facts, something which can disadvantage some students[18].

What is important here is that all in-class assessment is rigorous and consistent[19]. If decisions are being made about what students should be at what level, the assessments being used must be consistent, and consistently applied. A member of the team giving excessive support or guidance to students during an assessment where another teacher gives none can unduly punish either student group and give a false impression of a student's knowledge, ability and understanding.

This can even be extended to the environment in which assessments are held – if one group completes assessments in silence, with another completing assessments to background music in a class resembling a workshop, we build inherent inequality into our processes. This is not to say that in-class assessments should resemble exam halls or that some support should not be given, but there has to be a happy medium, and this happy medium has to be reflected in all classes, at least in the opening weeks and during the following assessments. Without this, we run the risk of calling the validity of assessments into question, and this validity is central to the process of evaluating student need[20].

Also, this is not to say that assessments should be lengthy, onerous affairs that instantly disengage students and leave staff with immense workloads – both students and staff are likely to burn out as a result, causing additional (long-term) challenges. No, assessments can be as simple as a ten-question long retrieval quiz, or a 20-minute writing exercise preceded by minimal teaching to set the scene and gauge knowledge retention skills[21].

The information during this period can either be taken to a second, much shorter, placement forum to move students to a different qualification or level, or discussed at English and maths team meetings, with student movement finalised after discussion with peers.

18 R.W. Cole (2008) *Educating Everybody's Children: Diverse Teaching Strategies for Diverse Learners*. Alexandria, VA: ASCD.

19 P.J. Black (1998) *Testing, Friend or Foe?: The Theory and Practice of Assessment and Testing*. Hove, East Sussex: Psychology Press.

20 A. Pollard, ed. (2002) *Readings for Reflective Teaching*. London: A&C Black.

21 C. Barton (2018) *How I Wish I'd Taught Maths: Lessons Learned from Research, Conversations with Experts, and 12 Years of Mistakes*. Melton, Woodbridge: John Catt Educational Ltd.

Adult Assessment and Enrolment

With adult education budgets increasingly cut back over the last two decades[22], colleges are often left trying to do more with less. A vital part of any community, the English and maths provision offered to adults can represent a real lifeline to adults who want a change of career, to begin Further Education or simply want to improve their skills. It is not difficult to see motivations behind this – research suggests an 'intense relationship'[23] between low literacy ability, poor health and a shorter life expectancy.

Clearly, correlation does not necessarily imply causation, but there is an obvious and clear link between employment opportunities and outcomes and literacy and numeracy skills. With this in mind, many adults can be fearful of entering colleges due to previous negative experiences of education[24]. As a result, we must provide additional support to defeat these barriers.

Initial and diagnostic assessments will of course take place, with additional discussion about prior learning at interview, but there are further steps we must take, if only to reassure and confirm our colleges as welcome environments, and foundations for second chances.

Firstly, invite potential adult students in for an informal discussion and group presentation about what is available, days and times of sessions, what will be required and what is covered in each qualification at each level. There will be students who will be surprised to learn that the grading system is now numerical, or those who have never heard of Functional Skills, and will need background information. This reassurance is also likely to fill students with confidence in the college, and can support retention and attendance in future. Ask English and maths staff to also attend a presentation on the topics and elements which will be covered at each level and for each qualification – when the presentation is finished, potential students should be given the opportunity to meet and get to know their potential teachers.

If possible, host several open evenings throughout the academic year – give them the information they need and provide details on potential pathways (i.e. Entry to Level 1 to Level 2/GCSE). Distribution of revision and introductory tasks can also be enormously beneficial. Receiving a revision workbook, a pack of work or access to online materials can give adult learners a valuable head start before the beginning of the course and can again aid retention and attendance statistics as learners feel better prepared and better supported by the college. Supplemented with regular communication ('keep-warm' emails

---

22 D. Luchinskaya and P. Dickinson (2019) *The Adult Skills Gap: Is Falling Investment in UK Adults Stalling Social Mobility?* London: Social Mobility Commission.

23 L. Gilbert, A. Teravainen, A. Clark and S. Shaw (2018) *Literacy and Life Expectancy: An Evidence Review Exploring the Link between Literacy and Life Expectancy in England through Health and Socioeconomic Factors.* London: National Literacy Trust.

24 S. Wallace (2017) *Motivating Unwilling Learners in Further Education: The Key to Improving Behaviour.* London: Bloomsbury Publishing.

giving information on developments at the college and potential revision websites and resources), adult learners can begin to develop a relationship with the college and potentially with the staff they will deal with when enrolled[25].

Induction and Beyond

So, initial and diagnostic assessments have been completed (as has free writing, where applicable), placement forums have been completed and students have been placed on relevant qualifications, at relevant levels.

One of the busiest times in the Further Education calendar: timetables will now be issued and students will generally begin to attend an induction week designed to give them a flavour of what is to come.

As well as being an important time for all vocational lecturers, who meet students for the first time and have opportunities to communicate expectations with both new and existing students, this is also an excellent time to embed the importance of English and maths college-wide. Induction sessions in English and maths too often hinge on what students *shouldn't* do and focus on continued assessment (immediately after students have just completed initial and diagnostic assessments, and have probably also completed assessment in vocational areas). It doesn't have to be this way.

Engage with Vocational Induction

Firstly, what is to stop English and maths teachers engaging with vocational induction sessions? Going into construction, hairdressing or engineering lessons and supporting students during these initial sessions is an excellent way to build relationships and get to know them before being seen through the lens of English and maths.

Many of our students have had previous negative experiences with English and maths, and whether this be through (perceived) prior failure[26] or a lack of guidance and support, (whether we like it or not) we must start to mend the relationships that we played no part in breaking. Though our students are highly skilled in vocational areas and passionate about learning their trade, at this point in the year they are being exposed to new skill sets and are unlikely to succeed in their first attempts – this shared, common ground is a golden opportunity to build relationships with students[27].

---

25 P. Jarvis and C. Griffin, eds (2003) *Adult and Continuing Education, Volume V: Adult Education – Viewed from the Disciplines*. London and New York: Taylor & Francis.

26 S. Wallace (2007) *Getting the Buggers Motivated in FE*. London and New York: A&C Black.

27 I. Lopez (2017) *Keeping it Real and Relevant: Building Authentic Relationships in Your Diverse Classroom*. Alexandria, VA: ASCD.

Many teachers feel a majority of students are extremely anxious about appearing to fail in front of their peers. In fact, it is what this failure represents[28] which primarily causes the response we see in students (refusal to answer questions, complete activities etc.). Students fear being mocked or openly ridiculed by other students, who become relieved that attention and focus is not on them. To counter this, if you engage in tasks while supporting students in a lesson, seeing a teacher failing miserably at mixing hair dye or creating a dovetail joint takes all focus from learners, and allows a more comfortable and safe environment – a key component in a successful classroom[29].

Having done this, when entering your lessons, the foundation of a strong and positive relationship has already been created, and learning can begin. It is important when supporting in vocational sessions that English and maths teachers do just that – support. This is all we are there to do – this can provide challenges at times and lead to a number of questions:

- What should you do if you see challenging behaviour?
- Should you step in?
- Will this undermine the vocational teacher?
- What if you don't step in – what does this suggest about behaviour standards in your own class?

In an attempt to avoid these scenarios, make sure you are introduced as an English and/or maths teacher at the beginning of the session and help to uphold college expectations by setting clear boundaries with the vocational teacher before the session. We are in their space, their curriculum and, in this instance, with their students, so respect is paramount.

If you are not confident in attending a vocational session and engaging with tasks, there is nothing stopping you giving a brief presentation during theory sessions in which you outline the positive aspects and impact English and maths achievement will have. More on this in Chapter 11.

Place Students Efficiently and Permanently

There is much above, and in academic writing elsewhere, about the tools required to effectively place students on relevant qualifications and at relevant levels. However, what if subsequent data or performance suggests a move to another qualification or level? The key here is to make sure that there is suitable evidence to make a change[30], and that this change will last for the remainder of

---

28 A. Martin (2010) *Building Classroom Success: Eliminating Academic Fear and Failure*. London: A&C Black.

29 Education and Training Foundation (2014) *Professional Standards for Teachers and Trainers in Education and Training – England*. London: ETF.

30 T. Allan, J. Rodger, M. Dodd and M. Cutmore (2016) *Effective Practice in Supporting Entry/Level 1 Students in Post-16 Institutions (2015/27)*. London: DfE.

the academic term. Additionally, we must make sure that any change is made in consultation with the student (though student opinion is obviously outweighed by data, current level or teacher evaluation) and best serves the student's career options and destinations[31].

Assess effectively (more on this in Chapter 8) and discuss any decisions with vocational tutors, while also discussing with peers and moderating any work which suggests a qualification or level move is the best course of action. Again, where possible, this needs to be completed before (or at the latest, by) October half term as any move after this date could disadvantage students who have missed too much teaching (i.e. a move in January from GCSE to Level 2, or vice versa, means a student has missed 40 per cent of the relevant qualification teaching for that academic year).

All student qualification or level movement which occurs after October should ideally be scrutinised and signed off by the head of department (or equivalent) to ensure that this is the right move for the student. This may seem excessive, but it will allow leaders and managers to identify any issues or challenges with qualification or level movement, and mitigate against these. There are also some occasions when a student or parent/carer may challenge a qualification or level move, and involving the Head of Department provides a back-up for such situations.

SEND and Access Arrangements

In best cases, any SEND or access arrangement information should be captured at enrolment (and even before if solid links with schools are established). We are all aware that testing to identify any additional need (and in turn access arrangement) should be completed as early as possible, but what steps do we need to take to ensure this happens?

As with the majority of ideas and strategies in this book, high-quality initial training is the first and one of the most important steps which we need to see happen. Are staff on enrolment desks fully aware of their role and the actions they must take? Is enrolment and accompanying paperwork able to capture the range and depth of information that teachers need to be effective? Does it capture previous grades, exam board, special educational needs, required support or further arrangements that will support learning? And, more importantly, is this information then properly communicated?

And this is how we must think about enrolment and associated processes. At times, paperwork and administration can seem unimportant, and that the really important stuff starts when we first meet students and begin to teach. However, the paperwork, the administration, tells a story about our students and so it is vital we capture the information accurately and efficiently.

---

31 R.M. McGill (2015) *Teacher Toolkit: Helping you Survive your First Five Years.* London: Bloomsbury Publishing.

Firstly, ensure all enrolment paperwork captures the information which is needed for effective placement, teaching and learning – draw together key staff (administrators, teachers, leaders, support staff etc.) and ask the question: does this paperwork do what we need it to do? If the answer is 'no', make the changes[32].

Next, do staff know how to use it? A simple question, but with the range of activities occurring during enrolment there can often be staff shortages (due to holiday, induction lessons, planning, external commitments etc.), and there can be times when there are staff carrying out induction who do not have a full picture of the requirements. All staff who will eventually carry out enrolment should be identified as early as possible and be given training on what processes should occur, and why they should occur in that way. This training does not need to be onerous, and can be as simple as modelling an example via online training, or producing a short example of how to effectively complete paperwork.

Completing these two initial steps will save a lot of time later. Once students who require access arrangements or who have additional needs have been identified, testing can now be completed by those responsible for SEND. Another vital step here is confirming in what area these needs present themselves. For example, a student may well need support in English, but not maths or their vocational area (or vice versa) – it is important to make this distinction for many reasons.

Remember here that asking students what assistance they required in school will not give us all of the information we need (or be totally accurate), but it is a good starting point until we get to know our students.

Try as we might to normalise support, additional support can be perceived as a weakness by other students, and lead to the spread of challenging behaviour at times (in many forms, but usually exhibiting in the form of bullying)[33]. Students can also often still feel the stigma of requiring additional support in lessons[34], so we must attempt to give as much support as possible while also minimizing the appearance of support.

Transition should identify all students with an Education, Health and Care Plan (EHCP) and the paperwork to confirm support and additional arrangements should be going on in the background as we continue enrolment. However, any students who aren't picked up here should be a priority during induction and initial sessions.

After this, as this book will espouse, communication is absolutely key. An additional need has been identified and confirmed via relevant testing – do all relevant teaching staff know about this? Whether the additional need only refers to English, maths or a vocational area is irrelevant: all staff who teach that student should know about it. Log it on relevant systems (ProM etc.), make

---

32 G. Hornby (2016) *Inclusive Special Education*. New York: Springer-Verlag.
33 K. Rigby (2007) *Bullying in Schools: And What to Do About it*. Victoria: Australian Council for Educational Research.
34 E. Goffman (2009) *Stigma: Notes on the Management of Spoiled Identity*. London: Simon & Schuster.

paperwork available on shared areas and give staff time to access and read these documents.

Recording everything so everyone can see it is key, as is monitoring this. Do all staff know? If not, we're letting our students down.

The final step in this process, as students become settled into their programmes of study, is to ensure continuity. So many SEND and access arrangement processes change so often. Get the processes right early, train everyone and communicate.

Arranging Intervention

Though an extremely busy time, during enrolment and the opening weeks of the academic year is the perfect time to begin to put interventions in place for those who may need additional support. Early intervention is often touted as a pillar of Primary Education[35] – why can't we take these same principles and apply them to Further Education? With successive governments seemingly constantly discussing future allocation of specialist funding for FE, in an attempt to help students 'close the gap', the sector has seen some funding given for intervention. In 2020, in response to the Covid-19 pandemic, an additional £96m was ringfenced for post-16 education intervention[36].

In planning to use this funding, initially, suitable returning students should be identified – this could potentially happen through the placement forum, or in a more informal discussion during a team meeting. Through collaborative discussion, teams should identify what resources are available for intervention (i.e. do teachers have the capacity to complete some sessions? Are there online resources to help with this?) and then decide what parameters will need to be met for students to receive intervention.

The detail around the Department for Education's additional funding informally acts as excellent guidance around what and how intervention should take place[37]:

- Intervention (or 'catch-up' sessions) should be held with three to five students.
- A record should be kept of the resources (staff time, any resources or materials used etc.) that are planned and used for each session.
- Continuity of setting and environment should be maintained for student well-being and to help reduce any challenging behaviour[38] – interventions should be held in the same, suitably sized and resourced room.

35 B. Persky and L.H. Golubchick, eds (1991) *Early Childhood Education.* Lanham, MD: University Press of America.

36 www.gov.uk/government/news/every-pupil-in-england-to-see-another-rise-in-funding-in-2021 (accessed 11 January 2021).

37 www.gov.uk/guidance/coronavirus-covid-19-catch-up-premium (accessed 11 January 2021).

38 Cowley, *Getting the Buggers to Behave.*

Of course, a record of resources doesn't need to be too strict or formal, just a log which can be seen by teachers to identify and confirm what additional work has been completed to inform future planning.

With the above in place, the next issue is when intervention will take place. This can be difficult as students may have full days without any timetabled slots and every other day is filled with English, maths and vocational sessions. A potential solution could be to timetable an additional slot in collaboration with vocational teams and use this time to identify and run intervention sessions. However, this can be difficult due to the complexity of vocational timetables (more on this in Chapter 7), so a further option could be using tutorial time to run micro-teaching sessions[39] to develop knowledge around English and maths basic or foundation principles. Furthermore, offering this intervention online, or through recorded sessions (with support available through the chat feature of the online tool used) can be enormously impactful.

Retention and Attendance – First Steps

In the early stages of the year, many vocational teams are concerned with the challenges presented by retention and early attendance. As this retention has an enormous impact on English and maths, what solutions can we put in place which will complement and support vocational areas?

A compromise which benefits both English and maths and vocational courses is what is needed here. As planned residential/enrichment activities (often announced at very short notice due to availability) impact English and maths attendance later in the year, there is the opportunity to kill two birds with one stone. Asking vocational areas to complete residential and enrichment activities in the first half term, though initially difficult to organise, will boost retention and attendance in vocational areas[40] and, ultimately, achievement[41]. Again, pointing out the benefits of changing some elements of the vocational academic calendar with the head of department and senior leaders can give them a greater understanding of the challenges faced in English and maths, and also highlight how small changes they can make can have a massive impact.

Making this change removes issues with unannounced trips later in the year (which can result in missing key sessions in English and maths) and can ultimately garner more support from vocational teams. This also takes the onus off English and maths staff to accommodate residential and enrichment activities later in the year and gives responsibility back to students – if students attend English and maths, they attend residentials and enrichment.

---

39 D.W. Allen (1967) *Micro-teaching: A Description*. Stanford, CA: Stanford University.
40 K. Reid (2013) *An Essential Guide to Improving Attendance in your School: Practical Resources for all School Managers*. Abingdon: Routledge.
41 J. Hodges, J. McIntosh and M. Gentry (2017) The effect of an out-of-school enrichment program on the academic achievement of high-potential students from low-income families, *Journal of Advanced Academics*, 28(3): 204–24.

Conclusion

With students, teachers and leaders facing more challenges than ever before, it is vital that we are able to support all students, teams and staff from the first moment students enter post-16 education. The initial actions detailed above are by no means an exhaustive list, but are certainly starting points which should be taken into account and can easily be adapted, adjusted or extended depending on context.

Either way, the key to ensuring students are successful (and how we measure this success) is gathering the information we need to support them. We must set students up to have high attendance and engagement, to achieve academically and to flourish and develop as individuals. Without the right information, and without communicating this information effectively, we cannot facilitate this.

Get the processes right as early as possible; train all staff and communicate.

Summary

- Setting, support and standards are vital to high-quality initial and diagnostic assessment.
- Use placement forums as an additional monitoring step in placing students on the right qualifications at the right levels.
- Use in-class assessment to compliment the initial assessment and placement forum to create a truly holistic assessment experience.
- Engagement with vocational induction (theory and practical) aids relationship building between students and English and maths teachers.
- For enrolment, SEND and access arrangements, remember: get the processes right early, train everyone and communicate.

Reflection

- Are baseline assessments efficient and effective?
- Do all relevant teachers (vocational and English and maths) use BKSB (the most prominent tool used to assess students) to inform teaching?
- How do you share initial and diagnostic assessment results with students?
- Do all staff know their responsibilities around initial and diagnostic assessment?
- What is being done to ensure students are efficiently placed on the right qualification, at the right level?

2 Leadership in English and Maths

'As long as you're trying your best and doing the things I'm asking of you, I'm happy.'
A hopeful leader (2018)

Though the terminology, roles and titles may change, the majority of educational settings in primary and secondary have fairly simple, straightforward management or leadership structures[1]. Broadly speaking, they follow a similar structure to Figure 2.1.

As with the structure itself, the majority of these roles are fairly simply defined – the Principal or Headteacher and deputy head or Vice Principal will have whole-school and overall accountability, with Assistant Vice Principals or Assistant Headteachers reporting to them and being accountable for an element of whole-school practice (behaviour, data, SEND, or quality of teaching, learning and assessment). Next, middle leaders or heads of department will take responsibility for individual curriculum areas and report in to Assistant Vice Principals or Assistant Headteachers.

In best cases, this structure lays the foundation for solid systems of accountability and best practice, and allows individual responsibilities to be delegated, leading to the best possible outcomes for students. Where this fails, it is as a result of too much structure (What is a junior Assistant Vice Principal? Do we need a head of key stage 3 literacy?), too little accountability or too much accountability – hyper-accountability[2].

Though structures in Further Education can share many, many similarities with the above, in some cases the hyper-accountability can remain in colleges where structures have adapted and diversified since the 1992 funding reforms[3]. As a result, and since the changes relating to resits of English and maths[4], English and maths has the unique position of sitting at once everywhere and nowhere in many college structures.

Despite English and maths departments usually comprising the highest number of students in a college, and their vital importance recognised throughout

---

1   A. Gold and J.M. Evans (1998) *Reflecting on School Management.* Hove, East Sussex: Psychology Press.
2   L. Starkey (2012) *Teaching and Learning in the Digital Age.* Abingdon: Routledge.
3   D. McTavish (2003) Aspects of public sector management: a case study of Further Education, ten years from the passage of the Further and Higher Education Act, *Educational Management and Administration,* 31(2): 175–87.
4   A. Wolf (2011) *Review of Vocational Education, 2011. The Wolf Report: Recommendations: Final Progress Report.* London: DfE.

Figure 2.1

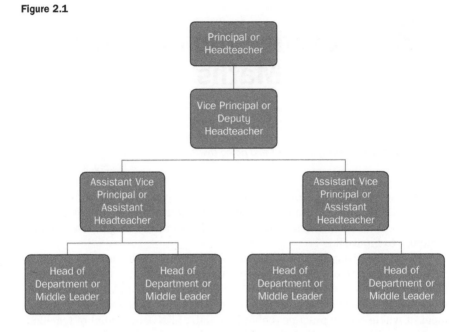

post-16 education, English and maths are not always in the foreground of whole-college decisions as other areas take immediate priority: funding, specification changes, staffing[5] and the importance of generating additional funding due to a lack of funding reform[6].

As a result, English and maths resit provision can mirror health and safety in many post-16 institutions – it is constantly on the agenda, there needs to be consistent and high-quality provision, but it is not the most pressing priority. Until it is.

Because of this, and because of the prominence English and maths can be given by Ofsted during inspections, the responsibility for English and maths is often distributed along a sliding scale of whole-college superiority (or power) and subject-specific knowledge. This means that the more whole-college responsibility the individual responsible for English and maths has, the less subject knowledge they will tend to have. In other words, the more whole-college responsibility the individual responsible for English and maths has, the less experience and fewer subject-specific, relevant qualifications they are likely to hold. Put simply, the more power, the less experience in English and maths.

This chapter seeks to discuss and explore the potential leadership options for English and maths, and debate the pros and cons associated with each. As in other chapters, due to the diversity and range of contexts in Further Education, this will by no means act as a definitive guide, but it will provide a background

5   D. Greatbatch and S. Tate (2018) *Teaching, Leadership and Governance in Further Education*. London: DfE.

6   J. Britton, C. Farquharson and L. Sibieta (2019) *2019 Annual Report on Education Spending in England*. London: Institute for Fiscal Studies.

Table 2.1

Management	Leadership
• Planning against existing strategies and practices to achieve needed results • Monitoring current strategies to gauge success • Organizing staff and staffing so existing practices are completed • Ensuring the efficient completion of existing processes • Delegating and organizing	• Establishing direction and strategy • Facilitating and producing movement and change to achieve a successful vision • Bringing people together to achieve these strategies • Creating more effective processes • Motivating and inspiring

to the prevalent leadership structures in English and maths and give context to those structures.

However, first, before looking at the potential structures and roles involved in leading English and maths, it is important that we can define the characteristics of effective leadership in this area.

Effective Leadership in English and Maths

Though, much like post-16 education itself, the titles and roles associated with leadership in English and maths can change, there are two fundamental practices: leading and managing.

As John Kotter outlined in his excellent book *Force For Change: How Leadership Differs from Management*, and as in all other sectors, the characteristics associated with the two are very different[7]:

The differences between leading and managing English and maths can be profound. With the challenges associated with post-16 English and maths (detailed throughout this book), a mix of knowledge, understanding and skill in leadership and management is vital. However, such is the diversity within Further Education that it may be necessary to apply one while learning the other.

With this in mind, whether applying leadership or management techniques, there are certain traits that are required in those responsible for English and maths in post-16 education. Though these traits are obviously seen throughout education, there are specific elements which are unique to English and maths:

- **Accountability**

  Accountability is enormously important in any manager or leader as, without it, it is enormously difficult for trust to develop between peers, colleagues or team members. However, if we can only be accountable for the

---

7 J.P. Kotter (2008) *Force for Change: How Leadership Differs from Management.* New York: Simon & Schuster.

things we can control, accountability becomes a truly unique beast in post-16 English and maths as there are so many uncontrolled variables (prior knowledge, availability of resources, funding etc.). With this in mind, we must focus on being accountable for and facilitating inputs, rather than staunchly penalizing outcomes. In developing trust, leaders must facilitate what Andy Buck calls 'managing up'[8] – teams must develop high-quality relationships with managers and leaders in order to pass things 'up' to them for resolution. English and maths leaders must recognise they have to take overall accountability, and remove undue burden from teams as a result.

- **Adaptability**

  As successful educational environments have a strong learning culture[9], adaptability for all staff is key. This is never more true than for English and maths leaders and managers. With changes to legislation, qualification reform and the range of challenges in post-16 English and maths, being adaptable is vital to supporting staff and giving a team the resources they need to produce a supportive learning environment. Research suggests it is easier to change teaching style than to adapt a curriculum[10] – as leaders are likely to have to do both and collaborate with all stakeholders throughout the college structure, adaptability is key.

- **Resilience**

  With the national average for grade 4+ in GCSE sitting below 30 per cent for English and maths for the majority of the life of the new specification[11], resilience is vital. It can be enormously difficult for a team to give their all, control and manage all inputs, hold additional sessions, provide constant support, negotiate and collaborate with vocational teams, and still see more than 70 per cent of students fail to achieve the grade they had hoped for. As a leader, this disappointment can feel all the heavier, and this is before discussing and evaluating results with your team or senior leaders, let alone with students themselves or parents and carers. With challenges in attendance, behaviour and engagement, we must be enormously resilient, because without this we cannot fully support our staff.

- **Empathy**

  There are many parts to a successful English and maths department, with trust, collaboration and positivity just a few of the elements required for an effective team. However, as much as leaders are there to celebrate the

8   A. Buck (2016) *Leadership Matters: How Leaders at all Levels can Create Good Schools.* Melton, Woodbridge: John Catt Educational Ltd.

9   B. Robertson (2020) *The Teaching Delusion: Why Teaching in Our Schools isn't Good Enough (and How we can Make it Better).* Melton, Woodbridge: John Catt Educational Ltd.

10 C. Chan, M.L. Chang, P. Westwood and M.T. Yuen (2002) Teaching adaptively: how easy is differentiation in practice?, *The Asia-Pacific Education Researcher*, 11(1): 27–58.

11 www.aoc.co.uk/news/gcse-results-day-2019-aoc-comment (accessed 11 January 2021).

successes, we must also be able to offer support and guidance[12]. A professional extension of the support and guidance we offer to students, we need to predict (where possible), identify and attempt to resolve the challenges our teams face. This can be extraordinarily difficult if we have not faced these challenges ourselves, but judging people is not part of the role of a leader and manager. Simple questions will help here: What is the challenge? How is it impacting the individual? How can the impact be minimised? Solutions can range from taking on small additional workload (covering a lesson, marking a set of books etc.) to seeking external help (counselling, job-sharing, extended leave from college), but the priority, as it is elsewhere, is to support.

- **Communication**

  Intelligent leaders understand they are there for all of their staff[13], not just those they have a good relationship with and, so, communication is key. This is clearly true for all leaders, in all sectors, but with the number and diversity of students seen in English and maths in FE, communication must be effective, clear and timely. This is often difficult as leaders and managers collate and filter what messages are important and which are necessary[14], and so a range of approaches and styles must be used to communicate. Whether communicating one-to-one, with a small group or the whole team, clarity is key. Always have an agenda, stick to it and leave anything that is additional for a later date and time, and inform all relevant staff[15].

- **Providing time and resources**

  As important as any leadership characteristic, being able to provide a team with the time and resources they need to operate effectively is invaluable. This can mean anything from effectively balancing budgets so additional teachers can be taken on or existing staff can complete external training, to developing new assessment and feedback strategies to cut workload (as described in Chapter 8), to streamlining existing processes to focus on new initiatives. Key to facilitating more time and resources is replacing the existing whenever the new is introduced. Any new strategy or process should always replace, or plan to replace, an existing one. If leaders continue to add workload, they dilute the effectiveness of our staff, and ultimately leaders are accountable for the results of this workload increase. Leaders are also responsible for facilitating staff at all times.

---

12 E. Turner (2019) *Be More Toddler: A Leadership Education from our Little Learners.* Melton, Woodbridge: John Catt Educational Ltd.

13 M. Myatt (2016) *High Challenge, Low Threat: Finding the Balance.* Melton, Woodbridge: John Catt Educational Ltd.

14 S. Gill (2002) *Successful Difficult Conversations in School: Improve your Team's Performance, Behaviour and Attitude with Kindness and Success.* Melton, Woodbridge: John Catt Educational Ltd.

15 National College for Teaching and Leadership (n.d.) *Managing meetings and communication* [online]. Available at: www.inspiringleaderstoday.com/ILTMaterials/ LEVEL1_MSP-v4.0-2014_08_08-12_18_0/managing-systems-and-processes/msp-s7/ msp-s7-t3.html (accessed 15 January 2021).

- **Accessibility**

  Simply put, leaders cannot complete any changes or manage any existing processes if they do not communicate with teams, leaders and other relevant staff, and this can't be achieved if they are inaccessible. Obviously, this does not mean that leaders should be at the beck and call of staff throughout the working week, but there must be key times when leaders will be available to offer support, guidance and advice. Quite honestly, when first entering Further Education (and to this day), I regularly hounded line managers and leaders for counselling and advice, and developed much more quickly as a result. Were it not for the availability and accessibility of these leaders, my development as a teacher, leader and colleague would have undoubtedly been greatly stunted. Sometimes just being available to listen is enough to support staff. Regardless, leaders must be available and they must be accessible simply because of the many, and ever changing, challenges that come with English and maths in Further Education.

This list of characteristics and traits is certainly not exhaustive and there are elements which have not been discussed in nearly enough detail. However, this book is concerned with best practice in all elements of post-16 English and maths and the elements required for effective leadership could easily fill an entire library. As a conclusion to what is needed to be an effective leader in this field, leadership in post-16 English and maths is more about developing positive, collaborative relationships than any other field or sector. Due to the often challenging circumstances, teachers rely on colleagues and leaders rely on peers for more than just support. In truly excellent colleges, a community of practice develops, and this is in no small part down to the relationships which are formed.

As a result, the above traits are more vital in post-16 English and maths simply because they will more quickly and more effectively help to build the foundations of excellent relationships – relationships which help leaders navigate and negotiate the many roles they must play.

The Roles of an English and Maths Leader

The 2018 report *Teaching, Leadership and Governance in Further Education*[16] suggests (via Lambert in 2013[17]) that 'there are three dimensions to the role of the Principal in FE colleges: an external-public, an internal-public and an internal-private.'

Clearly, managers and leaders in English and maths do not face the challenges of a Principal or CEO, however there are comparisons to be made with the above quote and the dimensions and roles English and maths leaders must

---

16 Greatbatch and Tate, *Teaching, Leadership and Governance.*
17 S. Lambert (2013). Defining a tri-dimensional role for leadership in Further Education colleges, *Management in Education*, 27(1): 39–42.

play by simply adapting and extending the existing roles and dimensions. Firstly, if we change the use and definition of 'public' to mean vocational teams when discussing these roles in the context of English and maths leaders, they take on an entirely different, yet relevant, meaning.

External public: the role played in front of all stakeholders in relation to English and maths – this is the message and the communications which are broadcast to everyone: leaders, students, teachers, vocational teams, parents, external agencies etc. As it is broadcast to a wide audience, this message is likely to be simple and clear, but will give some information on the goals and values associated with English and maths.

Internal public: similar to external public, but with a greater focus on *how* these goals will be achieved, this role relates to communication of the steps that will need to be taken, accountabilities, responsibilities and evaluation processes for all internal stakeholders involved with English and maths.

External private: the characteristics of this role are seen in the discussions between English and maths leaders and vocational leaders about the priorities, strengths, weaknesses and performance of English and maths in their particular area. The information and communications performed as part of this role will stay internal to the college – information is given external to the English and maths team, but keeps some degree of privacy as it is not shared outside of vocational leaders and teams.

Internal private: this role relates to the role English and maths leaders play with their own team and in discussions with senior leaders about all matters relating to English and maths. It is used to communicate within the English and maths team, but these communications rarely go beyond the confidentiality of the team.

As leaders and managers of English and maths must switch between and juggle these roles when dealing with students, parents, carers, colleagues, peers, senior leaders, teachers and all other stakeholders, is it really any surprise that there is no dominant structure of leadership within FE English and maths?

Consequently, it is important to consider what leadership and management structures are currently in use. Again, this is not an exhaustive list, as there is such diversity in Further Education that flexibility is vital[18] and many of these models may be used in part or not at all, but the leadership structures in the next section are the most prominent and prevalent models used.

Leaders in English and Maths

Each of these structures has its own strengths and weaknesses, and each has at its heart the student experience and giving students the best possible opportunity

---

18 B. Lenon (2018) *Other People's Children: What Happens to those in the Bottom 50% Academically?* Melton, Woodbridge: John Catt Educational Ltd.

to achieve. This is not to say they will work in all Further Education contexts – again, the diversity in this sector means it is not possible to make blanket statements about leadership structures. With this in mind, let's look at these structures in more detail.

Assistant Principal or Similar Post

It is common in post-16 education for an Assistant Principal to hold account-ability for English and maths. Often, giving responsibility and accountability to such a senior figure in the college can reflect the importance of English and maths in a setting, and identifies English and maths as a priority area which receives much focus (and, potentially, the resources to match).

More often than not, an Assistant Principal is unlikely to have taught English and maths in post-16 education, and this can cause issues with the English and maths practitioner team, who can feel that a lack of specialism will impact decision making (i.e. without specialist knowledge, how can truly informed decisions be made?) This can potentially also impact team morale, as it is unlikely English and maths will be the Assistant Principal's only responsibility and so their time is constantly being split between English and maths and their other responsibilities. As explained above, this lack of accessibility can be dam-aging to teachers' trust in a leader. Monitoring and evaluation of the team also then becomes a challenge and this can further impact staff morale as teachers feel they are professionally stagnating.

Having said this, the role of Assistant Principal inherently brings whole-college responsibility in a host of areas, and this means English and maths is fully promoted as a result[19]. In other words, with an Assistant Principal holding responsibility for English and maths, whole-college changes which benefit English and maths can be made quickly, effectively and with little challenge[20].

In short, there is a leader with the power to alter college policy, strategy and processes to benefit English and maths. The downside is that, though passion-ate and supportive, an Assistant Principal is not a dedicated leader in this area, but spends their time focusing on a range of college-wide priorities.

There are variations below this initial level, with there often being a lead teacher for each subject appointed to look after the day-to-day management of that subject. Though there are a range of titles for this role, 'Curriculum Lead' is often the preferred moniker.

A potential outcome of this leadership model is that consistent results are achieved for GCSE and Functional Skills, but teaching, learning and assessment quality may suffer – if there is no one to consistently monitor, evaluate and sup-port, how do we improve classroom practice? There can also remain a core of students who repeatedly fail to achieve their goals as they are overlooked in preference for those students who are closer to achieving a pass or grade 4[21] – the

---

19 Myatt, *High Challenge, Low Threat.*
20 Greatbatch and Tate, *Teaching, Leadership and Governance.*
21 www.ascl.org.uk/Our-view/Campaigns/The-Forgotten-Third (accessed 11 January 2021).

rationale being that if teachers focus on those who are more likely to pass, achievement figures are guaranteed.

Curriculum Lead/Lead Teacher or Similar Post

A Curriculum Lead (or Lead Teacher) will often take control of the day-to-day management of the English and maths team. This will include completion of English and maths administration, answering queries from a range of stakeholders (from vocational leaders to English and maths staff) and ensuring the overall effectiveness and success of existing processes is consistently achieved on time.

This can be a very challenging role – there is no inherent power attached to the role and vocational leaders and teams can sometimes have to wait for the phone call, meeting or email to come from an Assistant Principal who sits above them in a college hierarchy. There can also be a lot of responsibility attached to the role, and though there is no in-built accountability (which sits with the Assistant Principal), expectations are high nonetheless.

A positive of this structure is that Curriculum Leads or Lead Teachers do have some freedom to shape the English and maths curriculum, assessment methods and styles (to a certain extent), and the nuts and bolts of teaching, learning and assessment with little interference. This model is especially preferable where this freedom is needed – as the author and motivational speaker Simon Sinek states, 'The role of a leader is not to come up with all the great ideas; the role of a leader is to create an environment in which great ideas can happen'[22].

With this role, it can be inferred that the English and maths team has the majority of its processes and strategies embedded and there is little need for wholesale changes (hence responsibility being given to a senior leader, who is unlikely to have the availability to complete change management strategies[23]).

Unlike other leadership roles in English and maths, a Curriculum Lead or Lead Teacher is also likely to have a significant teaching timetable in addition to leadership or management responsibilities. Though this can act as an excellent barometer for the strategies which are being enacted, it can also provide unique workload challenges.

Head of Department or Similar Post

A more traditional leader in the majority of contexts (specifically secondary[24]), this is one of the more popular leadership structures in post-16 English and maths. Lower in the college hierarchy than the Assistant Principal, and a stage

---

22 S. Sinek (2009) *Start with Why: How Great Leaders Inspire Everyone to Take Action.* London and New York: Penguin.

23 K. Thompson (2016) *A Systematic Guide to Change Management.* Great Britain: CreateSpace Publishing.

24 M. Brundrett and I. Terrell, eds (2003) *Learning to Lead in the Secondary School: Becoming an Effective Head of Department.* Abingdon: Routledge.

above a Curriculum Lead or Lead Teacher, an English and maths department head is tasked with the majority of major whole-college decisions in relation to English and maths, and as a result is accountable for the outcomes these decisions drive.

There are certainly benefits to using this leadership style in a college structure: parity with other vocational heads at middle and senior leadership forums is assured, and as decisions sit with one individual, all English and maths stakeholders know where accountability is centred and who they must collaborate with. In addition, clarity of communication and the vision for English and maths is much easier to define as it comes from a single individual, whereas this can sometimes be lost when dealing with an Assistant Principal and potentially multiple Curriculum Leads or Lead Teachers.

Having said this, where there is parity with vocational heads of department, there can be additional challenges. It can be difficult to embed whole-college practices when attempting to overrule a colleague who sits at the same hierarchical level – simply put, one head of department can't overrule another as they are at the same level and doing the same job. Any issues at this level between English and maths and vocational heads must be referred to senior leadership and there is no guarantee that English and maths will be the priority in all contexts[25].

As much as accountability sits with one individual, it is unlikely this individual will lead and manage the department without delegation to a second or deputy head of department. Again, this role can have many titles, including second in department, deputy Head of Department, Curriculum Lead or Lead Teacher (which can become confusing when compared to the above descriptions) or quality co-ordinator. The staff that inhabit these roles are often invaluable sources of advice, support and feedback for any English and maths leader, and the mix of staff who take these roles is as diverse as Further Education itself.

The majority of English and maths heads of department will likely only have a specialism in one area (i.e. either English or maths). As a result, it is vital that there is a complementary force within the team to give guidance and support[26] in the area which is not their specialism. In other words, a head of department specializing in English should probably look for a maths specialist as a deputy (and vice versa). Where this is not possible, it is beneficial to have a deputy head of department who has superior knowledge of the non-specialist area, or an unofficial deputy should be identified to complement the deputy head of department. In other words, a leader with an English specialism and a deputy head of department with an English specialism will probably rely on the same maths specialist to give advice and support in that area.

Monitoring and feedback in this model is much more effective, due to the proximity of staff to the English and maths team, and the inherent knowledge and understanding a specialist will hold. Consistent, high-quality monitoring

---

25 Greatbatch and Tate, *Teaching, Leadership and Governance.*
26 M. Coalter (2018) *Talent Architects: How to Make Your School a Great Place to Work.* Melton, Woodbridge: John Catt Educational Ltd.

(such as regular, low-stakes meetings to set data-driven achievable targets[27]) will also develop an organizational culture and, therefore, outcomes.

The impact of this model will offer a much more holistic approach to consistency and improvement – all areas will be monitored and evaluated at once while bespoke intervention is considered for key areas. There will of course be a focus on improving achievement statistics, but improvement in teaching, learning and assessment will form a key part of this. Improvement will be made *with* teachers[28], not *to* them.

Non-specialist Leadership

Especially interesting in English and maths departments in Further Education, is where a head of department is not a specialist in either English or maths. This provides a range of unique challenges and occurs for a number of reasons.

For many reasons (shortages in specialist staff[29], funding[30], available training[31]), there are leaders in Further Education who hold accountability and responsibility for English and maths but have a specialism in neither English or maths.

For example, due to timetable changes (i.e. a shortage of hours and a willingness to teach on an English or maths programme) a teacher can find themselves teaching English and/or maths, enjoy this experience and slowly develop a full timetable of English and/or maths teaching before moving into leadership.

The primary reason behind this is funding and national staff shortages. For example, if there are 3 hours of Functional Skills maths teaching for which there are no staff, and an engineering lecturer has 3 free hours on their timetable and a history of teaching a maths unit, the solution is obvious. Once having taught Functional Skills, the engineer may find they teach 6 hours the year after, 12 hours the year after that, and then they are suddenly asked to lead the department.

This profile of leader creates a unique set of benefits and challenges for senior leaders, English and maths teachers, vocational teams, vocational teachers and students. Having spent time working in vocational teams, vocational leaders of English and maths teams are then adept at communicating and working collaboratively with vocational staff. Further to this, consistency in embedding English and maths in vocational areas is suddenly much smoother as a result of the leader's fundamental vocational knowledge.

Leaders of this type also have a solid understanding of the inner workings of a Further Education college, which might not be the case with specialists brought in from outside FE (i.e. a leader in secondary making the transition to

27 J. Hattie (2012) *Visible Learning for Teachers: Maximizing Impact on Learning.* Abingdon and New York: Routledge.
28 Buck, *Leadership Matters.*
29 Sibieta, L. (2020). *Teacher Shortages in England: Analysis and Pay Options.* London: Education Policy Institute.
30 Britton, Farquharson and Sibieta, *2019 Annual Report.*
31 Greatbatch and Tate, *Teaching, Leadership and Governance.*

Further Education will likely need an adjustment period – a vocational leader will not).

An additional challenge here can be the investment from English and maths practitioners, who may not feel confident in the knowledge and understanding a non-specialist may exhibit. This can prove a sizeable initial hurdle, especially if significant change management is required. Regardless, there is likely to be a settling in period with transition from a vocational area to English and maths.

The impact of a non-specialist is very much dependent on the buy-in[32] which is generated among vocational staff and English and maths staff, because without this very little positive change can occur[33]. If buy-in is achieved in both teams, improvement in all areas is possible. However, if it is not achieved, with even minimal challenge from teachers or vocational staff, an English and maths team can stagnate, and results, achievement and quality with it. In elite sport as it is in English and maths – if we stand still while everyone else moves forward, we regress[34].

Leadership in Large Centres

With all of this taken into account, there are still additional challenges for Further Education English and maths leaders which are perhaps not seen in other sectors: the size of the college, provision and/or cohort. Whether an English and maths leader is taken from senior or middle management, specialist or non-specialist areas or even recruited from another sector (HE, secondary or even primary), English and maths leadership models can change significantly when student numbers increase.

With GCSE and Functional Skills student numbers ranging from double figures to 3500+ students per qualification[35], leadership models can often change dramatically at inner city colleges with enormous resit cohorts. As a result of this, a head of English and maths can hold a role more comparable to an Assistant Principal at a smaller college, often with each of their deputy heads or curriculum leads overseeing English and maths at a satellite campus which may in itself have a cohort larger than most normal colleges.

This is when a deputy head or Curriculum Lead must make the move from manager to leader, as they are likely to have a cohort of staff working underneath them who will hold responsibility for hundreds of students. It can be difficult to apply consistency here as the majority of teachers may spend little time in the company of their line manager. Consequently, the training and guidance the deputy head receives must be of high quality and the overall strategy

---

32 M.S. Walton (2004) *Generating Buy-in: Mastering the Language of Leadership*. New York: AMACOM.

33 Thompson, *Systematic Guide to Change Management*.

34 S. Madsen (2019) *The Power of Project Leadership: 7 Keys to help you Transform from Project Manager to Project Leader*. London: Kogan Page.

35 www.tes.com/news/how-hold-gcse-exam-3700-students (accessed 11 January 2021).

and vision from the leader of English and maths must be clear, well communicated and open to regular feedback and challenge[36].

The larger the college, the more clarity is needed[37] in how we will achieve our aims, goals and overall vision.

Choosing the Best Leadership Models and Structures

Though there are a range of structures, organizational features and possibilities in the way an English and maths team can be managed and led, there are too many variables at work across the diverse landscape of Further Education to identify one overall 'best' method. Similar to the potential models which are trialled for the placement of English and maths teams (i.e. together in a central location, fragmented and in vocational areas, or a mixture of the two), which is covered in greater detail elsewhere in this book, the quality of leadership is always more about people than systems[38].

Effective leaders can thrive in an ineffective system; however, there are many more challenges when ineffective leaders attempt to thrive in an environment, even when the system is effective[39].

A head of English and maths model, with support from a high-quality deputy head for each subject area, offers the best compromise of accessibility, availability, subject knowledge and whole-college standing, but as detailed above, there are challenges with this model. This is also without discussing the possibility of an ineffective leader holding the role.

Conclusion

Regardless of the structure, the most important element in everything that has been discussed in this chapter is communication. Without it, individuals in any leadership model are powerless and those looking to them for guidance are rudderless. At first, this will manifest as missed deadlines or a lower quality of work than has been requested and expected. If continued, and unchecked, a lack of communication will morph into much more serious challenges: staff

---

36 M. Evans (2019) *Leaders With Substance: An Antidote to Leadership Genericism in Schools*. Melton, Woodbridge: John Catt Educational Ltd.

37 S. Walker (2017) *The Captain Class: A New Theory of Leadership*. New York: Random House.

38 B. Dive (2008) *The Accountable Leader: Developing Effective Leadership through Managerial Accountability*. London and Philadelphia: Kogan Page Publishers.

39 B. Kellerman (2004) *Bad Leadership: What it Is, How it Happens, Why it Matters*. Boston, MA: Harvard Business Press.

absence, recruitment issues[40], a toxic culture, inequality in workload distribution and a lowering of expectations.

The priority for communication is not only to make sure that everyone can be heard, but that they can be heard equally within the confines of the leadership structure, by the relevant leader. This can take the form of collaborative meetings with the entire team, one-to-one informal discussion and even the use of student voice data[41] (the effective use of which can bring great insight).

The most effective leadership structure will ultimately be the model which allows for effective collaborative discussions with vocational teams[42] (as well as English and maths staff) as this is the most effective route to developing college-wide accountability in English and maths. We are all teachers of English and maths, after all.

Summary

- The most effective leadership model is that which promotes existing college strengths.
- To support effective leadership in English and maths, a balance of subject knowledge and whole-college reach must be achieved.
- Leadership and management require different skill sets, but are equally important for English and maths.
- The individual is as important as the role for Further Education English and maths, due to the many challenges and hurdles inherent in English and maths.
- Collaboration is key to success in English and maths leadership.
- The tier beneath the overall leadership of English and maths must be nurtured and guided to fully achieve student potential.

Reflection

- Is regular collaboration occurring between English and maths leaders and vocational leaders?
- Are there systems and processes in place for regular and clear communication within the English and maths team?
- Is best practice being modelled by English and maths leadership?
- What is the purpose of the college English and maths structure?
- Why has this structure been identified as the most effective? Is it effective?

---

40 Coalter, *Talent Architects*.
41 M. Fielding (2006) Leadership, radical student engagement and the necessity of person-centred education, *International Journal of Leadership in Education*, 9(4): 299–313.
42 Greatbatch and Tate, *Teaching, Leadership and Governance*.

3 Student Expectations and Classroom Management

'Erm, excuse me ... can you put your mobile phone away?'
Teachers (the advent of mobile phones – present day)

At some point, all teachers encounter challenging behaviour. Evidenced by everything from a simple lack of awareness to consciously attempting to sabotage lessons, these behaviours happen because of everything from apathy to issues outside of college. Additionally, they can be directed at any number of targets from an individual teacher, topic or unit to other students or even the college itself.

At its worst, challenging behaviour can stop all learning and so it's vital that teachers and leaders are equipped to respond. Having met teachers and leaders from across the country, common complaints are broadly similar:

- mobile phones
- low-level disruption
- lack of equipment (particularly in maths)
- discussing taboo topics
- swearing
- punctuality
- attendance
- bullying
- serious 'events' (fighting, racist or homophobic language etc.)

A further issue is that we too often negatively prioritise and focus on this behaviour and forget to pay attention to the majority of positive, motivated and hard-working students.

So, how should we deal effectively with challenging behaviour? Well, firstly, we need to know the causes – why do students misbehave?

As Susan Wallace details in her book, *Motivating Unwilling Learners in Further Education*, there are fewer motivations behind this behaviour than you might think. Susan identifies these factors as 'The Four Big Demotivators'[1]:

---

1   S. Wallace (2017) *Motivating Unwilling Learners in Further Education: The Key to Improving Behaviour*. London: Bloomsbury.

1 **Fear**

Fear of staff and the questions we ask; fear of failing and what this represents; fear of other students and being perceived as 'different' or weak – this fear can remain well into adulthood[2].

2 **Boredom**

Work isn't challenging enough or is too challenging; topics are uninteresting or poorly presented and lessons are too long or there isn't long left in a lesson – there are a host of reasons why students cite boredom as a reason why they challenge teachers.

3 **Previous negative experience**

Either from school or previous resit involvement, students often show signs of previous negative experiences – removal from classes, detention, suspensions and a plethora of unsuccessful sanctions. Many students in FE English and maths classes also feel they have 'failed'. Which leads us to …

4 **Loss of hope**

'What's the point? I can't do it' – unfortunately, words to this effect are often used in FE classrooms. For a range of reasons, students have simply given up. They feel they will never achieve, so why try? Consequently, they look for distractions and, if none are present, create them.

Addressing Challenging Behaviour

Common throughout education, why aren't these elements always addressed? Some feel teachers are unprepared due to too little focus on classroom management during teacher training[3]. However, this is not the only issue with effective behaviour management.

'The Four Big Demotivators' can just as easily apply to teachers:

1 **Fear**

With students surrounded by their peers, or even physically imposing, some teachers may not feel confident enough to tackle challenging behaviour.

2 **Boredom**

Much less prominent, though still seen, this can take the form of teacher apathy or passive acceptance of usually low-level disruptive behaviour. This is generally caused by a combination of the next two factors.

3 **Previous negative experience**

When teachers try and fail to tackle challenging behaviour, they can feel less motivated to try and tackle it in future. They tried, and nothing changed – which leads us to …

2 M. Myatt (2018) *High Challenge, Low Threat: Finding the Balance.* Melton, Woodbridge: John Catt Educational Ltd.
3 T. Bennett (2010) *The Behaviour Guru.* London: Continuum.

4 **Loss of hope**

'What's the point? It won't change anything' – unfortunately, these words, or words to this effect, echo around staffrooms in FE colleges. Due to lack of impact, or support, some teachers simply give up and accept challenging behaviour.

Having been contacted by FE English and maths teachers from across the country, some feel behaviour issues in English and maths are not taken as seriously as they would be in vocational areas – or worse, minimised if students are vocationally successful: 'I know he's disruptive, but he's a good bricky …'.

This not only undermines English and maths teachers, but it sets a dangerous precedent.

Behaviour Management – Strategies and Approaches

As any doctor will tell you, prevention is better than cure. In light of this, we need to look at how to prevent challenging behaviour, starting with a framework of sanctions, that's complemented by simple and clear rewards (more on this later). However, before, during and after these policies are applied, is what happens in the classroom.

So, how do we promote positive behaviour? As the saying goes, those who fail to prepare, prepare to fail – the first step is preparation.

Though there are many experts on behavioural psychology, the single greatest advice ever imparted on behaviour management comes from the eminent philosopher Patrick Swayze, in the 1989 tour de force, *Roadhouse*. In the seminal masterpiece, Swayze plays a head bouncer charged with turning around the fortunes of a failing bar in America's Deep South.

On visiting the bar, he witnesses the depraved behaviour of the regulars (and staff), before meeting with all staff at closing time to deliver three 'golden rules' to 'fix' the bar. These golden rules, though adapted, are just as applicable in education, and work in any context, with any student:

1 Never underestimate your opponent – expect the unexpected.
2 Take it outside – never start anything in the classroom unless it's absolutely necessary.
3 Be nice.

Loosely translated:

1 Treat students with respect and set high expectations – students will meet the expectations you place on them (whether high or low).
2 Don't ever get drawn into an argument or make challenging behaviour the focus of the lesson.

Table 3.1

Teacher exterior	Communication	Teacher behaviour(s)	Care
How you come across	*Deliver messages*	*Setting expectations*	*Empathy*
• How do my students view me? • How do they perceive me? • What 'vibe' do I give off?	• How do I communicate? • Do I communicate effectively? • What am I saying without saying?	• Do I treat all students with respect? • Do I meet the expectations I set for students? • Am I accountable?	• Do my students trust me? • Am I fair? • Do I show genuine care for my students?

3 *Be nice!* No matter what behaviour is presented, always remember that there are likely to be external motivators for this behaviour[4] and *it's not personal.*

Using these golden rules as our starting point, we must then look at the behaviours they drive. Adapted from Jim Roberson's *The Discipline Coach*[5], Table 3.1 shows four key behaviours and questions we need to reflect on while preparing to promote positive behaviour.

What to Do; When to Do it

So, using Swayze's golden rules and Roberson's reflections, let's see how this translates in the classroom.

Before a Lesson Starts

Always be there before the students. *Always.* Arriving late leaves you unprepared, and students will sense this. Also, make sure you have all resources prepared and ready to use, with the room layout prepared. Few in FE have their own classroom, so the layout may have been rearranged – change this if possible, and if not, ask students to do this on arrival. Make sure there is enough room to comfortably move around the classroom; have a 'disco space' (leave enough space for 'a dance' at the front, middle and back of the classroom). NB: don't actually dance!

Do: arrive before students, be fully prepared, prepare the room for your needs
Don't: be late, be rushed, tolerate another teacher's room plan

---

4 P. Dix (2017) *When the Adults Change, Everything Changes: Seismic Shifts in School Behaviour.* Carmarthen: Crown House Publishing.
5 J. Roberson (2012) *The Discipline Coach.* Carmarthen: Independent Thinking Press.

Setting Expectations

A vital part of classroom culture: let students know as early as possible what is and isn't expected in your classroom by setting the rules collaboratively. Not all rules need to be collaborative (there are college-wide rules after all) and this can take an entire lesson, but you must communicate expectations as clearly, simply and obviously as possible. Keep it simple and remind them that these are the rules for everyone in college (staff included).

Some students may respond with, 'They don't make us do this in other lessons.' If so, don't dwell on it and let them know your primary interest is what happens in your classroom. If possible, observe these same students in vocational lessons to find out for yourself.

Do: create rules together, clearly communicate expectations, discuss 'why' these rules exist

Don't: create rules you can't uphold, compromise standards, be drawn into an argument

Students Arrive and Enter the Classroom

Greet all students positively at the door. Ask them questions about their day, their week, their interests – get to know them! Great classroom management is about creating relationships and routines, and this is your opportunity. Get to know names quickly and make sure you speak to everyone in your class at least once from this point until the end of the lesson. Have books set out where you would like students to sit and have spare equipment with you at the door. If students don't have pens etc. hand them out here – they then enter the room ready to work. Pick your battles – don't sanction for lack of equipment: it immediately creates a negative environment; you may well be the fifth teacher who's sanctioned them that day (leading to an aggressive response).

Have an activity ready for them to complete as soon as they walk in – if you don't have something for them to do, they will find something to do (likely on their phones). Your expectations and standards start here.

Do: greet students warmly and positively, have spare equipment, set tasks for all students, monitor your body language, control the environment

Don't: be tied to your desk or laptop, appear negative, give students too much freedom

Mobile Phones

Asking students to turn phones off on entering the classroom, or a quick reminder of the impact phones have on memory and even brain function[6], can work on some students, but not all. Asking students to hand phones in can work, but it only takes one refusal and then no one will – and, with phones

---

6 J. Firth, J. Torous, B. Stubbs et al. (2019) The 'online brain': how the internet may be changing our cognition, *World Psychiatry*, 18(2): 119–29.

costing up to £1000, why take the risk? Instead, use non-verbal techniques like walking around the class or standing/sitting next to students as you start your lesson. They don't want you to see their phone screens and (when you are circulating) they can't always see where you are so won't take the risk.

For repeat offenders, lightly and deliberately tap on their desk as you pass (signifying you've 'caught' them) and if they still don't comply, talk to them outside or after lessons (more on this later).

Do: remind students of expectations at the start of lessons, remind them of consequences in employment, give students an opportunity to remove their phone
Don't: be drawn into an argument about phones, change focus to mobile phone use during lessons, try and confiscate a phone

Know your Place

Considering the work it takes to be a teacher, be proud of yourself and your role. Be confident in your ability and authority and communicate this. Though friendly, you are not their friend, so don't act like it. Being their friend may placate students in the short term, but they will have little respect for you in the long term, and behaviour and achievement will suffer. Again, set rules, boundaries and expectations and don't blur these lines – be consistent or students will continue to test you.

Do: be friendly, remind students of expectations and rules
Don't: be their friend, stray from expectations, overshare

Groups and Individuals

Challenging behaviour from individuals and groups should always be handled differently. For individuals, the techniques and suggestions in this chapter will serve you well; however, for groups (or even pairs), you must take a different approach. Firstly, divide and conquer. Do not challenge a group – they will feel confident when with peers and probably fear looking weak in front of their peers if they comply. Ask students to switch seats/tables, discreetly remind them of expectations and invite them outside for a brief chat about their behaviour. If they refuse to comply, deliver sanctions after the lesson.

Do: deal with behaviour individually, be discreet, celebrate those who are complying, ignore requests from defiant students
Don't: challenge a large group or pair, be drawn into an argument

Repeated Non-compliance

When non-compliance or defiance happens, it has the potential to destroy learning. Here are a number of effective steps to resolution through restorative discussion[7]:

---

7   Dix, *When the Adults Change, Everything Changes.*

- When defiance first happens, praise the work and contribution of those around defiant students.
- Next, reiterate expectations to everyone – don't single out students (they can thrive on this).
- Continuing defiance? Approach the student, and at desk height, to avoid looking aggressive – quietly and discreetly remind them of expectations then walk away.
- If continuing, ask students to step outside for a quick chat. If they refuse, sanction them at lesson end.
- When outside, ask students to explain why they think you are both there. Remind them of expectations and sanctions if they continue this behaviour, and what they are capable of – leave on a positive note.
- If defiance continues, have one final out-of-class conversation and repeat expectations and sanctions.
- Finally, ignore the defiance as best you can and sanction at lesson end. If this behaviour can't be ignored, ask the student to leave the lesson.
- Follow this up with a relevant tutor or head of department.

Do: be fair, consistent and balanced, reiterate expectations to everyone, be calm, give opportunities for students to improve their behaviour
Don't: threaten, promise impossible sanctions or rewards, lose your cool

Low-level Disruption

Very similar to phone use and repeated non-compliance, try positive reinforcement and continued reminders of expectations. Move around the classroom while you are explaining tasks by buying a presentation controller (a simple remote control to move slides remotely via USB), meaning you can teach while circulating. Again, don't single individuals out, and try non-verbal techniques such as looking at those who are causing the disruption, sitting or standing next to them or even asking them questions about what has been covered so far.

Do: be discreet, repeat expectations, be consistent and fair
Don't: overreact, single students out, make the disruption the focus of the lesson

Continuous or Major Disruption

You have tried a range of strategies: non-verbal techniques, repeating expectations, praising students, changing seating, restorative conversations and a final warning. None of these have been successful. More seriously, a major event may have occurred (severe bullying or violence). Under these circumstances, it may be appropriate to ask a student to leave the classroom for the remainder of the lesson. A last resort: remember that this will permanently damage teacher–student relationships and you will have to put the work in to restore the relationship. This will mean contacting home, the relevant tutor and potentially the head of department. Though it instantly solves issues, it can create many more.

Do: exhaust all other options, be fair, be calm, highlight why a student is being asked to leave

Don't: shout, threaten, remove a student for anything other than a serious behavioural incident

Stay Cool, Calm and Collected

Obvious, but don't scream; don't shout. It's ineffective and gives students the entertainment they may have been trying to trigger. Many students will have seen and heard it all before from parents, carers, siblings, partners and friends so it will have little impact other than to detract from learning.

Do: keep your cool, remember it's only one lesson, use a range of strategies

Don't: lose your temper, shout, threaten

Language and Mindset

Though not everyone agrees with Dweck's Growth Mindset[8] theory, remaining positive and using positive language is vital in an FE setting[9]. Adapt the language you use when in classrooms – students have not 'failed', they have simply not hit their target yet. If we enter classrooms expecting challenging behaviour, we may be part of the problem. Support students to achieve, stay fair and be calm[10] – you are the personification of your classroom. If you are manic, angry and reactive, so too will your students be.

Dealing with challenging behaviour isn't just about responding and confronting it. Teachers are responsible for establishing a positive environment – for promoting positive behaviour.

Rewards and Incentives

Though sanctions will help to promote positive behaviour, again prevention is always better than a cure. With this in mind, students need to know beforehand that positive behaviour will be rewarded. Too often, teachers spend a disproportionate amount of time focusing on challenging students and so we don't give nearly enough time and attention to conscientious, hard-working students who consistently try their best.

---

8   C. Dweck (2015) Carol Dweck revisits the growth mindset, *Education Week*, 35(5): 20–4.

9   Wallace, *Motivating Unwilling Learners*.

10 J. Thom (2020) *A Quiet Education: Challenging the Extrovert Ideal in Schools*. Melton, Woodbridge: John Catt Educational Ltd.

Some teachers will insist that students 'should just work' or that 'passing is a reward' – this won't motivate students. Asking students to give 100 per cent in October because a reward *may* come in April to August won't adequately motivate most students, and, without rewards in the short term, students who *are* motivated will likely do the bare minimum and not much more. It's also very easy to forget that just as we want good behaviour, so do students[11].

To properly motivate students, we have to offer carrots as well as sticks. To motivate students with rewards of any type, there are basic principles that all teachers should follow. Let's look at how (and what) rewards can be offered to prevent challenging behaviour in the first place.

Simplicity

If *consistency* is king, then *simplicity* is prime minister. Any reward, or reward system, should be simple to understand and straightforward to apply. At all times, teachers and students should know what actions will lead to what rewards, and this should be performed consistently. Don't make promises you can't keep, or students won't trust you and challenging behaviours will increase.

Consistency and Clarity

Students should be constantly reminded of the rewards on offer – do this throughout lessons and throughout the year and always follow through with any promised rewards. If you promise a voucher, the student gets the voucher, or all students lose faith in the system. If one student gets a voucher for 100 per cent attendance, all students must get a voucher for 100 per cent attendance or the system fails[12]. It's also important to stay excited and positive about what you are teaching[13]. In contradiction, some evidence suggests rewards work best when more unpredictable[14]. For this, use your judgement.

Flexibility and Familiarity

Reward systems should be flexible for staff *and* students: not all students want the same reward, and not all staff feel comfortable giving the same reward. Also, not all students want to *receive* rewards in the same way. Some want to be celebrated in class and college-wide; others want quiet rewards slipped into exercise books or posted home. Perception among peers is a massive student motivator, so it's important to make sure you know their preferences.

---

11 S. Strickland (2020) *Education Exposed: Leading a School in a Time of Uncertainty.* Melton, Woodbridge: John Catt Educational Ltd.

12 Bennett, *The Behaviour Guru.*

13 M. Pinkett and M. Roberts (2019) *Boys Don't Try? Rethinking Masculinity in Schools.* Abingdon and New York: Routledge.

14 B.F. Skinner (1965) *Science and Human Behavior.* New York: Simon and Schuster.

It sounds simple, but to effectively reward, we must know students' hobbies, interests and personalities. A football-themed reward for a rugby fan (with no interest in football) wastes resources and can weaken teacher–student relationships. Knowing students helps teachers to decide *how* and *when* to reward. Also, students appreciate that you have taken the time and effort to give rewards on their terms.

Chronology

Though it will motivate some, end-of-year rewards won't motivate *all* students. This is why it's important to give rewards at different times. Where possible, rewards can be offered every lesson/week, every half term and every year. 'That's not possible! It will cost too much, take too much time and add more work', I hear you cry. Well, improving behaviour actually cuts workload (no warnings, emails, meetings, phone calls etc. to do), and which would you rather be doing? Also, once routines are established, and rewards bulk bought, rewards become embedded throughout your practice. As for the financial cost ...

Affordability

Students often ask for highly expensive rewards for simple tasks (I was once asked to buy a student an iPad because they had started regularly bringing a pen to lessons). Despite this student's protests, we must remember that rewards don't need to break the bank.

Rewards will take on the value of the importance you give them – if you are passionate about rewards, excited about rewards, students will invest in them, and the opposite is also true. Take the time to build up rewards, to promote them, to discuss their value, and students will invest emotionally and academically.

Equality and Fairness

Like sanctions, we must be fair and equal when giving out rewards. If two students complete all their work in a lesson, but one did so within 10 minutes and did nothing else, while the other worked diligently from start to finish, both would not receive the same reward (student 1 shouldn't receive any reward). Outcomes should be rewarded *after* being balanced against inputs. Put simply, if a student isn't giving their best, no matter what they achieve, they shouldn't be rewarded.

Examples of Rewards

These are our defining principles. But what about examples? Below are a range of examples to use in all classrooms – but remember, rewards will take on the value of the importance you give them. Be enthusiastic about rewards and take liberties with the truth! Convincing a class that a free pen from a conference once belonged to Jay Z will give it more importance than anything you buy!

- **Vocational rewards** – vocational teams will buy the tools and materials they need at the start and throughout the year. However, they will also receive freebies and samples from local and regional companies – tending to be shoved away somewhere in a filing cabinet. Why not ask vocational teams if they have anything that you can offer as a reward in English and maths lessons? A tile cutter, spirit level or scissors can mean the world to a student in relevant classes, and it costs nothing.

- **Stationery** – always a popular option! Often arriving without equipment, giving stationery as a reward will help them and you. A pen, pencil, ruler, rubber or compass is cheap to buy, and after suitably stretching the truth ('it once belonged to the Queen') becomes a much sought-after object. Items such as a journal or maths set can also be used outside of the classroom.

- **Stickers** – Bear with me! It may seem like something for much younger students, but stickers work just as well with all types of learners on all types of courses. Again, give it relevant value, talk up the value and importance, and students will want them. You can even acknowledge the ridiculousness of giving stickers as rewards – this helps build positive relationships.

  'That was an excellent piece of work in our last lesson, Matthew. How do you know it was an excellent piece of work? Because you've got a massive unicorn sticker next to it.'

  Ridiculous. But it works.

- **Vouchers** – if there is a budget in the department, tap into this and offer vouchers where you can. These don't need to be massively expensive, and letting students choose the voucher (within reason) can again help build relationships. As little as £10 a month is sufficient across a cohort and will motivate a surprising number of students. When vouchers are then given and word spreads, more students can be motivated.

No Budget? Try these Rewards

- **A raffle or lottery** – giving regular rewards isn't cost-effective for everyone. So, what do you do when you can't spend? Don't. Setting up a simple raffle system (online, via a simple tracker or teacher planner) delays having to spend while still motivating students. Having given a raffle 'entry' for outstanding work, draw this raffle weekly, monthly, termly or annually and remind students that you value their hard work.

- **Intangibles** – we've already covered the (potentially morally dubious, yet effective) approach of truth stretching ('This is Paul McCartney's ruler'), but humour is a very effective motivator[15]. Regardless of academic achievement, students are education savvy – they know funding is tight, so play on this. Create an in-class in-joke. Offer prizes worth tens or hundreds of thousands of pounds, offer teacher 'points' for performance which are exchanged for Lamborghinis and yachts and then provide IOUs at lesson, week or term end.

---

15 B. Rogers (2002) *Classroom Behaviour*. London: Sage.

'Well done Sarah. Excellent work and definitely worth 15,000 points. Do you want to exchange them for a Ferrari, or roll it over for next week? You want the Ferrari? Fine, but it's parked out of town, so I'll have to bring it next month, okay?'

Ridiculous. But effective.

- **In-lesson rewards** – as discussed in 'The Four Big Demotivators', students are often frightened of being perceived by peers as too eager or as foolish (e.g. answering teacher questions or reading aloud). Use this. Reward excellent work or effort by giving students the option to 'pass' on reading aloud or answering questions. Absolutely pick this up with them later (quietly question them afterwards; ask them to read answers at their desk etc.), but forcing them to do either could potentially embarrass them and harm the teacher–student relationship as well as their confidence. Allowing this small compromise strengthens relationships, and you can slowly build up to students answering questions or reading aloud (once trust is built, start with a word, a sentence, then a paragraph etc.).

- **Communication** – communicate with home or vocational tutors to celebrate a student. A quick call or text home actually moves any potential workload burden to parents/carers, and vocational teachers can pick this up in tutor time. Do this at the start of the week with vocational tutors (giving them a week to mention it) or the end of the week for parents/carers (students can then be rewarded over the weekend). If or when students are rewarded, they will know you were the cause and positive relationships will develop. For a small expense, this can be done via postcard or letter and give students something tangible.

- **Use freebies** – just like the free tools and toys vocational areas are routinely given, use the freebies you are given at training events, conferences, meetings and outside of college as rewards. Key rings, pens, pencils, rubbers, cuddly toys (really) and even USB sticks are all interesting and sought-after rewards. Again, stretch the truth and make this an in-class in-joke – offer the Premier Inn pen with the claim you were given it by Tom Hanks when you attended the 2017 Oscars.

What to Remember with Rewards and Incentives

There is a lot of flexibility with rewards, but the key is making rewards practical, repeatable, functional and cost-effective. They must also be necessary – don't offer students rewards they do not need. They will invest no value in them and won't work for them. Students must need, or be made to think they need, what you are offering.

Also remember that rewards are tools and that these too can have a negative impact if used incorrectly[16]. Make sure that students aren't *only* completing tasks for rewards, or motivation may degrade when rewards are removed[17].

---

16 M. Lepper, D. Greene and R. Nisbett (1973) Undermining children's intrinsic interest with extrinsic reward, *Journal of Personality and Social Psychology*, 28(1): 129–37.

17 D. Didau and N. Rose (2016) *What Every Teacher Needs to Know About … Psychology*. Melton, Woodbridge: John Catt Educational Ltd.

Also, use verbal praise wherever appropriate, but never use this as a tool to manipulate or influence (e.g. 'if you finish your questions, then ...')[18]. Again, students are more savvy than you think and they will see straight through this attempted manipulation, damaging the student–teacher relationship.

End-of-year Awards

In the majority of colleges, end-of-year awards ceremonies are held, with the best and most conscientious students officially rewarded for their efforts and achievements. Too often, English and maths is not represented at these awards. To make sure that English and maths has parity with all other courses and subjects, it must have relevant, comparable awards.

Whether this be Student of the Year, Most Improved Student of the Year, or any other award, we must make sure that students are officially recognised for their efforts. This is the perfect opportunity. It can be difficult to initiate this at times, so an effective method is to have the award sponsored by a local organization or use funding from English and maths budgets to offer a voucher or physical trophy.

Sanctions: A Whole-college Approach

Promoting positive behaviour starts with teachers and students developing strong and respectful relationships[19]. For this we need clear boundaries[20] and expectations. Simply put, if students don't know where the line is (what is and isn't acceptable), they will cross it. To set these boundaries, we need to set expectations as early as possible in classrooms and we need a whole-college policy on rewards and sanctions. To be fully effective, our expectations and the whole-college policy should be:

- succinct and clear
- easily communicated, highlighting expectations for all
- flexible, when needed
- created through collaboration and adhered to
- as focused on rewards as sanctions.

Students can easily exploit a policy which doesn't follow these guidelines, and they will. So, what should a successful college policy look like?

Table 3.2 sets out a policy that is simple to follow which can quickly be adopted by any college.

---

18 Didau and Rose, *What Every Teacher Needs to Know*.
19 B. Rogers (2002) *Teacher Leadership and Behaviour Management*. London: Sage.
20 B.S. Parsonson (2012) Evidence-based classroom management strategies, *Kairaranga*, 13(1): 16–23.

Table 3.2

Stage	Behaviour(s)	Action	Staff to complete/attend	Appeal to:
Stage I Persistent	Persistent low-level issues such as lateness, lack of readiness, phone use, distracting others.	Verbal warning given one-to-one. Warning and action plan confirmed and relevant staff informed (Head of Department, tutor etc.).	Warning completed by subject teacher (vocational or English and maths).	Head of department
Stage II Deliberate	Deliberate or escalating low-level disruption and behaviour detailed.	Written warning given one-to-one. Warning and new action plan confirmed in writing with head of department and tutor informed.	Warning completed by relevant head of department.	Senior leader
Stage III Continued/major	Continuous disruptive behaviour after Stages I and II. Student now moves to a formal disciplinary meeting.	Meeting held. Written confirmation of new action plan and date of review. Progress towards action plan discussed. Potential suspension if satisfactory progress not made.	Meeting chaired by senior leader with attendance from parent/guardian/employer, head of department and pastoral rep.	Principal
Stage IV Final	Final stage. Major incident. Deteriorating behaviour since Stage III, or action plan(s) not satisfactorily completed.	Student (and representative) attend final meeting with Assistant Principal and/or Principal. Outcome via letter with verbal confirmation of either renewed action plan, suspension or withdrawal.	Meeting chaired by senior leader and/or Principal with attendance from parent/guardian.	Governors

As the stages of the policy are completed, all staff should be informed or 'tagged' via the college's in-house system (ProMonitor etc.), which should be the primary method of communicating and updating staff (not email).

To complement this process, all staff should also receive training in applying each stage, with templates of all documents (verbal/written warning paperwork etc.) circulated and modelled. With a consistent approach, students quickly understand when and how sanctions will be applied.

Though implementation of this policy will take buy-in from senior leaders, it can have a transformational effect on English and maths behaviours, outcomes and achievement. Common arguments against implementing it are that it will simply take too much time to complete relevant notes on college systems or to hold meetings. If this is the case, surely this is a tacit admission that there are issues with challenging behaviour, and that a functional, coherent system is more needed than ever?

Again, to generate buy-in from senior leaders, it is worth communicating that this system actually transfers some of the workload created by dealing with behaviour to English and maths. It empowers staff, and reiterates that English and maths staff are able to apply consequences. Though there is additional workload in the beginning, once the system is up and running, and a minority of students have fallen foul of it, all students will know the boundaries they must abide by, and challenging behaviour will lessen.

Summary

- Outline expectations, rewards and sanctions at the earliest opportunity and continue to do this when appropriate.
- Use a range of approaches to develop strong teacher–student relationships.
- Remain fair, treat students equally and 'wipe the slate' when lessons finish.
- Remember the motivators for challenging behaviour in all interactions.
- Work *with* vocational teams to develop positive behaviour.
- Say 'thank you' instead of 'please' at the end of a request. 'Thank you' suggests compliance is guaranteed – 'please' suggests there is an option to say no.
- Be nice.
- Keep calm and carry on.

Reflection

- How are relationships being built in each classroom?
- What choices are students given during and around their learning?
- Could any behaviour/classroom management issues be resolved before teaching or outside of the lesson?
- How am I perceived by students? Why? Does this need to change?
- Are high-quality behaviours modelled in all areas of a student's journey? What can I do to make sure they are?

4   Student Motivation

'I don't care. I've already got a job working for my uncle; I'm never going to use English and maths.'

16-year-old catering student (2018)

Having failed to achieve the required grade (often on multiple occasions), students can be apathetic towards academia in general (let alone English and maths). This leads to apparently inevitable challenging behaviour, non-attendance and a lack of engagement at all levels of English and maths in Further Education.

With up to 60 per cent of students who sit the exam going on to receive a lower grade than at their previous attempt[1], statistics suggest that the longer students continue to resit, the less chance they have of achieving their desired grade; therefore, it becomes more challenging to motivate them.

This issue is further exacerbated by statements made before students even reach Further Education. Variations on the following statements are regularly made by teachers during KS4:

1. 'If you don't get a grade 4 in English or maths, you won't be able to go to college.'
2. 'You need to get a grade 4 in Y11 because you won't get it at college if you don't get it at school.'

These statements are problematic for many reasons. Firstly, statement 1 simply isn't true in many cases. Like no other sector, Further Education teachers and leaders work to offer opportunities to all students from all backgrounds. In FE, every student is welcome and the hard work of college staff is testament to that.

While seen as a highly trustworthy profession[2], the issue then is that when the above statements are proven untrue, student trust begins to evaporate. With this statement eroding trust from the time it is uttered to the time students enrol, many start college with a 'trust deficit', potentially leaving them feeling vulnerable in future English and maths lessons[3]. This 'trust deficit' then leads to

1. www.cambridgeassessment.org.uk/Images/476535-which-students-benefit-from-re-taking-mathematics-and-english-gcses-post-16-.pdf (accessed 11 January 2021).
2. CV-Library (2019) *The 10 least and most trusted professions in the UK*. Available at: www.cv-library.co.uk/recruitment-insight/10-least-trusted-professions-uk/ (accessed 11 January 2021).
3. A.S. Bryk and B. Schneider (2003) Trust in schools: a core resource for school reform, *Educational Leadership*, 60(6): 40–5.

an active distrust in teachers and increases the amount of work needed to rehabilitate students into trusting teachers.

Put simply, having seen these statements constantly proven wrong, a counter-narrative formulates with students: 'My Y11 English and maths teachers either lied to me or they were wrong so there's now a chance that all teachers could be wrong or lying to me.'

Statement 2 presents additional problems. As anyone witnessing results day will tell you, when students don't achieve, they truly are devastated. This can lead to students becoming wary of exposing themselves to potential future failure and they can emotionally and cognitively[4] disengage as a result. Add what students perceive as a lack of faith from teachers, and after hearing these statements, students can easily slip into one of the 'Four Big Demotivators'[5] – loss of hope. This then translates into statements such as, 'I don't care if I fail' – a phrase which is more about protecting self-esteem than anything to do with English and maths.

So, how do we motivate our learners? Many of the students we encounter in FE display challenging behaviour due to their previous negative experiences. Therefore, we must build respectful and trusting relationships between and with students[6]. Research suggests that teachers who believe relationships are a key ingredient in promoting positive behaviour are more likely to receive greater trust from students with a history of behaviour issues[7].

The issue here is that trust is difficult to gain and easily lost. Trust can be lost after any number of changes, for example moving from KS4 to FE, or moving from one teacher to another. It also suggests that after distrust develops, any subsequent incident is seen through a lens of distrust[8]. With many students experiencing challenges before reaching Further Education[9], trust can be the difference between teachers making an impact or continued apathy.

Mike Bottery, Emeritus Professor of Education at the University of Hull, has suggested that trust can be developed in three different ways[10]:

4   P.T. Balwant (2018) The meaning of student engagement and disengagement in the classroom context: lessons from organisational behaviour, *Journal of Further and Higher Education*, 42(3): 389–401.
5   S. Wallace (2017) *Motivating Unwilling Learners in Further Education: The Key to Improving Behaviour.* London: Bloomsbury.
6   C. Bergin and D. Bergin (2009) Attachment in the classroom, *Educational Psychology Review*, 21(2): 141–70.
7   A. Gregory and M.B. Ripski (2008) Adolescent trust in teachers: implications for behavior in the high school classroom, *School Psychology Review*, 37(3): 337–53.
8   K.S. Louis (2003) Trust and improvement in schools. Paper presented at BELMAS annual conference, Milton Keynes, October.
9   B. Lenon (2018) *Other People's Children: What Happens to those in the Bottom 50% Academically?* Melton, Woodbridge: John Catt Educational Ltd.
10 M. Bottery (2004) Trust: its importance for educators, *Management in Education*, 18(5): 6–10.

Table 4.1

Trust principles	What this means in FE
1 Sharing agreed principles and priorities	An agreement between teacher and student that ensures: • The goal of the teacher is to support student achievement • Teacher priority is plugging gaps and providing exam preparation • Teacher and student will work to the best of their ability
2 Individual integrity	• To simplify, each (teacher and student) will stay within agreed rules • This requires equality and reliability on each side
3 The demonstration of competence	• The requirement that teachers are perceived as experts at all times • Teachers model professionalism • Sharing of feedback to help students feel competent in their studies (if students think they are failing, they will emotionally withdraw)

1   Sharing agreed principles and priorities
2   Individual integrity
3   The demonstration of competence

But how does this translate into FE English and maths? Well, let's add more detail to these points – see Table 4.1.

With the tools and strategies in Chapter 3 helping to build a foundation of trust, we need to go further to motivate all students; however, to develop trust and high-quality relationships, we need to use strategies which develop aspirations[11]. The strategies in this chapter look to do that and also add additional tools for managing challenging behaviour, and will empower both students and teachers[12].

With that in mind, let's get to it.

Contextualising Resources

Often pinpointed as a universal remedy in FE English and maths, contextualising resources can certainly make an impact. For the uninitiated, this usually means basing English and maths resources around vocational course topics. In English, this could mean analysing a health and safety extract when teaching

---

11   S. Blandford (2017) *Born to Fail?: Social Mobility: A Working Class View*. Melton, Woodbridge: John Catt Educational Ltd.
12   J. Davison and J. Moss, eds (2002) *Issues in English Teaching*. Abingdon: Routledge.

engineering students, or in maths using hair dyeing as a basis to teach ratio to hairdressers.

When studying these topics in English and/or maths in isolation, students can struggle with the knowledge, skills and topics being taught. However, if framed around students' vocational programmes, student engagement improves, as does the likelihood of effective and authentic modelling[13] and more effective education-to-industry transition[14]. Another benefit is the necessary collaboration between English and maths teams and vocational teams, as working collaboratively gives further insight to all areas of a student's experience.

A highly popular form of contextualisation is project-led learning as it asks students to complete projects around vocational topics by using English and/or maths skills. This type of activity is easily replicated once the initial resources have been created (in collaboration). For example:

- Budgeting in healthcare – students are tasked with creating a balanced budget for a care home (using maths skills)
- Report writing – health and safety report writing in construction, engineering, automotive etc. (using English skills)
- Creating promotional materials – a brochure for travel and tourism or a social media campaign for a new gym (English)
- Business planning for a new salon or restaurant (budget, investment, expected turnover/profit, staff salaries etc.) (maths)
- Completing logistical projects for building a new stadium or hotel – capacity, resources and building materials required, timescales etc. (English and maths)

Though highly effective, this can prove difficult due to the workload required (i.e. collaborating with vocational teams and creating resources around a teacher's non-specialist subject etc.). To cut workload, this can also be done without the need to create mounds of resources by using contextualised learning.

Contextualised Learning

Very similar to contextualised resources, but without the need for lots of bespoke resources. This approach centres around giving students relevant English and maths examples which occur in their day-to-day lives and then comparing the skills used to the skills they need to use in the classroom. Below are two simple examples which can be used in any classroom:

---

13 T. Sherrington (2019) *Rosenshine's Principles in Action*. Melton, Woodbridge: John Catt Educational Ltd.
14 B. Harreveld and M. Singh (2009) Contextualising learning at the education–training–work interface, *Education and Training*, 51(2): 92–107.

1 *By the age of 10 years old (or even younger), you can independently cross a road near where you live. To do this, you gauge the speed of every car and pedestrian within an approximate distance (which you also estimate), estimate weather conditions, your own speed, any changes in direction or speed of cars/pedestrians and incorporate variables such as overtaking people, changes to terrain (potholes, kerbs, obstacles) and do all of this while concentrating on tasks such as chatting to friends or checking your phone. You do all of these highly complex calculations, successfully, within a fraction of a second. If you can do all of this at the age of 10, you can 'do' long division.*

2 *You're at a cafe with some friends. While chatting about a film you saw recently, you realise your friend has not seen it. Using your phone, you search for the main actor's Instagram profile and, as you scroll through Instagram, you notice a picture of them in pyjamas, with tissues, and the caption, 'Wish I was at the party now!' You show your friend the picture and discuss the actor's condition. During this conversation, you have used emotional intelligence to identify that your friend is interested in the film, inference and deduction to identify that the actor is ill, and then communicated all of this to your friend (while also analysing their reactions and responding). If you can do all of this in a couple of minutes, you can ace a GCSE English language exam.*

Usually, teachers use examples like mortgages, car payments, the price of holidays etc. to contextualise learning. Though effective, and students are often motivated by these topics, for some these life events are inaccessible. To truly motivate, students must realise that they already have these skills and that they are using them[15].

We must also remember that, as much as contextualisation engages and motivates, there will come a time when we have to return to lesson content, and students can then revert to their original state. Simply put, it's great to base an algebra lesson around going on holiday, but when students realise they still have to complete algebra tasks, they may lose motivation[16]. The point here is to always remember that as much as we want to engage students, well-paced, solid teaching is still required, regardless of content.

The Benefits of English and Maths

Regularly used in classrooms up and down the country, listing English and maths' benefits can have an enormous impact on motivation and can easily link to student aspirations. Statements which are usually used to motivate are similar to this:

---

15 D. Didau and N. Rose (2016) *What Every Teacher Needs to Know About … Psychology.* Melton, Woodbridge: John Catt Educational Ltd.

16 M. Pinkett and M. Roberts (2019) *Boys Don't Try? Rethinking Masculinity in Schools.* Abingdon and New York: Routledge.

'If you get a grade 4 in your English and maths GCSEs, you'll get a better job and make more money.'

Convincing, to an extent, but the issue with this statement is that it isn't linked to any concrete outcome. To make this statement more effective, we need to engage statistics in order to make these outcomes more tangible:

- Good maths skills (and a relevant qualification) can add as much as £2100 to annual earnings[17].
- The same is true of good reading skills[18].
- Government research shows that achieving a grade 4 or above in both GCSE English and maths can add up to £80k to a student's lifetime earnings[19].
- Getting good grades in English and maths significantly increases the likelihood of gaining a university qualification, which adds up to £100k more in lifetime earnings[20].
- Higher literacy and numeracy levels have been linked to better health and longer lifespans[21].

Hopefully, these statistics will resonate with students, and they can even be used as a starting point to discuss the generic topics, for instance how students would spend their additional earnings.

Growth Mindset and the Power of High Expectations

The old classic. There are those who swear by growth mindset and also those who see it as pseudoscience. Growth mindset theory states that skills and abilities can be developed through hard work and consistency, and that the skills and abilities people are born with are a starting point not an end point. Developed and popularised by Carole Dweck, she maintains that a growth mindset is vital to develop resilience and to achieve notable accomplishments[22]. Whether

---

17 www.telegraph.co.uk/finance/personalfinance/9918813/Maths-skills-add-2100-to-your-salary.html (accessed 11 January 2021).
18 C. Crawford and J. Cribb (2015) *The Link between Childhood Reading Skills and Adult Outcomes: Analysis of a Cohort of British Children.* IFS Briefing Note BN169. London: Institute for Fiscal Studies.
19 www.gov.uk/government/news/school-success-adds-140000-to-wages-research-reveals (accessed 11 January 2021).
20 www.channel4.com/news/factcheck/do-graduates-earn-100000-more-than-non-graduates (accessed 11 January 2021).
21 L. Gilbert, A. Teravainen, A. Clark and S. Shaw (2018) *Literacy and Life Expectancy: An Evidence Review Exploring the Link between Literacy and Life Expectancy in England through Health and Socioeconomic Factors.* London: National Literacy Trust.
22 C. Dweck (2015) Carol Dweck revisits the growth mindset, *Education Week*, 35(5): 20–4.

teachers believe in this or not, it is vital that we communicate the basic principles of growth mindset to students – we must let them know that achievement is linked to effort, and that with enough consistent hard work it is a matter of *when* and not *if* they achieve.

Additionally, we must have high expectations. It is terrifying to hear teachers say they won't set certain work for certain students because 'they won't be able to do it'. If you think they won't be able to do it, break it down, streamline tasks, give additional support or time for tasks. Derived from a study by Rosenthal and Jacobson, the *Pygmalion* (or Rosenthal) *effect*[23] has shown that high expectations lead to improved achievement and, conversely, there is a *Golem effect*: lower expectations lead to weaker achievement. In other words, the expectations you place on your students can directly impact their performance; students will meet your expectations.

Embedding English and Maths College-wide

Though there is more on this later in the book, embedding English and maths college-wide is a key motivational tool. From simply asking for continued promotion and verbal support of English and maths, to asking vocational teams to use resources which are used in English and maths classes, showing solidarity with English and maths teachers is a simple and effective method of using Bottery's principles for building trust[24] (sharing agreed principles/priorities, individual integrity and demonstrating competence).

As previously mentioned, offering English and maths continuing professional development (CPD) to vocational tutors and leaders also further develops the impact of embedding English and maths and helps vocational teams to communicate its importance by using vocational and contextually relevant examples.

Motivating Introverts

When reading this chapter, there is likely to be a specific *type* of learner that teachers think about (and hope to motivate): apathetic towards academia, potentially displaying challenging behaviour, lots of potential (though rarely used) and generally quite confident (which presents additional issues). With consistency, there are many strategies which will have an impact on these students. But what about those who are quieter, less confident, or introverts?

When motivating students, it is important to remember that classrooms are full of students who exist somewhere along what Jamie Thom calls the

---

23 R. Rosenthal and L. Jacobson (1992) *Pygmalion in the Classroom: Teacher Expectation and Pupils' Intellectual Development*, newly expanded edn. Carmarthen: Crown House Publishing.

24 Bottery, Trust.

introvert–extrovert continuum[25]. There are students who can't be stopped when in discussion with friends, but spend entire academic years in silence. We must motivate them too. As Jamie details in his book *A Quiet Education*, there is often a stigma around quiet students, and it can be difficult for them to express themselves as a result. So, we need to plan tasks which boost their self-esteem and give them opportunities to shine.

For example, give introverts solo tasks to complete: they can work best individually – give them the space to do this. Whether in lessons, through homework or through remote/distance learning opportunities, it is important we recognise introverts on their own terms. With this in mind, reward and shine a spotlight on introverts as discreetly as possible. Assigning tasks which require attention to detail can help (for example, tasks such as planning, organizing and problem solving can be very effective) and tasks such as silent debates are excellent for this. To create a silent debate, students are given a question or topic to discuss, but they can only give opinions by writing them on a large piece of paper (which sits in the middle of a table). This means all students give their opinion without fear of being interrupted or intimidated.

Structured, timed tasks are also enormously effective in helping introverted students to feel like key members of the group.

We must remember that all of our students are unique, and introverts are no different. To motivate introverts (just as any other student), discreetly talk to them. Ask them what would make them comfortable in your class – take the time, and you'll reap the rewards.

Motivating Extroverts

Though motivating introverted students provides unique challenges, managing and motivating extroverted students can be more problematic. Unmotivated extroverts have the capability to distract scores of students and, coupled with challenging behaviour, can potentially sabotage learning.

A step towards motivating extroverted students can be to give them additional responsibility in the classroom. This doesn't necessarily need to be a massive responsibility. For example, questioning students while an extroverted student writes notes for each answer on the whiteboard can be enormously empowering. The extroverted student receives attention, while on task, and students become more engaged as they observe the extrovert in an unfamiliar role (at the front of the class). Even, turning this on its head, asking the extrovert to write notes, can make introverted students feel more comfortable as their more confident peers are engaged with tasks.

Other examples include asking extroverts to question other students (with pre-agreed questions) or using hot-seating activities (giving a student the role of a character with others questioning them). Even showing that you value

25 J. Thom (2020) *A Quiet Education: Challenging the Extrovert Ideal in Schools*. Melton, Woodbridge: John Catt Educational Ltd.

their opinion can help to form a meaningful relationship between teacher and extrovert student, and this will help to win over peer groups.

Extroverts can also thrive from working under pressure – setting time-sensitive tasks (while giving introverts the space they need) to challenge extroverts will motivate them to want to succeed. It can also be beneficial to give extroverts greater flexibility and freedom in their work. Where introverts can enjoy structure, extroverts often enjoy being in control – give them this opportunity. However, it is wise to keep all of these tasks highly structured and timed to mitigate against challenging behavior.

Links to Employment and Careers

Loosely tied to contextualisation, this is a great way to show students what they can achieve with the relevant English and maths skills. In collaboration with vocational teams, and using local, regional and national industry, contacting leading figures and giving them the opportunity to speak about how English and maths have aided their success can work wonders. This is also even easier to facilitate if done remotely. For example, a former student who now runs his own company can speak to current students in the same field and detail how he achieved his success and how English and maths skills created a valuable road map to success. This also helps students to perceive English and maths in a completely different light, develops shared priorities and showcases the competence of English and maths teachers. Doing this with active servicemen and women, professional athletes and nationally successful tradespeople will have a similar impact.

To have a truly widespread impact on students, professionals should have links to individuals, careers or projects with which students are already familiar. As a result, they will be viewed with greater integrity (and by extension, so will the college, the vocational teachers and English and maths staff).

Educational Trips

Many will read this and focus on the challenges: the paperwork, insurance, staffing and permission issues (not to mention the cost). All completely understandable. However, with the potential to produce an enormous impact, a trip lasting just a few hours can be enormously beneficial.

When attending a workshop on motivating disengaged students, I was fortunate to hear a fantastic example of the simple way this can be achieved[26]. The speaker, an Assistant Headteacher, told a story about a discussion he had with a student about why he always wore a suit. The teacher answered that wearing a suit made him feel more confident, and this confidence made him better at his

---

26 J. Roberson (2019) Strategies for engaging students. Paper presented at the mE+ Conference, Middlesbrough, February.

job. The student replied that he'd never worn a suit and thought he never would. Obviously saddened by this, the teacher organised a trip to a fashion outlet a few weeks later and took the entire class.

Spending a few hours in the store, students tried on every suit they could. For many, it was the first time they had done anything like this and the experience built solid foundations between teacher and students. It was an example to students that they could achieve anything, and they became more engaged as a result. The teacher and his students then more visibly shared priorities; the teacher appeared highly competent and the teacher's integrity was showcased.

To do this in an FE setting, make links with local businesses and business people, and local and regional industry – visit them with English and maths as the focus. Discuss the importance of English and maths with staff, show students the importance and relevance of the subjects, and these targeted and personalised opportunities will be rewarded with engagement[27].

Help Students Help Themselves

As teachers, we are constantly telling students that English and maths are vital to successful careers. We model this in classrooms every day, so why don't we go further? With minimal effort, it is possible to create bespoke workshops to support students with everyday English and maths challenges, instantly contextualising English and maths and also supporting students to make informed and considered choices.

For a limited time each week, teachers can offer support with CVs, application forms (for any number of contexts: an application for the armed forces, for a job, for benefits etc.), help with car finance, credit or store cards (though obviously with heavy caveats!) or discuss how mortgages work to help students in the years to come. Obviously, there are potential safeguarding issues here, but this can facilitate better communication and relationships with parents/carers. These sessions can be held as starter activities, finishing tasks or additional sessions (anywhere from 5 minutes to an hour). With so much provision moving online, these sessions can also be held remotely or online with relative ease.

It gives teachers excellent opportunities to build relationships, discuss student interests (and concerns) and then plan lessons around these topics.

Offer Choices

Many students present challenging behaviour or a lack of engagement in FE simply because they feel they have outgrown the teacher–student model (with

---

27 C. Fuller and T. Macfadyen (2012) 'What with your grades?' Students' motivation for and experiences of vocational courses in Further Education, *Journal of Vocational Education & Training*, 64(1): 87–101.

the teacher in charge, and the student subservient). You can see their point – at 16 or 17, they have much more freedom than they did in school, and so students can feel as though they should be treated as adults[28]. Research suggests challenging behaviour is more likely to develop in students who view themselves as older[29], so we must give students choices.

From a vote on topics or extracts, to the focus of a lesson, there are many ways this can happen. Even with just a simple reading exercise, there are a number of ways choice can be provided:

- Do you want to read first or last?
- Do you want to read a full paragraph or X number of sentences?
- Do you want to read it now or look at the task first?
- Do you want to identify key words with a highlighter or underline them?

These suggestions are simple and easily applied, and as students feel they are being respected (as their opinion is canvassed), engagement follows.

Low-stakes Journals

Erin Gruwell was a teacher in 1990s Los Angeles who achieved remarkable results with disengaged students against a backdrop of gangs, violence and drugs. But how did she help her students to achieve when few gave them a chance? Low-stakes journals. On realizing she knew very little about her students' lives, she gave them blank journals and asked them to write about any topic they liked for a short time each lesson. Initially reluctant, students eventually got involved and began to further engage with lessons and with Gruwell.

There is obviously more to the strategies Gruwell tried (and I would urge you to read her story[30]), but low-stakes journals are a cost-effective way to build relationships with minimal workload. Teachers read student journals but never leave feedback, and as a result, students take more personal risks when writing[31]. This then offers opportunities to get to know students better than we normally can in the time we have with them.

Again, it is difficult at first to ask students to write in journals, but initial modelling and a range of topics to inspire them will help. Once students engage with the journals, research has shown that short writing tasks based around a

28 N.L. Galambos and L.C. Tilton-Weaver (2000) Adolescents' psychosocial maturity, problem behavior, and subjective age: in search of the adultoid, *Applied Developmental Science*, 4(4): 178–92.

29 A.M. Hubley and R.G. Arim (2012) Subjective age in early adolescence: relationships with chronological age, pubertal timing, desired age, and problem behaviors, *Journal of Adolescence*, 35(2): 357–66.

30 E. Gruwell (2007) *The Freedom Writers Diary: How a Teacher and 150 Teens Used Writing to Change Themselves and the World Around Them*. New York: Broadway Books.

31 D. Foster (2015) Private journals versus public blogs: the impact of peer readership on low-stakes reflective writing, *Teaching Sociology*, 43(2): 104–14.

student's personal values (and why these values are important to them) can improve achievement by up to 25 per cent[32].

Giving Additional Support

There are many strategies in this chapter which will inspire and support students to engage in English and maths; however, giving additional support is potentially the most effective. For obvious reasons, personalised, flexible interventions allow teachers to focus on immediate student needs and can also help students to develop resilience (which is consistently linked to better outcomes[33,34]). Generally low cost[35], this doesn't have to be a long-term solution, and it can be used to plug gaps in knowledge before reintroducing students to their original classes.

Students often show greater engagement in these sessions as they are a much more suitable environment for breaking down the complex barriers many students need to overcome in FE[36]. Also, students in FE often view themselves as ineffective learners[37] and intervention gives them the time and space to develop these skills. This support can come in the form of one-to-one or small group intervention or as a semi-regular meeting to discuss progress in English and maths and what further support may be required.

Tap into Peer Groups

Whether targeting individual students or whole groups, motivating students is more effectively achieved when harnessing the power of peer groups[38]. Motivating an individual student can be much more difficult if your message or overall goal is at odds with the message coming from the student's friends. As a result, it is important that we incorporate this aspect of the classroom

32 S. Hume, F. O'Reilly, B. Groot et al. (2018) *Improving Engagement and Attainment in Maths and English Courses: Insights from Behavioural Research.* London: DfE.
33 A.L. Duckworth, C. Peterson, M.D. Matthews and D.R. Kelly (2007) Grit: perseverance and passion for long-term goals, *Journal of Personality and Social Psychology*, 92(6): 1087–101.
34 A.L. Duckworth, D. Weir, E. Tsukayama and D. Kwok (2012) Who does well in life? Conscientious adults excel in both objective and subjective success, *Frontiers in Psychology*, 3: 356, doi: 10.3389/fpsyg.2012.00356.
35 Audit Commission (2010) *Against the Odds: Re-engaging Young People in Education, Employment or Training.* London: Audit Commission.
36 K. Kettlewell, C. Southcott, E. Stevens and T. McCrone (2012) *Engaging the Disengaged.* Slough: National Foundation for Educational Research.
37 S. Hume, F. O'Reilly, B. Groot et al. (2018) *Retention and Success in Maths and English: A Practitioner Guide to Applying Behavioural Insights.* London: DfE and Behavioural Insights Team.
38 Hume, O'Reilly, Groot et al., *Improving Engagement and Attainment in Maths and English Courses.*

dynamic into our plans, as without the support of their peer groups, previously disengaged students can face pressure to revert to their previous behaviour.

Though not always easy, there are some simple strategies which can be used to make peer groups active collaborators in motivating even the most disengaged student. Firstly, identify a core group of disengaged learners who you will focus on attempting to motivate. Next identify their friends and the peer groups in which they socialise. Praise and reward the positive actions and behaviours from these individuals, support them in vocational sessions if you can, discuss interests and hobbies with them at the start or end of lessons and get to know them and, slowly but surely, the dynamic of the group will change. It is very likely the core of disengaged students in this peer group will begin to engage and at times this can have the impact of changing whole-class behaviour.

Tied to behaviour and classroom management, it is vital that you remain fair with these students as they will likely pounce on any inconsistency or inequality and use this as proof that their teachers lack integrity (which then gives them motivation to disengage). Take away the reasons for disengagement, and students will have little choice but to engage.

Keep Lessons Relevant, Well Paced and Structured

Though all of the above strategies and techniques (and those detailed in Chapter 3) will impact student motivation, it is important to remember that at the foundation of student engagement is good teaching. You will also note the lower case 'g' – there are no discussions of Ofsted gradings here. By 'good teaching', I mean remaining consistent, planning well-paced and relevant lessons with clear structures that students can engage with.

Consistency is vital both in and outside of the classroom, and making sure there is a consistent structure to lessons is very important to building relationships with students and developing trust. As I have previously mentioned, if there is little trust in the student–teacher relationship, it is unlikely students will engage.

Whenever consistency is discussed in this book, it does not mean to constantly do the same thing, but instead to constantly uphold the same standard, expectation or level. Vary topics, timings, questions, activities, feedback methods and other elements of your lessons when you need to. If students tell you that lessons are boring, briefly discuss this and take their suggestions on board.

This is not to say that students should dictate lesson content or style, but (as for vocational teachers) there must be some collaboration as the lessons are ultimately for students and we can assure greater engagement through collaboration.

Conclusion

The approaches in this chapter, like those throughout this book, are intended as tools to be used as and when teachers see fit (as they are described here, or heavily adapted). The one key ingredient which is needed for all of these strategies is teacher resilience. It can be enormously frustrating to be confronted with disengagement on a daily basis, no more so than when seeing the impact this has on the most conscientious students, but we must make sure that we don't give up.

One of the many challenges seen as a result of specification reform in GCSE and Functional Skills (and exam disruptions in 2020 and 2021) is that students achieving a grade 3 or below are exhibiting less trust for practitioners as a result of their prior experiences. We are seeing, and will potentially continue to see, a wave of students in Further Education English and maths who feel let down by the system they have trusted throughout their time in education, and this will impact their motivation, behaviour and attitude when entering Further Education to resit English and/or maths.

Furthermore, students who have already attempted resits in Further Education will suffer a range of emotions – as discussed earlier in this chapter, many students have (at this point) already developed a distrust of academia as they feel it has let them down. This is likely to be further exacerbated due to the impact of Covid-19. With this in mind, it is now more vital than ever that we are able to motivate and support students to succeed, achieve and reach their potential.

Though additional funding and intervention will go some way to closing achievement and attainment gaps, it is clear that we need more than this moving forward. To truly motivate and support our students, we must develop high-quality environments and embed the routines which will lead to success.

Motivating students is about routines and creating a positive and safe culture in the classroom. With these strategies and techniques, we make it abundantly clear that we value our students and we want them to succeed (shared priorities), we are experts in our field (competency) and we are passionate about helping young people (integrity).

Summary

- Contextualise, and use it as a valuable tool, but don't rely solely on contextualisation.
- Use the resources at your disposal whether they be internal or in local, regional or national industry.
- Link learning to the outside world, and visit that world if you can.
- Be creative to reach the most disengaged students – help to support them in the way they want to be supported.
- Give students choices in what and how they learn (when you can).
- High expectations are vital in helping students to aspire.
- Keep going – you are making a difference.

Reflection

- How can I better understand what motivates my students? What do students want?

- Am I modelling best practice in my attitude? Do students see that I am motivated?
- What can I do to make sure students understand expectations?
- What can I do to give students additional choices in lessons?
- How can I more clearly communicate end goals and the 'why' to students?

5 Staff Behaviours and Development

'Do I have to go on this course?'
An English lecturer before a CPD workshop (2019)

'I can't wait for this – there will be so many ideas and practical tips.'
Another English lecturer before the same CPD workshop (2019)

At all levels of education there is a range of discussion about student behaviour and the motivation which drives it (good and bad). As both positive and highly challenging behaviour has a huge impact on student experience, progress and mental health[1], there are also clear links between challenging behaviour, lower academic achievement and safeguarding[2].

What is given less coverage, however, is the impact staff behaviour can have on students. With Further Education funding having seen little increase since 2010[3], and continual professional development less prioritised as a result[4], this chapter will focus on the methods and strategies needed to help English and maths teachers develop their practice and create a positive, reflective culture within English and maths teams.

As the two statements that open this chapter suggest, no two teachers are the same in terms of development, attitude or impact, so it is important that we are able to define the different professional needs that they have.

With such a wide scope, this chapter will be split into three sections: the first section will focus on the causes of some staff behaviours and the motivations for those behaviours; the second will then look at how English and maths teachers can evaluate their own needs, become more reflective and ultimately develop into more effective teachers; and the final section of this chapter is aimed at English and maths leaders and managers.

As discussed elsewhere in this book, there are a range of titles and roles with responsibility for English and maths. From Head of Department, to Curriculum

---

1   Department for Education (2018) *Mental Health and Behaviour in Schools* [Departmental advice]. London: DfE.
2   T. Bennett (2017) *Creating a Culture: How School Leaders Can Optimise Behaviour*. London: DfE.
3   J. Britton, C. Farquharson and L. Sibieta (2019) *2019 Annual Report on Education Spending in England*. London: Institute for Fiscal Studies.
4   D. Greatbatch and S. Tate (2018) *Teaching, Leadership and Governance in Further Education*. London: DfE.

Leads, to Assistant Principal and everything in between, this section offers insight and strategies to best develop teachers within English and maths teams and the approaches needed to make teams and staff more effective.

Section One: Staff Behaviours and Motivations

Like no other educational sector, Further Education draws on all walks of life to create a truly diverse professional body. From those who have spent a lifetime in industry and want to 'give back' or support future tradespeople, to those who have only ever wanted a career in teaching, FE is a rich tapestry of talent.

However, as a result of this mix of experience and backgrounds, consistency can be difficult to achieve and maintain, especially in English and maths. With more and more students resitting[5] (and the challenges associated with this), training needs and opportunities for development can be difficult to identify.

As a result of ever shrinking budgets in Further Education, even when training needs are identified, the pool of CPD options can be small. With minimal additional budget available for regular external CPD, training is regularly split into two categories: in-house and 'one size fits all'.

In-house training tends to be organised by senior leaders, a lead teacher or teaching team, and it consists of pleas for members of staff to voluntarily run sessions based on existing knowledge. At its best, this type of training helps to forge excellent links and facilitates collaboration across the college – making a real impact. However, this type of training can also prove problematic.

Firstly, if quality collaboration already exists, the ideas and strategies shared may already have been covered. Also, if the practice of using in-house training is used too often, there is the possibility that 'the well will run dry' (there is a lack of new volunteers to host workshops or not enough time to develop new innovation). Additionally, there is the risk of inconsistency with this style of CPD[6].

To mitigate this, teachers should attend external training and then roll this out in-house, but as discussed, there are many barriers to this, including funding, teaching commitments and inconsistency during roll-out.

Consequently, colleges can ask CPD speakers or specialists to run in-house training for all staff, with sessions completed in as little as a morning or over several days. Though much more cost-effective (as all staff can attend), rewarding and impactful, this training will likely be 'one size fits all' in approach.

---

5   https://ffteducationdatalab.org.uk/2020/06/gcse-results-2020-a-look-at-the-grades-proposed-by-schools/ (accessed 11 January 2021).

6   C. Whitehouse (2011) *Effective Continuing Professional Development for Teachers.* Manchester: Assessment and Qualifications Alliance.

As with our students, no two teachers have the same strengths, developmental areas or even qualifications[7]. In any training of this nature, there are likely to be teachers attending who are experts on the training topic, as well as novice teachers who need additional trainer support (and don't receive it). An additional side effect can be the resentment felt by some staff who feel they do not need to be there – we've all attended training with a highly experienced teacher who would rather have been marking or planning lessons – and the impact this has on other staff can be profound (and can potentially endanger the impact of the training). Also, research suggests a 'one size fits all approach' is far from the most beneficial, to say the least[8].

This is without even discussing the fact that all training has the potential to be ineffective – whether too focused on theory with too little attention to practical application, or training is simply not contextually relevant. The best training must have the right mixture of both[9] as, if it does not, just as students can lose confidence in teachers who deliver lacklustre lessons, the same can happen with teachers and CPD[10]. This can lead to previously exemplary staff accidentally mimicking stereotypical student complaints: 'What's the point? We never learn anything!'

Eventually, this negativity will have a lasting impact on teacher and team morale – this is why it is important to identify this behaviour in ourselves, in others and in teams and remedy it quickly.

Unfortunately, damaging staff behaviours can be evident in teams for many more reasons than just a lack of high-quality CPD. Challenging behaviour, attendance issues, lack of government investment and feelings of inadequacy in comparison to vocational areas (whether real or imagined) can test the resilience and spirit of even the best staff. All of these challenges are hallmarks of English and maths in the post-16 landscape, and they can take their toll.

Additionally, with the ever changing nature of FE English and maths, simply 'standing still' can be difficult. In the last five years alone there have been curriculum overhauls and reforms in all English and maths qualifications at a majority of levels. This is also without taking into account historical changes like Ofsted's move to replace 'Satisfactory' with 'Requires Improvement' or any number of government reports, reviews or white papers.

Taking all of this into account, it is perhaps understandable that some teachers in FE English and maths do not reach the expectations which are set. If this

7   A. Noyes, D. Dalby and Y. Lavis (2018) *A Survey of Teachers of Mathematics in England's Further Education Colleges: The Mathematics in Further Education Colleges Project: Interim Report*. Nottingham: University of Nottingham.

8   Department for Education (2016) *Standard for Teachers' Professional Development*. London: DfE.

9   B. Clay and D. Weston (2018) *Unleashing Great Teaching: The Secrets to the Most Effective Teacher Development*. Abingdon: Routledge.

10 D. Pedder and V.D. Opfer (2011) Are we realising the full potential of teachers' professional learning in schools in England? Policy issues and recommendations from a national study, *Professional Development in Education*, 37(5): 741–58.

section has described some of the motives behind these negative staff behaviours, then we must now look at how to remedy them.

Section Two: Evaluating Needs, Reflecting and Becoming More Effective

Diagnosing Needs

The first step to developing your own teaching, learning and assessment practice is to identify your own needs. This can be difficult at times, and even cause anxiety, but it is vital that we are able to reflect and identify developmental areas. In diagnosing your own needs, the way in which you receive feedback is absolutely critical. If feedback is too positive, you may come away from a discussion feeling you have nothing to improve. Too negative, and it may be difficult to take the feedback on board, or you may dismiss it due to your own adverse reaction.

However, diagnosing your own needs can be easily and quickly accomplished. Using the following tools, you can receive effective feedback to help you see how you are perceived (which can be vital) and also what your needs are.

Anonymous survey

An excellent method to get effective and efficient feedback: asking colleagues, peers and/or managers to complete an anonymous survey on your skills, strengths and areas for development. This can be a great way to start the reflection process. It can be done as simply as completing a questionnaire (and asking those who complete it to leave it on your desk when you are away from the office) or via online survey websites which some find easier to complete.

As much as you may want to focus on each individual response as you receive it, it is best to collate all of the responses and look at them at the same time so that you can get a more rounded view on how you are seen.

It's good to talk

Often overlooked, another method to receive quality feedback to help you reflect is not dissimilar to asking for survey feedback: have a conversation. Again, this can be done with a peer, a colleague or a middle/senior leader. This does have the potential to be slightly more uncomfortable – after all, you are sitting opposite someone who is explaining your perceived weaknesses – but can be extremely powerful as you have the opportunity to ask questions about the feedback and also discuss potential solutions.

Best completed with an immediate or senior manager, this is likely to be very valuable and can also give you insight into college operations and where you sit within that structure.

Even more often overlooked, have a conversation with teaching/support assistants or non-teaching staff to discuss what they perceive as your areas for development. They see much more teaching than most professionals and should be deeply respected for the role they play[11]. Again, it can be a tough conversation, but it is a fantastic start on the road to identifying your needs. Further still, this practice can be completed with students. It very much should be completed with the right classes (i.e. not those who may have taken a dislike to you for following college procedures), in the right way (keep it anonymous where possible), but can have a massive impact. This can also act as a precursor to any student voice survey and so the feedback can be invaluable.

Me and my shadow

Again, potentially uncomfortable at times, but asking to shadow an immediate or senior manager can be enormously useful in helping with reflection and identifying needs. This aids reflection through two main processes: firstly, there is the potential to identify strengths in others that you would like to exhibit and, secondly, we can sometimes identify weaknesses in others that we would like to avoid exhibiting.

As a result, we can complete this process and have a better understanding of the teacher or leader we would like to be, identify what traits this professional does and doesn't have and then begin the exercise of developing and shedding the relevant skills/traits in ourselves.

This can be done over a full day, a morning or afternoon, or even just some key meetings with agendas around an area of interest to English and maths or teaching, learning and assessment.

A key part of this process is holding a reflective catch-up after shadowing has been completed: What did you learn? What skills have you identified as strengths/areas for development? What are your next steps? Discussing this with a manager or leader is extremely valuable as they are in a position to help you develop. Speak to leaders about this and explain how and why you would like to shadow – leaders recognise the importance of these opportunities, and it will also benefit the college.

Identify department needs

A simple, though slightly more generic approach – what does your department need? What are the skills or areas of knowledge and understanding that are lacking within your department? Again, this can be diagnosed through discussions with leaders and managers, or you can spend time looking at results and data trends over the previous two or three academic years.

If students are performing poorly at the same topics or tasks over a number of years, it is likely the teaching of this area needs refinement or innovation. Be

---

11 M.A. Morehead (1998) Professional behaviors for the beginning teacher, *American Secondary Education*, 26(4): 22–6.

that innovation! Discuss this with your head of department or a senior leader (if you can) – let them know that you are eager to support department weaknesses and help your colleagues. Offering to share the results of any training you attend can also strengthen a case for CPD.

What do your numbers say?

On this theme, why not look at your own data? Are students performing below expectation in any areas? Why? Is this a result of the cohorts you have taught (students who get lots of maths teaching in their vocational areas will likely receive better results in resit maths) or due to areas that you can develop in your own teaching?

If possible, it is also a good idea to compare your areas of weakness to your peers. This is best done anonymously if possible, or you could add this to the discussion with your immediate line manager or a college leader.

Start on a flexible qualification

Though this can come at a financial cost, starting a qualification which facilitates reflection through flexibility can be enormously rewarding. For example, the National Professional Qualifications (in Middle Leader, Senior Leadership and Headship) are all accredited by the Department for Education and are structured to allow for a flexible focus (*you* decide the topic of your final assessment portfolio) and the course provides a range of relevant reading to engage with.

A Masters in Education can be enormously beneficial as well. Though expensive, this will facilitate some excellent collaborations and also allow engagement with a range of relevant reading. As neither of these routes require an immediate decision on an assessment focus, there is time here to use the reflective tools they employ to make a decision on your areas of development.

With funding available for qualifications (and qualifications like this) through bursaries, external funding or grants, this route can provide excellent opportunities for reflection. Again, highlight with leaders the benefits this will have for the college and for students in the immediate future – link this to outcomes and potential improvements to achievement to strengthen your case.

I Know My Needs – What Next?

Whether using the ideas in the previous section as tools to identify your development needs, or you already know what you want/need to develop, the next stage is to identify how you will do this. It is important to start thinking about how you will address these developmental areas and over what timescales.

The first stage, however, is to decide if you want to see direct or indirect improvement[12]. Outlined in the Department for Education's standards for teach-

---

12 Department for Education, *Standard for Teachers' Professional Development.*

ers' professional development, direct improvement is any action or training which will directly and immediately impact student outcomes or achievement. Conversely, indirect improvement focuses on enhancing the processes around these improvements (administration, the running of the college etc.).

When this decision has been made, it's time to choose the right CPD for you. But what options are there? Let's take a look.

Need to read

With so much literature on professional development, teaching and pedagogy, it can be difficult to know where to start at times. Thankfully, having bought this book, you have proven yourself to be a connoisseur! In all seriousness, firstly, try to identify the topic or area that you feel will make the biggest impact on your practice. Then make sure you have a genuine *interest* in this area. If you aren't interested in the reading, it won't get done.

Keep a broad base here – read books, blogs, articles, websites, magazines, pamphlets, government documents and anything else you feel is relevant. Sites such as Twitter and LinkedIn or apps such as Teacher Tapp (where thousands of teachers answer three or four questions each day with results collated and shared the following day) can be wonderful tools to help you to identify high-quality literature.

Action research

If you want to engage with academic literature without completing a qualification, you could consider starting an action research project[13]. For those who have not encountered action research, it can develop along these rough guidelines (though obviously this is not an exhaustive list)[14]:

1 Choose a focus – what do you want to improve or develop?
2 Check the theory – what does the existing research say? What does existing research tell you will be found?
3 Your questions – what questions do you want to be answered as a result of the project? This gives much greater ownership of the project[15]:
4 Collect the data – whether this is through assessment, questionnaire, survey or generated by monitoring attendance etc., collecting accurate and relevant data is vital.
5 Analyse the data – what does the data show? What are the results of your project?

---

13 C. Scutt and S. Harrison, eds (2019) *Teacher CPD: International Trends, Opportunities and Challenges.* London: Chartered College of Teaching.
14 R. Sagor (2000) *Guiding School Improvement with Action Research: ASCD.* Alexandria, VA: ASCD.
15 S. Allison (2014) *Perfect Teacher-led CPD.* Carmarthen: Crown House Publishing.

6 Report your results – it is vital to share your results with all relevant staff.

7 Take action – What are your next steps? How will you remedy any issues you have found?

As they require collaboration with a range of colleagues and leaders, action research projects can be enormously rewarding and prove an extremely engaging method of reflection as well as focusing on the developmental journey[16] – rather than a qualification. Leaders will quickly lend support to action research projects, as they are usually of low (financial) cost and high reward, and can trigger whole-college change.

Webinars and online conferences

Though action research projects are enormously rewarding, they can take time to implement, and this means there may be a wait to reap the rewards. If you're looking for a quick hit of training or CPD, webinars are perfect.

From the Education and Training Foundation's range of webinars[17] to the Association of Colleges' pre-recorded[18] and live[19] sessions, there are hundreds of potential training sessions which can be easily and flexibly accessed.

With the changes to remote and distance learning as a result of Covid-19, there are also more and more teachers, leaders and trainers heading to online meeting platforms like Microsoft Teams and Zoom to create and host their own training (and at greatly reduced prices). Traditionally expensive and large-scale conferences are also making the move to the small (computer) screen and this provides the perfect opportunity to engage with innovative training methods.

Triangulated observations

Discussed in further detail in Chapter 9, triangulated observations can be enormously beneficial. This approach consists of forming a group of three teachers and regularly collaborating and observing each other. This observation does not have to last long (it can be as little as 10–15 minutes per week), but it gives valuable insight into how others teach similar topics and what techniques and strategies are embedded in their practice.

Like some of the other strategies here, it can be uncomfortable at first (there are few who like being observed), but once this hurdle has been cleared it opens the way for collaborative reflection, and sharing this load with colleagues proves a more efficient method of producing new resources or trialling new

---

16 B. Burstow (2017) *Effective Teacher Development: Theory and Practice in Professional Learning.* London: Bloomsbury Publishing.

17 www.et-foundation.co.uk/supporting/professional-development/maths-and-english/ (accessed 11 January 2021).

18 www.aoc-services.co.uk/events-and-training/learningweek/ (accessed 11 January 2021).

19 www.aoc-services.co.uk/events-and-training (accessed 11 January 2021).

approaches. This isn't just a tool for celebrating successes, but also for identifying the challenges teachers experience[20]. These approaches can include joint resource development, or simply using a colleague's methods and asking them to observe.

Local, regional and national collaboration

An effective and easily implemented method for developing practice, using local, regional and national collaborators is often easy to initiate and gives real insight into the joint challenges colleges face and the range of strategies used to solve them.

With a simple phone call or email, a visit to another local or regional college, to discuss the strategies they use to combat the challenges faced in all FE English and maths departments, can be quickly arranged. Why not organise a joint training day or a sharing good practice event? Better still, with the recent advances in remote and distance learning, all of this can be done for free online, with online communities springing up as a result. As a teacher, involve line managers and your Head of Department, who will probably already have existing links at a range of colleges.

As ever, this can take a little bit of work to initiate, but once up and running this provides massive scope for sharing, reflective feedback, critical friendships and exchanging good practice. By simply talking to practitioners who face the same challenges, great ideas and innovation are easily shared. Again, you might try to persuade your manager by highlighting the benefits of any collaboration and using training days or administration days to collaborate and look to develop innovation.

Extend collaboration to all key stages

With the obvious parallels between KS4 and post-16, using local secondary schools as sources of collaboration and training can be extremely beneficial.

There is generally an argument that these are different students who are operating in different environments, but there are so many more similarities than differences. Sharing training or collaboration on lesson pace, differentiation, questioning, assessment, behaviour and workload management and developing a rich curriculum could be beneficial to both settings.

As above, this could take the form of local or regional collaboration, teach meets, sharing good practice events and online conferences, or a simple visit and some brief observations. Either way, discussion with highly skilled teachers (in both sectors) will benefit all.

Furthermore, with phonics becoming an integral part of Functional Skills in the recent Functional Skills reform and the requirements for Functional Skills entry assessments, making use of local primary school provision should also

---

20 D. Lemov, E. Woolway and K. Yezzi (2012) *Practice Perfect: 42 Rules for Getting Better at Getting Better.* San Francisco, CA: John Wiley & Sons.

be seen as a viable training and collaborative outlet. Highlight to leaders that this also builds and develops relationships with potential students of the future, as well as strengthening links with the community and aiding CPD, and they are likely to fully support this move.

Become a mentor or coach

What better way to reflect on your own training needs than to support a newly qualified teacher who's making their first steps in the profession? A fantastic reflective opportunity[21], mentoring a new member of staff can facilitate observation of potentially new and innovative ideas. Additionally, this provides regular opportunities for discussion around planning, teaching and assessment with input from a new perspective. Research suggests new teachers are not immediately accepted in school or college culture[22] and so the invaluable insight they provide as an outsider can be a real strength.

This is also an opportunity to collaborate with other mentors and engage with a range of coaching approaches, helping you to look at what elements of your own practice can be refined or further evaluated.

What does Effective CPD Look Like?

Whatever CPD method you choose, it is important to interrogate whether it is effective and whether it has had the desired impact. With so many courses, webinars, blogs, conferences and books out there, it can be difficult to identify what will make the difference.

With this in mind, effective CPD should fall within the following guidelines:

- **Explanation of goals:** do you know what you will be covering and why? The potential and intended outcomes for students should be outlined from the start.
- **Appropriate and focused:** is the training relevant to those attending? Is it what you need? Is it appropriate for all?
- **Impactful:** do you know that this training could have an immediate impact? How do you know this? What does the research say? Have the authors been involved in the research process at any point?
- **Interesting:** simply put, does the training hold your attention? Are you interested to find out more? Would you attend follow-up training?
- **Author credibility:** are the presenters/trainers/authors experts? Do they have relevant experience, skills, knowledge and understanding in this particular area? How do you know?
- **Next steps:** what happens after the training is over? Are there additional sessions, resources or support? What are the next steps?

---

21 Allison, *Perfect Teacher-led CPD.*
22 Morehead, Professional behaviors for the beginning teacher.

Ultimately, being an outstanding practitioner and developing as a practitioner are very similar. Both are focused around initiating the right routines to best support your students. A continual process, it is about how you can keep getting better to make the most difference. Taking ownership of your professional development is development in itself.

Section Three: How Leaders can Develop Individuals and Teams

Having covered behaviours, development needs and potential CPD, it is time to discuss what middle and senior leaders can do to embed and engender high expectations and the right culture in English and maths departments. As above, this doesn't need to take the form of expensive external training, or time-consuming in-house CPD, but can be completed incrementally, in everything we do.

Below are just some of the ways English and maths teams can be developed through proactive leadership.

Modelling Outstanding Practice

Simple and easily applied, continually modelling outstanding practice can have a positive, long-term impact on staff[23]. Whether evidenced by arriving early or staying late, beating deadlines or leaving outstanding feedback for students, the importance of modelling outstanding practice cannot be overstated[24].

More than anything, continually modelling outstanding practice means that routines are formed and excellent practice becomes normalised within the department. Or, to put it much more succinctly, 'practice makes permanent'[25].

Although we cannot control outcomes in English and maths (too many variables are provided by just the exam), we can and must control the inputs. English and maths leaders should leave all areas of their work open to scrutiny by their staff – this will help to develop trust while also implicitly communicating expectations.

Among all things, be visible, and don't ask anything of your team that you would not do yourself.

The Importance and Power of Communication

If trust is one of the key drivers to a high-performing team, then communication is the catalyst for establishing a culture of trust[26]. As discussed, we must

---

23 J. Dean (2013) *Making Habits, Breaking Habits: How to make Changes that Stick*. London: Oneworld Publications.

24 A. Buck (2016) *Leadership Matters: How Leaders at all Levels can Create Good Schools*. Melton, Woodbridge: John Catt Educational Ltd.

25 Lemov, Woolway and Yezzi, *Practice Perfect*.

26 K. Thompson (2016) *A Systematic Guide to Change Management*. Great Britain: CreateSpace Publishing.

remember that (like students) no two teachers are the same. As an extension of this, we cannot communicate with all staff using a narrow base of methods and expect that messages will all be received loud and clear.

Open communication can very quickly lead to improvement[27] so it is important that forums are created in which all staff can share concerns, anxieties and grievances (whether they are justified or not). To do this, use email and whole-team briefings to get across simple messages as efficiently and clearly as possible (fielding all questions) and use small group, pair or one-to-one meetings to clarify anything further. A key part of high-quality communication is about knowing when to be 'big' and when to be 'small'. Be 'big' (college- or team-wide, large groups or posters/banners and other marketing) when starting to communicate and clarifying new ideas or processes, and be 'small' (one-to-one, small groups, programme teams, discussion) when needing to differentiate or personalise communication.

We can't develop teams and individuals if they don't know the expectations, strategy or vision[28].

Defining Responsibilities and Delegation

Too often, teaching is viewed as 'the lonely profession'[29]. As a result, it is vital that leaders properly delegate and define responsibilities so that teachers can support each other to create department communities.

It is important to clearly define and communicate who is responsible for what within departments. Asking staff to take ownership and accountability for the things they want changed (which they are passionate about) is also a simple and effective measure to ensure high standards and expectations are complied with. Simply put, it matters more to staff when they are personally invested.

Have informal meetings at the beginning of the year, discuss priorities with staff – Where do they feel their strengths lie? What do they want to improve? What would they like responsibility for and what changes do they want to drive? Support them throughout this process and you can fully utilise a diverse set of teachers.

There may be some who complain about any additional responsibility or workload, but we must remember that teachers who aren't committed to professional learning aren't committed to improvement[30]. Communicate this, and find a solution collaboratively.

---

27 S. Walker (2017) *The Captain Class: The Hidden Force that Creates the World's Greatest Teams*. New York: Random House.

28 M. Myatt (2016) *High Challenge, Low Threat: Finding the Balance*. Melton, Woodbridge: John Catt Educational Ltd.

29 M. Fullan and A. Hargreaves (1991) *What's Worth Fighting For?: Working Together for your School*. Toronto: Ontario Public School Teachers' Federation.

30 B. Robertson (2020) *The Teaching Delusion: Why Teaching in Our Schools isn't Good Enough (and How we can Make it Better)*. Melton, Woodbridge: John Catt Educational Ltd.

Evaluate and Diagnose your own CPD

As discussed earlier, asking peers and leaders to anonymously complete evaluations of your strengths and areas of development can be enormously beneficial. As a leader, it is vital to know how you are perceived and why you are seen in that way. It can be difficult (very difficult), but it is enormously important.

Just because we are leaders does not mean we are above evaluation of our own knowledge and skills and working with our teams to develop ourselves. There will be those in your team who excel in areas in which you need support – ask for this support. This is where making links with local, regional and national colleges can also be a vital tool in diagnosing your own CPD needs. Use tools such as LinkedIn or Twitter to develop a network that you can discuss challenges with and potentially seek advice from (as well as sharing your own good practice).

Make links wherever you can; collaborate and share the load.

Growing your Own

Though there has been some progress made on addressing teacher shortages in English and maths in Further Education, there is evidence that shortages are increasing[31]. A potential solution, the 'grow your own' model, has many benefits.

This term is generally used to describe recruitment or promotion from within to fill staff shortage areas, and in the UK it usually means recruitment of future leaders[32]. The definition in this chapter is closer to the US definition, where established 'Grow Your Own' programmes look to resolve teacher shortages, retention problems and issues in teacher diversity[33].

In using this method to identify relevant staff and fill staffing shortages in English and maths, the process is similar to that used to identify leaders in industry. As Byham et al. detail in *Grow your own Leaders: How to Identify, Develop, and Retain Leadership Talent*[34], the first stage is to cast the net far and wide, as we can't afford to miss out on good staff. Identify any staff currently working in areas other than English and maths (vocational areas, supporting in classrooms or SEND) who you feel are suitable and motivated to teach in English and maths. Having done this, informally approach them and discuss this possibility.

Though those teaching vocational courses with healthy student numbers may be reluctant, those in SEND or support teams often jump at this chance. With relevant training (including potentially supporting a bid for a PGCE/

31 Association of Colleges (2020) *AoC English and Maths Survey January 2020.* Available at: www.aoc.co.uk/files/aoc-english-and-maths-survey-report-march-2020pdf (accessed 11 January 2021).

32 W.C. Byham, A.B. Smith and M.J. Paese (2002) *Grow your own Leaders: How to Identify, Develop, and Retain Leadership Talent.* Upper Saddle River, NJ: FT Press.

33 H.R. Milner IV and K. Lomotey, eds (2013) *Handbook of Urban Education.* New York and Abingdon: Routledge.

34 Byham, Smith and Paese, *Grow your own Leaders.*

PGDE (postgraduate certificate in education/professional graduate diploma in education) place) and bespoke CPD (one size fits all will not work), within a relatively short amount of time, any English and maths staff shortage can be filled with staff who will quickly grow into high-quality teachers.

Having said this, there should still be a number of criteria for identifying these potential English and maths teachers, including a minimum qualification requirement (Level 2 qualifications in English and maths, though a Level 3 in either is hugely beneficial), a minimum time working at the college and a willingness to complete additional training or qualifications. As a teacher, persuading managers and leaders to follow this effective and low-cost solution offers the very real opportunity to play an important part in English and maths recruitment and shape the English and maths team.

The process of 'converting' a support assistant should start with a full timetable of support in English and maths. Then, the fledgling teacher can move to small group support (for English and maths), eventually completing one-to-ones with English and maths students and small groups using collaboratively created resources. Finally, they will take responsibility for planning, teaching and assessing those groups. As the member of staff has previously supported in English and maths, they know the working practices, content, standards and expectations and will be able to hit the ground running.

This is also an excellent way to 'continue the cycle'. As in any organization, staff will come and go. However, there can be continuity issues when recruiting new staff – 'growing your own' is an excellent way to ensure this continuity and essentially train replacements before they are needed.

Beginning this process may need significant buy-in from senior leaders, but the benefits are obvious: significant savings in recruitment and initial salary, real buy-in from the member of staff recruited, savings on CPD (as the staff member is trained internally) and excellent relationships with students as the member of staff continues relationships they have already built.

Managing Change

From policy, to process, to staffing – changing anything in an English and maths department can be difficult due to the sheer number of variables that have to be dealt with. From changing timetables, to student numbers or funding, any plans can be altered (or even erased) quickly and definitely.

With this in mind, it is important to remember that influencing staff behaviours and development is one of the biggest changes which can occur in a department. It is a long-, medium- and short-term goal and every member of the team requires something different.

There will be some who will support the changes you are trying to make, and those who do not. It is just as important to collaborate with supporters as it is to get feedback from 'powerful opponents'[35]. When trying to develop any member of your team, make sure you are not trying to do too much too soon. If

---

35 Thompson, *A Systematic Guide to Change Management.*

you find you've given yourself too much to manage, delegate, collaborate and communicate with your staff. Rome was not built in a day, after all.

Conclusion

Above all else, it is important to remember that individuals and teams cannot develop without the right culture and an environment of trust. Like trust, team morale and a positive team culture can be difficult to develop and very easily lost. It only takes a very small minority of staff to lose it, so it must be safeguarded at all costs.

Consequently, to develop, it is vital that all staff exhibit and promote positive behaviours at all times – whether in front of students or colleagues. No teacher or leader is the finished article, so we must remember why continued development is important, and we must celebrate what it has helped us to achieve.

Remember that CPD should be viewed and communicated as an achievement which helps to give direction to our roles and enables us to complete the work we are passionate about. It makes us more effective and helps us to better serve students.

However we complete professional development, the journey is an ongoing one.

Summary

- Evaluate your own skills, knowledge and understanding (collaboratively if possible).
- CPD does not have to take any specific form – if it enables improvement, it is CPD.
- Use a range of methods to continue your professional development: books, websites, blogs, podcasts, discussion, courses etc. They are all valuable if they make a difference.
- Good CPD should be differentiated and specific to the needs of the user.
- Just as we evaluate our own needs, evaluate the effectiveness of the CPD. Did it support teachers to support students? If the answer is 'yes' the training was effective.
- Cost-effectiveness does not always mean financial cost.

Reflection

- How are staff supported to perform to their best?
- What communication is in place to assess, analyse and provide outstanding CPD?
- How can you identify who you can learn from?
- In what ways can you support the colleagues and peers who need support?
- How are you supporting your own CPD? What tools/resources do you use?

6 Staff Motivation

'I don't want to do that now; I'll finish it tomorrow ...'

Every teacher (throughout entire careers)

From losing those extra pounds and finally reading that literary classic to finishing a pile of ironing or planning a holiday, motivation is everything[1]. This is also absolutely true in education.

With British teachers said to be working amongst the longest hours in the world[2] (and roughly 12.1 hours' unpaid overtime per week[3]), motivation is key to success and helping our students to achieve.

However, if distraction is a fundamental vulnerability of the brain[4], how do we become and remain motivated in a challenging role in a challenging sector?

Many teachers point to the unpredictability of teaching as one of the most attractive parts of the profession – no two students, lessons or days are the same, and this leads to high levels of engagement throughout. Nonetheless, it can also bring additional challenges.

Often, this unpredictability leads to additional workload. From attendance at unplanned meetings (with peers, leaders, parents or external agencies) to covering lessons or additional planning, the consequence is that teachers report the highest levels of work-related stress, depression and anxiety in the UK[5].

Research suggests that student behaviour(s) and student–teacher interactions are both the principal motivators and demotivators for teachers[6]. Unfortunately, and try as we might, controlling all student behaviour all of the time is simply not possible so we can't always rely on what happens in the classroom for motivation.

As a result, it is vital that we have the right tools to combat these challenges. Motivation, of course, is at the forefront of our arsenal, but so too are resilience, mindfulness and adaptability. We need these tools to help us to manage

1 L.A. Iacocca and W. Novak (1986) *Iacocca: An Autobiography*. New York: Bantam.
2 P. Dolton, O. Marcenaro, R.D. Vries and P.W. She (2018) *Global Teacher Status Index 2018*. London: Varkey Foundation.
3 www.tes.com/news/teachers-work-more-unpaid-overtime-anyone-else (accessed 11 January 2021).
4 A. Gazzaley and L.D. Rosen (2016) *The Distracted Mind: Ancient Brains in a High-tech World*. Cambridge, MA: MIT Press.
5 Health and Safety Executive (2018) *Work-related Stress, Anxiety or Depression Statistics in Great Britain*. London: HSE.
6 R. Addison and M. Brundrett (2008) Motivation and demotivation of teachers in primary schools: the challenge of change, *Education 3–13*, 36(1): 79–94.

the challenges we face inside and outside of the classroom, and without them we are likely to burn out[7].

To stop this happening, this chapter will focus on how to deal with demotivating factors and how to strengthen motivators. Whether looking to motivate ourselves, those around us or the teams we lead, this chapter will cover strategies which can be used to develop perseverance, intrinsic motivation and the importance of creating a well-being-centred culture[8] in teams as well as classrooms.

What Motivates Us?

No matter the context, knowing how and by what means we are motivated is crucial to our development. Though it can be argued that there are many motivating factors for teachers in any sector, these factors can mainly be classified into two groups:

- Intrinsic motivation – the act of completing a task for the fundamental satisfaction attached to completing it. We are motivated because we enjoy the activity itself.
- Extrinsic motivation – the act of completing a task for external rewards or incentives (e.g. money, success, praise etc.).

Though it's likely that we are motivated by elements of both – we enjoy teaching, but it is unlikely we would do it for free – it is key that we become more intrinsically motivated. Simply put, in education, not only is there no guarantee of extrinsic reward, but studies also have suggested that rewards do not always improve engagement[9].

Consequently, intrinsic motivation becomes ever more valuable. So, what do we need for intrinsic motivation?

Daniel Pink, in his excellent book *Drive*[10], suggests that motivation is derived from three factors:

- autonomy – the need to independently make decisions
- mastery – the need to continue improving and developing
- purpose – the need to believe we are contributing to something bigger

7   J.G. Rankin (2016) *First Aid for Teacher Burnout: How you can find Peace and Success*. New York: Taylor & Francis.

8   M. Coalter, (2018) *Talent Architects: How to Make Your School a Great Place to Work*. Melton, Woodbridge: John Catt Educational Ltd.

9   E.L. Deci (1971) Effects of externally mediated rewards on intrinsic motivation, *Journal of Personality and Social Psychology*, 18(1): 105–15.

10 D.H. Pink (2011) *Drive: The Surprising Truth about what Motivates us*. New York: Penguin.

We are more motivated if we believe we are in control of our actions (i.e. what we do, when we do it, who we do it with etc.), when we want to continually improve or when we feel we are contributing to the greater good.

As teachers and leaders, then, it is important to facilitate conditions and circumstances which promote these factors. However, it is also just as important to identify and eliminate the demotivating factors in our classrooms, teams and colleges. But what are they?

What Demotivates Teachers?

Much discussed, the demotivating factors for teachers in all sectors are well known and well publicised. Additional workload, challenging behaviour, lack of funding and lack of parental support are just some of the many complaints shared at teacher conferences, union meetings, in the press and around social media.

Just as they can motivate, money and time are often attributes which also lead to demotivation. An excess allows more resources and more innovation; an insufficiency means the opposite. These are also the two attributes we often do not have, but need. Too much extra work to complete? Given more time, all work can be completed. Challenging behaviour? Extra funding means more interventions can be put in place and smaller class sizes are possible, so we can find and treat the root of the behaviour.

This is also before we look at or consider the impact of lesson observations, where research suggests that feedback is at best unreliable and at worst inaccurate[11].

So, with little change to funding or guided learning hours expected any time soon, how can we remain motivated and keep demotivating factors at bay? The next section offers a range of strategies and techniques which can be employed in any context to make sure our own motivation, and the motivation of those around us, can be kept high.

Developing Resilience and Managing Stress

It is important to remember that resilience is not simply about how we deal with setbacks, but also how we manage aspects of day-to-day life. As the mental health charity *Mind* states, 'Resilience is not just your ability to bounce back, but also your capacity to adapt in the face of challenging circumstances, whilst maintaining a stable mental wellbeing'[12].

---

11 J.N. Joe, C.M. Tocci, S.L. Holtzman and J.C. Williams (2013) *Foundations of Observation: Considerations for Developing a Classroom Observation System that Helps Districts Achieve Consistent and Accurate Scores*. MET Project, Policy and Practice Brief. Seattle: Bill & Melinda Gates Foundation.

12 www.mind.org.uk/information-support/types-of-mental-health-problems/stress/developing-resilience/ (accessed 11 January 2021).

By this definition, then, resilience is about our ability to adapt to changes. An inability to do this (for whatever reason) leads to stress, and if too much stress is allowed to build up, the impact is quickly seen. The issue here is that the majority of us do not see the stresses that are happening throughout our days, weeks, months or lives. As Dr Rangan Chatterjee outlines in his book, *The Stress Solution*, micro-stress doses (MSD) are becoming ever more prevalent in our lives as technology means we are taking on more and more work[13].

Where once we would go to the estate agents and be presented with a selection of homes, we must now find them ourselves and arrange viewing times; we are expected to check out our own food at the supermarket; in years gone by we would make a phone call to fix an issue, now we must do it ourselves via the internet. Each of these micro-stresses impacts our working lives before we have even taken on additional workload as teachers.

So, how do we build resilience?

Own Your Emotions

It may sound a little 'new age', but research has shown[14] that students who regularly practise expressive writing show improved anxiety[15] and exhibit significantly improved exam outcomes[16]. If this works so well for students, the benefits for teachers are obvious.

Writing for just 10–20 minutes per day and exploring your feelings on a particular topic can massively help to reduce anxiety and stress about that topic. The writing doesn't have to be a masterpiece, nor does it even have to be kept – feel free to dispose of your work as soon as you have finished if you want to. The writing is the important process, not evidence of it.

It's Good to Talk

Though the world can feel a very lonely place when we are overloaded or suffering from anxiety, talking to peers, leaders, friends and family can also act as an important method of release. Having said this, it is important that we do this with the 'right' people – this means prioritizing relationships. Make sure you connect with compassionate and empathetic people who you trust, who may have experienced something similar or who can suggest concrete actions to help deal with your situation. It is also important to make sure there is structure

13 R. Chatterjee (2018) *The Stress Solution: The 4 Steps to a Calmer, Happier, Healthier You*. London: Penguin.

14 J.W. Pennebaker, J.K. Kiecolt-Glaser and R. Glaser (1988) Disclosure of traumas and immune function: health implications for psychotherapy, *Journal of Consulting and Clinical Psychology*, 56(2): 239–45.

15 D. Park, G. Ramirez and S.L. Beilock (2014) The role of expressive writing in math anxiety, *Journal of Experimental Psychology: Applied*, 20(2): 103.

16 J. Frattaroli, M. Thomas and S. Lyubomirsky (2011) Opening up in the classroom: effects of expressive writing on graduate school entrance exam performance, *Emotion*, 11(3): 691–6.

to your discussion – focus on solving or developing solutions to problems, and next steps. There is also a tendency to want to self-isolate when stressed or feeling anxious – resist this. Even if you have to complete projects or tasks as part of a group, stay connected to those around you.

Look After Yourself

This element of teaching is never given the focus it deserves: get enough sleep, eat the right food, try and get some exercise and know when to switch off. Even sleeping for as little as 6 hours per night can have severe consequences including cognitive impairment equivalent to being drunk[17]. Working for too long each day will also eventually lead to burnout and can have lasting health consequences[18].

A simple rule for better self-care is to have at least one day during the weekend and two evenings per week (Friday should be one) where you do no work. If you find you are struggling to complete your workload in the remaining time, you are likely doing (or being asked to do) too much work. Make and work with connections at work to discuss alternative strategies to cut workload or work more efficiently (or use the ones in this book!)

Avoid Negativity and Act

Unfortunately, it is nearly impossible to avoid negativity altogether. There will be those who will look to put a negative spin on all events – avoid or quickly shut down these individuals and move the conversation forward as quickly as you can.

Also, filling your time with helping others, completing projects and generally being proactive will leave a sense of accomplishment and even release dopamine, a hormone associated with happiness. Focusing on your personal qualities, facilitating challenge in these tasks and thinking about what you can gain from these actions can also help to build resilience[19].

Keep Perspective and Stay Positive

Though this can be enormously difficult at times, try and keep a positive mindset and remember to look at the bigger picture – identify when you are catastrophizing[20] and try to detect areas of unreasonable thinking and take time to analyse why you are thinking that way. Take your time, reflect on the source of

---

17 A.M. Williamson and A.M. Feyer (2000) Moderate sleep deprivation produces impairments in cognition and motor performance equivalent to legally prescribed levels of alcohol intoxication, *Occupational and Environmental Medicine*, 57(10): 649–55.

18 A.J. Krause, E.B. Simon, B.A. Mander et al. (2017) The sleep-deprived human brain, *Nature Reviews Neuroscience*, 18(7): 404–18.

19 D. Fletcher and M. Sarkar (2016) Mental fortitude training: an evidence-based approach to developing psychological resilience for sustained success, *Journal of Sport Psychology in Action*, 7(3): 135–57.

20 B. Busch and E. Watson (2019) *The Science of Learning: 77 Studies that Every Teacher Needs to Know*. Abingdon: Routledge.

the anxiety, and return to it later. A very simple way to do this is to focus on previous achievements: research has shown that persistent people are much more likely to focus on what they have previously achieved[21].

As much as we can become obsessed with supporting and guiding our students, we must remember that without self-care, we can't do this effectively.

Practise What You Preach

Think about all of the strategies, tactics and processes we put in place to help students to build resilience. Why can't we use these to develop our own resilience? Scrutinise and explain successes and failures, act with purpose, control what can be controlled and focus less on things you can't control, and resilience will be built incrementally and permanently.

It's the Little Things

We are regularly told that 'it's the thought that counts'. However, are we using this advice to its fullest advantage? With educational funding a regular topic of debate over the last decade, there is little remaining budget for anything deemed 'non-essential'. However, the cost-effectiveness of opening the purse strings for colleagues is quickly felt – when purchasing anything for motivational purposes, we don't need to 'break the bank' to inspire.

It goes without saying that the size and timing of gifts is absolutely essential, as is the relationship with the person receiving it (turning up to work with a diamond ring for someone you've met once in admin is not a good look). It's best to keep gifts small and for the entire team:

- Stationery – an oldy, but a goody. Pens, pencils and highlighters are all extremely valued in the world of education, cost very little and will be enormously appreciated.
- Food and confectionary – an easy one this. Whether breakfast, chocolates, doughnuts or even fruit, this simple gesture can work wonders for motivation and team morale. Putting time aside to enjoy this (a team breakfast for example) can also help to build and develop great relationships in a team.
- Books – on the theme of developing relationships within a team, bringing in old books or starting a team book club is a great way to get to know members of your team. This can also be a great way to facilitate CPD if educational books are swapped.

As leaders, it is also important that regular opportunities are scheduled for staff to bond and motivate each other. Keeping these tied to seasons or holidays can

---

21 D. Niven (2002) *The 100 Simple Secrets of Successful People: What Scientists have Learned and how you can Use it*. New York: Harper Collins.

be a great way of developing a positive team culture. For example, initiating Secret Santa (or Secret Easter – look it up, it's a thing), an end of term breakfast or bringing sweets and chocolates to weekly meetings will all be appreciated and raise team morale.

Of course, this doesn't mean that you have to put your hand in your pocket. It has been suggested that the two most important words we can use in a team are 'Well done'[22], but there are obviously others. If there is any challenge to 'well done' as the two most important words, 'thank you' is surely in the running.

Thanking and praising those around you is one of the easiest and most impactful things we can do as teachers or leaders, and we must make sure we do it regularly. If praise increases instances of appropriate behaviour in students[23], it has a similar impact with teachers and we must remember this.

As with praising students, it doesn't need to be a grand gesture. Something as simple as an email or passing comment in the canteen can have enormous benefits. If, as a leader, you want to go further, this can be extended to a letter, postcard or an email to senior leaders for a mention in whole-college briefings. As with praising students, it is important to know your team when giving praise.

Know Your Team and Your Colleagues

This does not simply mean knowing how they operate at work or in a classroom. This means knowing your colleagues or team members as people: What keeps them going? What are their hobbies? What are their interests? What do they do of an evening or a weekend? What are their future plans?

Simply put, you cannot fake caring. It is not enough to appear to care – you actually *do* have to care! This will of course take time, but the suggestions in this section will give opportunities to learn about your colleagues and you will come to know them as a result.

Find out their motives; find out why they want to teach. Getting to know their future plans or dreams, or even fears, can be hugely beneficial when motivating people. If you can find out potential intrinsic motivations, you can become a facilitator, improving relationships and motivating staff.

And remember the little stuff – where Adam's daughter goes to uni, that Jenny's boyfriend is having an operation, how many kids people have, where they live and (potentially most importantly) try and remember birthdays. Always remember birthdays.

22 A. Ferguson (2015) *Leading: Lessons in Leadership from the Legendary Manchester United Manager.* London: Hachette UK.

23 B. Simonsen, S. Fairbanks, A. Briesch, D. Myers and G. Sugai (2008) Evidence-based practices in classroom management: considerations for research to practice, *Education and Treatment of Children*, 31(3): 351–80.

CPD as Motivator

As discussed in Chapter 5, CPD is an extremely powerful motivator as it helps teachers to achieve their personal goals, while also empowering them to develop as practitioners and support students.

Confronted with few chances for promotion or pay increase, it can be easy for teachers to feel they are stuck in a career rut. CPD and training then become the perfect tool to give focus to teachers who feel this way. As discussed, CPD can take many different forms: a course, conferences, a workshop, an external/internal qualification, a project or simply reading a relevant book.

It is just as important to empower as it is to facilitate. CPD doesn't need to rely on enormous budgets – many conferences are reasonably priced, and many are free, and held at various points during the academic year (and on Saturdays for practitioners who can't attend during the week).

We mustn't forget that CPD can be multipurpose. It can and must be part-reward, part-motivator; a team morale-building tool and an opportunity to refine culture and build confidence. In short, everything needed to develop staff motivation and effectiveness.

Communicate

As teachers, we spend the majority of our time communicating with everyone from students, to parents and carers, to colleagues, to admin teams, to leaders and everyone in between. This leaves us uniquely placed to best make decisions for young people, but the downside is that we tend to spend too much time emphasizing completing tasks and becoming as efficient as possible.

Listening

As we remember 'the little things', and take the time to build relationships, we must place special emphasis on positive communication. Whether this means facilitating or engaging in collaboration or just making sure your team know why you are teaching topics in a certain way, communication is key to motivating colleagues or the team you lead.

Part of this is helping to develop an environment where your colleagues or team feel they will be listened to on any topics they give feedback on. Do you take their opinions seriously? Do you plan on acting on their feedback? Are all teachers given equal weight in discussion? If the answer is 'yes' to each of these questions, chances are communication is effective, and staff are motivated.

Speaking

Of course, communication is not only about listening, but also adding to the debate. With this in mind, to motivate yourself and the people around you, it is equally important to make sure you communicate your own messages.

Whether student, teacher or leader, to stay motivated, it is important to communicate with those around you. This can mean something as small as collaborating with team members during planning, to communicating key messages and strategies to your team – either way, it is vital that we communicate.

This becomes ever more crucial during difficult times. There will come times during an academic year, and many during a career, when we need to ask for support. This can be difficult at the time, but conveying this message to those who can support you will act as an excellent motivator.

The Power of Choice

As mentioned earlier, autonomy is a very important ingredient when motivating anyone. To increase your own and team motivation, we must have autonomy, but we cannot have it without choices[24]. Also, even the illusion of control can massively reduce the risk of depression and other negative influences[25].

It is vital that we have as many choices as possible when completing any task so that we feel autonomous, and therefore in control. If we feel in control, we are more motivated as we invest emotionally.

Many times, I have heard teachers reply that they are not in control as they have been asked to complete a specific task in a specific way by a leader. It's important to remember that in the majority of instances, most leaders desire an outcome, and don't necessarily have much investment in the way it is reached. Put simply, as long as we get from A to B by a deadline, does it matter which road we take?

If directed to achieve an outcome, think about how you can achieve this outcome: what choices are important in the project? Do you need flexibility? What resources do you need? Think about the methods that you would like to use to achieve the outcome and communicate this with leaders – as well as the motivational impact, this also has the benefit of displaying initiative and innovation to those around you.

Setting Goals

Also vitally important, setting relevant, achievable goals can be enormously motivational[26]. Firstly, goals should be appropriately challenging and directly

24 C. Duhigg (2016) *Smarter Faster Better: The Secrets of being Productive in Life and Business*. New York: Random House.
25 P.K. Presson and V.A. Benassi (1996) Locus of control orientation and depressive symptomatology: a meta-analysis, *Journal of Social Behavior and Personality*, 11(1): 201–12.
26 L. Rouillard (2003) *Goals and Goal Setting: Achieving Measured Objectives*. Boston, MA: Cengage Learning.

relevant to you and your role[27]. Secondly, though it may seem strange in the digital age, writing down these goals and creating 'to do' lists can also prove enormously motivational[28].

As proof of this, we need look no further than the scourge of student well-being – computer games. Games such as Grand Theft Auto, Fifa or Call of Duty have been student responses to the teacher question, 'Why did you get to bed so late?' for years. These games are so successful because they use the right mix of long- and short-term goals (while also keeping them separate). Long-term goals help gamers to remain focused on why they are doing what they are doing, and they are cleverly intertwined with short-term goals which, when completed, give a dopamine boost to keep us motivated[29].

We can use this model to our advantage: create and review long-term goals (what role we would like, how we would like to be successful, what we want to achieve) while also regularly creating achievable short-term goals. These short-term goals can be weekly or even daily, but they must be achievable. If too few of these goals remain unachieved, demotivation can set in and you may not even attempt the remaining items on your list. Essentially, when we stop succeeding, we stop trying[30].

A simple way to counter this, and try and have 'goal positive' days (i.e. days when you have completed more goals than not), is to add highly achievable tasks such as eating lunch, answering a set number of emails or even washing the dishes. Either way, a good way to start is to set the big goals, and then break down each one into what you need to do every day and every week to achieve it. Make your list, try your best, and give yourself a break if you don't do everything all the time.

Be Flexible

Giving yourself a break should not only be for lists, but all aspects of practice, and being flexible is a large part of this. If you don't achieve what you wanted to achieve on any set day, try and deal with whatever stopped you, or attempt it the day after. This is not to say we should consistently put off goals or aspects of our role, but that we shouldn't punish ourselves for not marking the books, planning the lesson or answering every email.

This applies to both teachers and leaders – if asked to take on additional workload, what flexibility will you need to complete it? Communicate this, get the training you need and you will be motivated to complete the task.

27 D.T. Hall and L.W. Foster (1977) A psychological success cycle and goal setting: goals, performance, and attitudes, *Academy of Management Journal*, 20(2): 282–90.
28 Fletcher and Sarkar, Mental fortitude training.
29 B. Adamou (2018) *Games and Gamification in Market Research: Increasing Consumer Engagement in Research for Business Success*. London: Kogan Page.
30 K.E. Parker, C.E. Pedersen, A.M. Gomez et al. (2019) A paranigral VTA nociceptin circuit that constrains motivation for reward, *Cell*, 178(3): 653–71.

As leaders, we must be as flexible as our team require. Can we cover lessons to help staff? Are we available for staff? Can we change our priorities dependent on what our team need? If we can't be flexible, communicate so that our environment changes to allow us to change. Giving time in lieu, time off, moving deadlines (where you can) and supporting colleagues is an excellent way to help foster motivation.

Stay Positive and Trust

It is also vital that we are as positive as we are flexible, and at all times. This can be difficult, yes, but it does make a difference to everything from student outcomes[31] to relationships with colleagues[32]. Part of this is trusting the people you work with – give them the benefit of the doubt, and support them when they may appear to falter. This again will build strong relationships in the workplace, a key driver of motivation.

Trust managers, leaders, external teams and systems, and if they falter, give support to help them get back on track. A simple way to do this is to focus on prior achievements and successes by highlighting the progress which has previously been made[33].

No matter the situation, positivity is always a key characteristic. A student has never attended? We have the opportunity to make a difference! Student thrown a chair at you? At least they attended! You don't have a set classroom for the year? You have the opportunity to work in a range of creative environments!

All jokes aside, it is difficult, but staying positive will make a huge difference to student success, as well as your own mental health – there is no more compelling argument than that.

Be Wary of Overload

With relentless motivation and positivity, it is tempting to take on additional workload and be everything to everyone. Don't, because it won't end well. Everyone has pressure points and there will come a time when you will need to look after yourself. Don't commit to too many tight deadlines or large projects – focus on completing tasks well. Quality, not quantity and all that.

Communication, again, is a key player here – talk to those around you and to leaders, and discuss flexibility in completing workload (or even deadlines).

31 K. Wheldall and F. Merrett (2017) *Positive Teaching: The Behavioural Approach.* Abingdon: Routledge.

32 S. Ellis and J. Tod (2018) *Behaviour for Learning: Promoting Positive Relationships in the Classroom.* Abingdon: Routledge.

33 T. Amabile and S. Kramer (2011) *The Progress Principle: Using Small Wins to Ignite Joy, Engagement, and Creativity at Work.* Boston, MA: Harvard Business Press.

List making can again be a key support mechanism – make a list of what you *have* to do. Once these items are ticked off, you have the opportunity to reschedule or even remove anything that remains. Do the essentials first, and what remains can be completed with much more flexibility.

Staying Motivated

For some, staying motivated can be just as challenging as becoming motivated in the first place. Just ask any one of the estimated 43 per cent of people who don't continue their New Year's resolution into February[34].

So, how can we stay motivated over long periods of time? Very simple – three words: reminders, repetition and rituals[35].

But what do these mean in practice? Let's take a look.

Reminders

This is the first stage in remaining motivated – remind yourself why you are doing the things you are doing. As mentioned earlier, drawing up lists can be an excellent way to do this, but it should not be the only way.

Written reminders can be enormously successful (diary entries, planners, post-it notes etc.), but in the digital age, electronic reminders are just as useful. Apps, electronic calendars or even playlists are of great benefit. A bigger issue can be forgetting to set reminders – this is why it is important to automate wherever possible.

Even slightly adapting your environment (posters, your phone screensaver etc.) can lead to enormous benefits. Set reminders to mark books, observe colleagues, plan lessons or collaborate with peers and it will get done.

Repetition

Continued motivation can only occur if we continue to complete the 'right' actions. To do this, we must continue to repeat the actions which motivate us.

Automating reminders will make sure that the actions and tasks you complete are continually repeated. When repeated enough, these tasks and actions become embedded in everyday practice and you begin to see the changes you want[36].

To help this repetition, use your subconscious to force further reminders. Listen to set playlists whenever you are completing tasks (a friend recom-

34 www.sundried.com/blogs/training/tagged/new-year (accessed 11 January 2021).

35 A.D. Tian, J. Schroeder, G. Häubl, J.L. Risen, M.I. Norton and F. Gino (2018) Enacting rituals to improve self-control, *Journal of Personality and Social Psychology*, 114(6): 851–76.

36 A.H. Maslow (1981) *Motivation and Personality*. New Delhi: Prabhat Prakashan.

mended Hans Zimmer soundtracks and they are now my 'go to'), and then listening to these playlists will trigger reminders to complete set tasks.

As above, make sure that you are tracking your progress – remember, looking back on previous achievements is an excellent tool to keep motivation up[37]. Use a wall planner, your phone or any other means to quickly do this.

Rituals

As low-stakes quizzes and retrieval practice have shown[38], when actions are consistently repeated, we not only remember them, but reproduce them with greater consistency. By regularly completing actions, and reminding ourselves to complete them, we will improve. By regularly doing the 'right' things in our classrooms and in our teams, positive rituals will develop.

This allows us to place greater focus on more consistent success and we are more easily motivated. It is important to remember that workload does play a part here as well, and we should add to remind, repeat and ritualise incrementally – you will not transform your practice in a fortnight.

Conclusion

Motivating yourself and others can seem a difficult challenge at various points during the academic year. It can feel as though there is little respite to workload, or that there is never the right time to make the relevant changes. After all, change management can be difficult even in ideal circumstances[39].

On this point, we are regularly told that the workplace is an environment where emotion should be suppressed – that we shouldn't become emotionally invested. As far as motivation goes, and within reason, ignore this advice. For motivation, focus on emotions, on addressing feelings[40] and think about the steps you will need to take.

This is not to say that we should expect all staff to be jumping for joy or crying in the canteen every morning, but we do need to better identify and deal with the emotions that our roles can cause, and turn this into motivation.

As leaders, it is important that we focus on the 'how' and not necessarily the 'who'[41] to remain motivated. Simply put, our teachers will remain much more

---

37 Amabile and Kramer, *The Progress Principle.*
38 J. Webb (2019) *How to Teach English Literature: Overcoming Cultural Poverty.* Melton, Woodbridge: John Catt Educational Ltd.
39 K. Thompson (2016) *A Systematic Guide to Change Management.* Great Britain: CreateSpace Publishing.
40 C. Heath and D. Heath (2008) *Made to Stick: Why Some Ideas Take Hold and Others Come Unstuck.* London: Random House; C. Heath and D. Heath (2010) *Switch: How to Change Things When Change is Hard.* London: Random House.
41 Duhigg, *Smarter Faster Better.*

motivated if they know they will be treated with equality and respect in everything they do.

This can be difficult as we inherently use different strategies and approaches with different staff, but we must review how this is perceived by others. The key here is to communicate clearly and in a timely manner. If all staff know their roles, responsibilities and accountabilities, the equality comes in the level of support which is provided.

For equality to reign, we must provide an environment of equal opportunity, recognition and support or guidance. This is absolutely key to providing a secure environment for our staff.

Summary

- Identify and clarify what motivates (and demotivates) you.
- Setting goals is an important measure to keep focus and help you achieve.
- Communication is key – be open and honest with those you work with and clarify roles, responsibilities and goals.
- Use and appreciate 'the little things'.
- Create and develop choices to give a sense of autonomy within your role.
- Respect the science and work on becoming more resilient.
- Stay positive (no matter how difficult it may seem).

Reflection

- How do you motivate yourself to continue to perform to a high level?
- What intrinsic and extrinsic motivators do you rely on?
- What rituals can you put in place to remain motivated?
- How are you managing your workload and priorities to remain at your best?
- What time and/or resources do you put aside to care for your mental and physical well-being?

7 Timetabling and Attendance

'What's wrong with timetabling GCSE maths 1–4pm on Friday?'
Vocational head of department (2017)

'I don't go because it's 1–4pm on a Friday!'
Every student in the above lesson (2017)

One of the most challenging aspects of Further Education English and maths, attendance is an issue which plagues every college. Though there are no officially published statistics on attendance in Further Education[1], anecdotally, most colleges report anywhere between 75 per cent and 85 per cent. Frankly, even if national data was compiled and analysed, it may be difficult to identify trends because of the enormous diversity in students, college location, context and a host of other socio-economic factors.

For example, can we really compare overall student attendance at an inner city college (with public transport options including buses, trams, an underground or metro system, subsidised cycle schemes and pedestrianization) to a rural college without public transport before 7am or after 7pm? Can we compare overall attendance statistics at a college in an affluent area to those at a college in an area of high deprivation?

The bigger question here, is whether we need to compare at all. Though there is much competition around vocational recruitment, strategy and achievement, there must be collaboration around improving attendance – simply put, if students don't attend, we can't support them. Research suggests that high levels of absenteeism can significantly impact student achievement[2] (of students who missed 50 per cent of lessons or more, only 3 per cent managed to achieve five or more GCSEs at grades A*–C including maths and English).

So, how do we work to improve student attendance? First, we need to identify why students don't attend. Why are students absent for English and maths? As much as we would like one issue to take aim at, unfortunately there are many. Student absence occurs for a number of reasons. In Ross Longhurst's

---

1   Ofsted (2013) *Improving Attendance and Punctuality: Strategies, Approaches and Lessons Learned from London Colleges: An AoC/Ofsted Action Learning Project.* Manchester: Ofsted. Available at: www.ofsted.gov.uk/resources/130212 (accessed 3 July 2020).
2   C. Taylor (2012) *Improving Attendance at School.* London: DfE.

'Why aren't they here? Student absenteeism in a Further Education college'[3], he identifies many reasons for student non-attendance, many of which a majority of us will have encountered before (whether real or fictitious):

- Illness or medical appointments
- Weather conditions
- Completing college work or work commitments
- Transport problems
- Family obligations
- Holidays
- Social activities with a partner, college friends or non-college friends
- Dislike subjects and/or teachers

Though not an exhaustive list, Longhurst's work does cover an array of excuses and explanations which we are regularly treated to. With college funding little changed in 10–20 years[4], there are also a raft of internal challenges which can lead to attendance issues. Issues of quality and consistency with classroom allocation, staffing and internal communication often directly lead to issues with attendance, and these are caused or exacerbated by funding (or a lack of funding).

This is also before we delve deeper into these reasons and ask *why* they lead to non-attendance[5]. For example, a dislike of the subject can be caused by something as serious as an undiagnosed special educational need[6] and prior negative experiences in that subject[7], or something as trivial as simply disliking members of that class.

As much as there are many reasons for it, teachers and leaders have a range of tools to combat non-attendance – chief among these is timetabling.

On an annual basis, timetabling is without doubt one of the most arduous and painstaking tasks every leader must complete. Taking into account the range of units, modules and qualifications, leaders must incorporate hundreds of students, scores of teachers, room availability, class size, student numbers, and fit this all into a neatly packaged college week, comprising full days, half days and evening sessions (all while analysing previous attendance data and attempting to dodge the cursed Friday afternoon slot).

3   R.J. Longhurst (1999) Why aren't they here? Student absenteeism in a Further Educa-
    tion college, *Journal of Further and Higher Education*, 23(1): 61–80.
4   J. Britton, C. Farquharson and L. Sibieta (2019) *2019 Annual Report on Education
    Spending in England*. London: Institute for Fiscal Studies.
5   S. Sinek, S. (2009) *Start with Why: How Great Leaders Inspire Everyone to Take
    Action*. London and New York: Penguin.
6   M. Orenstein, M. (2000) Picking up the clues: understanding undiagnosed learning
    disabilities, shame, and imprisoned intelligence, *Journal of College Student Psycho-
    therapy*, 15(2): 35–46.
7   S. Wallace (2017) *Motivating Unwilling Learners in Further Education: The Key to
    Improving Behaviour*. London: Bloomsbury.

Unfortunately, because timetabling can be such an onerous task, the priority is often to complete vocational timetabling in the first instance, and then look to cater for the needs of English and maths. Considering the pressures that timetabling can bring, this isn't surprising. I once worked with a leader who was tasked with creating a timetable so challenging that he reported dreaming about rooming clashes in his own home – his wife refused to give access to his kitchen as it was her timetabled slot.

High-quality, curriculum-led timetabling is vital to supporting attendance across the curriculum, and even more so in English and maths.

However, though high-quality timetabling can facilitate positive attendance statistics, it is obviously not the only factor, and is also no guarantee of high levels of attendance. This chapter seeks to deal with the issues and challenges of timetabling (including timelines and the stages necessary for effective timetabling) as well as strategies to improve whole-college English and maths attendance.

There is no silver bullet for improving attendance, and so this chapter seeks to give a range of strategies as (to paraphrase assessment expert Dylan Wiliam) nothing works everywhere, but everything works somewhere[8]. As no two colleges, cohorts or teacher and leadership teams are the same, these strategies can be used individually or in unison (dependent on context, setting and need) to support teachers, leaders and students in improving attendance.

What is Best Practice?

So, what does best practice look like for FE English and maths timetabling? Firstly, because English and maths faces such a range of challenges, it must be the priority when timetabling. This can be difficult to embed at first, and there may be some opposition from vocational leaders, but once implemented, attendance in English and maths is likely to improve and better collaboration between departments is also facilitated.

But why the vocational opposition? There are many answers, but the most common is very simply gaps. Lengthy gaps. Large gaps between lessons (i.e. lengths of time without any lesson timetabled) can lead to students leaving site, socializing or completing any number of activities which may provide a distraction to attending the next lesson.

For example, if a construction student has a construction lesson from 9 to 10am, they are much more likely to attend an English lesson which starts at 10am than if it starts at 12:30pm. This 2.5 hour gap is a sizeable chunk of time, especially if it is also the last lesson of the day. This gap massively increases the possibility that a student won't attend.

Though there can be difficult conversations around English and maths taking priority in timetabling, the benefits are obvious and should be used to persuade

---

8   D. Wiliam (2013) Assessment: the bridge between teaching and learning, *Voices from the Middle*, 21(2): 15–20.

senior leaders of the importance of English and maths timetabling. With better attendance linked to better outcomes[9], any step to improve attendance will aid end-of-year achievement rates. Also, this will ultimately help with retention, as students are able to complete courses without the sanctions imposed due to poor attendance. This also aids progression, as students are more likely to achieve English and maths qualifications and enter and achieve on Level 3 programmes. Highlighting this with senior leaders will strengthen the case for English and maths curriculum-led timetabling, as well as supporting students.

Lesson Length

Before discussing the challenges of timetabling, there is a very simple question which many colleges have answered differently, for many different reasons. How long should lessons be?

For GCSE, this is generally split into three options:

- one 3-hour lesson
- two 1.5-hour lessons
- three 1-hour lessons

For Functional Skills, 2 main options are used:

- one 1.5-hour lesson
- two 1-hour (or even 45-minute) lessons

It is of course difficult to say which is 'the best' option here as each choice has many pros and cons. Having said that, let's look at them.

GCSE: One 3-hour Lesson

Pros: Very simple to timetable and vocational teams are generally more satisfied with this session length as a result, potentially leading to more collaborative approaches to improving attendance. Attendance can be improved as all efforts can be focused on supporting students to attend one lesson, and one lesson only for each discipline. Further to this, it is easier to assign a room and any support staff. These sessions are also much easier to staff from an English and maths point of view.

Cons: Student behaviour can be a real issue. As covered in previous chapters, students can enter college with a range of previous negative experiences in English and maths (as well as a fear of the subject) – asking them to sit for 3 unbroken hours can prove difficult for students. Though there is no

---

9   Taylor, *Improving Attendance at School.*

definitive research on attention spans[10], this is especially true of students with certain SEND (attention deficit hyperactivity disorder, oppositional defiance disorder etc.). If a break is provided, this is either timetabled in (giving a 3-hour, 15-minute lesson) or, if not, this is taken from the lesson teaching time – a 15-minute break is 15 minutes of missed teaching. Regardless, students will need breaks[11], and this will detract from teaching.

If students miss this one 3-hour slot, they have also missed an entire week of teaching.

GCSE: Two 1.5-hour Lessons

Pros: There are few places in world education where lessons exceed 2 hours[12] and two 1.5-hour lessons is a quick fix for the attention span challenges seen in a 3-hour lesson. This is still not an enormous challenge for vocational teams to timetable and the wrap-around mentioned below is of great support to these sessions. If a student misses one of these sessions, they still have the opportunity to attend another.

Cons: In some instances, few vocational sessions are 1.5 hours long, and so 2-hour blocks have to be used for vocational timetabling. This can cause a range of issues. Also, with two sessions being needed, consistency of rooming can be difficult if teachers do not have their own dedicated base. Attendance challenges can arise as students need to attend twice as many lessons as they do for a single 3-hour slot. This also means more vocational support is required to assist with attendance, there are now twice as many registers to complete and analyse, and workload for administrative teams is also increased.

GCSE: Three 1-hour Lessons

Pros: Engagement in three 1-hour sessions is much greater, and students have a much higher chance of attending at least one session as there are multiple opportunities for vocational staff to support attendance. There are also opportunities for teachers to attempt a much broader range of topics and tasks in lessons, and to take greater risks due to the shorter nature of lessons and greater probability of positive student behaviour.

Cons: These sessions are extremely difficult to timetable and there is likely to be much opposition to this format from vocational leaders as a result. A way around this, which does occur in some colleges, is to have two mandatory sessions with the third lesson invite only. Irrespective of the potential moral

---

10 K. Wilson and J.H. Korn (2007) Attention during lectures: beyond ten minutes, *Teaching of Psychology*, 34(2): 85–9.

11 P. Osborne, P. (2005) *Teaching English One to One*. London: Modern English Publishing.

12 K.J. Roth (2006) *Teaching Science in Five Countries: Results from the TIMSS 1999 Video Study: Statistical Analysis Report*. Washington, DC: US Department of Education, National Center for Education Statistics.

issue here (disbarring students from a third session would need an extremely good justification), intentionally depriving students of an hour of teaching should never occur. With the additional burden on vocational and admin staff, and the likelihood of being given the same room for all three sessions extremely low, more lessons really can mean more problems. These sessions can also prove very difficult to staff.

Functional Skills: One 1.5-hour Lesson or Two 1-hour Lessons

Similar to above, more lessons can equal more problems. However, with additional teaching time (with the obvious expectation that teaching is of a good standard), students are much more likely to achieve positive outcomes. Simply put, if they get more teaching, they should learn more, leading to improved achievement.

For Functional Skills, however, it can be difficult to secure this time in the first place, let alone taking into account the additional staffing needs two 1-hour slots will bring, the rooming issues two sessions represent and the attached support problems additional sessions can bring (as detailed above).

To summarize, the 'best' or most effective lesson length very much depends on the resources a college has at its disposal. For GCSE provision, three 1-hour sessions can be extremely effective, but this represents a big ask in terms of resources. With this in mind, and the obvious engagement challenges from 3-hour lessons, two 1.5-hour lessons does appear to be the most effective lesson length.

For Functional Skills, though, two 1-hour sessions would represent additional teaching time, while the drain on resources negates many benefits, and one 1.5-hour lesson can be just as effective if the time is managed well.

Timetabling

The answer? Wrap-around timetabling. If English and maths produce an initial timetable first, vocational leaders can then wrap their timetables around English and maths. For example, the head of department for construction receives the timetable for English and maths shown in Table 7.1.

The following sessions have been timetabled for English:

Monday: 9–10:30am: GCSE English
Monday: 9–10am: Functional Skills Entry Level English
Wednesday : 11–12:30pm: GCSE English
Wednesday : 11–12pm: Functional Skills Level 1 English

With the following for maths:

Wednesday: 1–2:30pm: GCSE maths
Wednesday: 1–2pm: Functional Skills Entry Level maths
Thursday: 9–10:30am: GCSE maths
Thursday: 9–10am: Functional Skills Level 1 maths

Table 7.1

	9–10	10–11	11–12	12–1	1–2	2–3
Monday	GCSE English					
	FS Entry Level English					
Tuesday						
Wednesday			GCSE English		GCSE maths	
			FS L1 English		FS Entry Level maths	
Thursday	GCSE maths					
	FS L1 maths					
Friday						

A timetable like this should be created and distributed to all vocational heads of department around February – this will give them plenty of opportunities to schedule slots before and after English. This is beneficial for many reasons. Firstly, vocational tutors can remind students of English and maths sessions, locations and expectations around attendance (with the potential even for escorting students who refuse to attend). Also, there are no gaps in a student's timetable and it becomes more convenient for them to attend.

With Functional Skills scheduled at the same time, there is the opportunity for student progression (i.e. both Entry Level and Level 1 lesson times will be free on vocational timetables – students can complete the Entry Level qualification and, depending on suitability, could then move to a Level 1 lesson, or even a GCSE session). With vocational heads of department completing their timetable around the English and maths timetable, a vocational timetable may look something like the one in Table 7.2.

This timetable offers students solid opportunities to attend English and maths: there are not too many early lessons or late finishes, lessons are seemingly built around vocational lessons (though the opposite is true), there is opportunity for progression if appropriate and (as there are no vocational sessions running during English and maths) vocational teachers have the opportunity to support English and maths.

This support can come in the form of checking attendance in the first 5–10 minutes, and making crucial phone calls to students/parents to remind them of attendance responsibilities, or it could simply be that vocational staff, tutors or pastoral staff check-in on the lesson to confirm attendance.

Again, these changes can take considerable seniority to make them happen, but the benefits far outweigh any negatives. Persuade managers of their

Table 7.2

	9–10	10–11	11–12	12–1	1–2	2–3
Monday	GCSE English / FS Entry Level English	Vocational lesson			Vocational lesson	
Tuesday	Vocational lesson					
Wednesday	Vocational lesson		GCSE English / FS L1 English		GCSE maths / FS Entry Level maths	Vocational lesson
Thursday	GCSE maths / FS L1 maths	Vocational lesson			Vocational lesson	
Friday						

importance by highlighting the potential for improved achievement rates, and the positive impact on the student experience.

Another vital aspect of timetabling is making sure there is continuity and consistency with rooming. This situation is different throughout the country: some teachers have their own year-round dedicated classroom, while others share a classroom, and some do not have a designated classroom and instead must use a different room for each lesson.

Ideally, each English and maths teacher will have their own designated classroom. This facilitates good practice in a number of ways:

- Student familiarization with the environment helps build teacher–student relationships in a 'safe space'[13].
- Consistent rooming can also improve attendance. If two weekly GCSE lessons lasting 1.5 hours each are taught over 33 weeks, each lesson equates to 1.5 per cent of attendance. Students regularly claim not to have known where lessons were held in the first few weeks of term (or if there is a room change later in the year). If we can eradicate this problem through consistent room location, this could be worth a significant increase in attendance.
- Effective use of support materials – spelling rules, common formulas, question timings, prompts, displays – all of these materials can be best utilized when teachers have access to a permanent base.

---

13 O. Dreon and D. Polly, eds (2016) *Teacher Education for Ethical Professional Practice in the 21st Century*. Hershey, PA: IGI Global.

- Workload – if a teacher has a different classroom for each lesson, and an office base, it can take anywhere between 2 and 10 minutes to reach classrooms and return. Over a weekly timetable (say eight 3-hour GCSE slots), even 2 minutes' travel time for each lesson can represent an hour and 20 minutes of dead time. Over a year, this equates to over a week of walking time.
- Better practice – if based in one room, teachers can have access to more resources to deliver more engaging lessons. Put simply, few teachers will carry 25 dictionaries to each room – are they able to transport a range of resources if not based in their own classroom?

Obviously, it is not always possible for teachers to have their own base. However, to assist with attendance and timetabling, having the same room for each session with a particular class is enormously beneficial. For example, take the above hypothetical construction class – if students have two 1.5-hour GCSE maths lessons, having each lesson in the same room provides consistency and a sense of ownership.

When I worked as an English teacher in a secondary school, occasionally an assembly would be held during lessons. Once, this happened during a Year 10 English literature lesson. As I led the class to the main hall, I realised I had forgotten my key fob. I asked a member of the class if he could return and get it for me. His response?

'Where is it Sir? In our room?'

'Our' room. Not 'the' room, not 'a' room, but '*our*' room. This sense of belonging, of a shared environment, can massively help to build relationships. If there is no familiar 'turf', building trust can be difficult. Lessons can feel transient as there is no base, no home, and it can be difficult for students to view teachers with integrity, as they haven't even been given their own classroom.

The only remaining issue is the timetabling of English and maths slots for apprentices. The main two models for teaching apprentices are either an in-house approach similar to that for all other students, or to have teachers travel to workplaces to deliver sessions there. The preferable method is of course to have apprentices come to college – this is cost-effective in terms of time, resources, staff and finances, and also means teachers have additional time to prepare (i.e. they don't need to travel anywhere).

However, this can provide issues for employers, who need to release apprentices from work. To get around this, schedule sessions at 8:30am or before, or after 5pm. This may prove initially difficult for apprentices to attend, but they may well be additionally motivated to complete English and maths courses as a result. Further to this, utilizing online resources is another option – there will be more on this later in this chapter.

Improving Attendance

So, timetables are agreed and session lengths are also confirmed. Timetables have been distributed to vocational teams and everyone is aware of the times and days to support with attendance in the coming academic year. However, with so many changes in comparison to school (new environment, new friends, new teachers, no uniform, just 3 or even 1.5 hours of English and/or maths instead of 5), students will need additional attendance guidance. Curriculum-led timetabling and vocational support are not enough – what other steps can we take to improve attendance and give students the best possible opportunity to succeed in English and maths?

Don't Mix Sessions

With so many vocational timetables, and potential challenges to find slots for English and maths, it can be very tempting to mix vocational groups. Some enormous challenges can be solved by simply mixing the GCSE English students from health and care with engineers, so why don't we do it? Though this solves many logistical issues (and is certainly easier from an administrative point of view), the inherent challenges here centre around classroom and student dynamics. Obviously, we can't just say that *all* health and care students are the same, that *all* engineering students are the same, and some excellent steps are being taken to ensure full equality and diversity in our classrooms. Having said that, it is a statement of fact that most engineering classrooms are full of young men, and most health and care classrooms are full of young women.

As an extension, mixing these classrooms can create anxiety among students. Students, just like adults, can very easily be afraid of anything new or different[14], and entering a classroom with five to ten students from another area very much qualifies under this criterion. This can lead to behaviour issues, challenges with contextualisation ('Why are we talking about engineering? We do sport'), potential bullying issues around identity[15] and a host of other problems which then manifest as additional workload and detract from what is important.

This is not to say this shouldn't happen at all (it can happen on a case-by-case basis or via infill into adult groups for the right students) but it should be infrequent. Though it may be challenging to timetable according to vocational area, it causes many more challenges to mix groups.

As an extension of this, though it can be tempting to place students in two different GCSE groups (i.e. group 1 with peers and group 2 with another vocational area) to navigate a challenging vocational timetable, the inconsistency the student will experience is potentially academically damaging[16].

Use the Data and Communicate

To actively and accurately monitor attendance, it is vital that the data is accurate and precise. It really is that simple. Registers need to be completed inside

14 www.anti-bullyingalliance.org.uk/news-insight/news/ahead-anti-bullying-week-new-poll-shows-children-england-worry-about-being-seen- (accessed 11 January 2021).

15 P.K. Smith (2016) Bullying: Definition, types, causes, consequences and intervention, *Social and Personality Psychology Compass*, 10(9): 519–32.

16 A. Critto (2000) *Consistency: Being Coherent*. Lanham, MD: University Press of America.

10 minutes of a lesson starting so that pastoral teams can begin the process of identifying where students are. Accurate registers are also vital as a means of safeguarding, and also for non-attendance data analysis further down the line.

Can we identify trends in the data? Do students from certain groups in certain areas miss certain sessions on certain days? Why? Are there hot spots for non-attendance? What can we do about this? Who can support English and maths? Without the data, we can't identify trends and we can't ask the right questions.

Attached to this, there must be a solid line of communication from teacher to leader to attendance administration to pastoral staff and everyone in between.

This data also gives us the ammunition we need when in meetings with students – it's easy to argue against 'your attendance has been poor', but less so against 'you've missed seven of the last ten sessions'. This also allows us to identify students who are most at risk of withdrawing or dropping out of college altogether and to put steps in place to support these students.

Accuracy is important, but not without efficiency. The faster we get this accurate data, the faster we can support those who most need it.

Regular Meetings

Though there are many leaders who would claim that there are already too many meetings in their calendar[17], done correctly, meetings on attendance can be enormously effective and impactful. Firstly, invite all stakeholders (that word again) – a representative from admin/data/exams, a senior leader, the head of department and a pastoral representative. Keep a tight agenda, and focus on what will make a difference or 'make the boat go faster'[18] and leave anything not directly related to identifying and solving attendance issues for another time.

Too often, a student is discussed who has poor attendance, and suddenly someone will launch into an anecdote about that student's behaviour. It is not the right setting – focus on how the student can be supported to attend. Focus on key statistics and data – are there any trends? Any sub-trends? What have we done so far? Are those actions scalable?

A former colleague sent out letters at the end of each half term, giving parents and carers information about students' performance. A fantastic idea, and it worked exceptionally well for that area, but was it realistically scalable to English and maths, which had over five times the number of students? The pay-off did not match the workload, so it was not used.

Identify small groups of students, target them, statistically monitor those around them, and improve their attendance. More often than not, if we identify and support the non-attendance leaders in peer groups, we can positively impact attitudes and then attendance[19]. These meetings should be held no more

17 S.G. Rogelberg (2018) *The Surprising Science of Meetings: How you can Lead your Team to Peak Performance*. New York: Oxford University Press.

18 B. Hunt-Davis and H. Beveridge (2012) *Will it Make the Boat Go Faster?* Leicester: Troubador.

19 S. Hallam and L. Rogers (2008) *Improving Behaviour and Attendance at School*. Buckingham: McGraw-Hill Education.

than fortnightly and no less than once a month, and make them meaningful through collaboration[20] – English and maths leaders: what are you willing to do for vocational teams, before they support you in developing attendance?

Sanctions and Rewards

Detailed at length in Chapter 3, sanctions and rewards/incentives are an absolute essential for developing outstanding attendance. Again, this does not mean that we deliver a gold-plated Ferrari every time John attends English and maths each week, but we must recognise those who are consistently attending (and meeting our expectations).

To leave students unrewarded for consistent high-quality behaviour is to risk them falling into the bad habits of those we sanction. It also gives those in the middle (not consistently attending, but not missing enough sessions to cause concern – those at 85–90 per cent attendance) little motivation to improve their attendance. They attend just enough to be left alone – this can be a sizeable group of students. Give them something to aim for (rewards) and something to avoid (sanctions) and all students' attendance is likely to improve[21].

Less discussed, is providing rewards for staff. Creating an informal league table to measure each vocational area's English and maths attendance (with the blessing of each area) can be extremely effective in supporting attendance. This should obviously be done in jest, and should clearly be communicated and approved beforehand, with weekly or fortnightly updates given with the promise of sensational prizes (£1, or a cup of coffee).

Texts

Most schools and colleges use texts to encourage and motivate students to attend, but are we doing it correctly? A 2017 study into attendance found a similar story to that found in most colleges – attendance was initially good, and then started to drop off[22].

To arrest this slide, the researchers sent weekly carefully worded motivational texts (starting around half term) to encourage and remind students of lessons, expectations and their responsibilities. Texts worded similarly to the following were sent at the beginning of each week:

- '[Student name] it never hurts to be prepared! Decide when you will practise and mark next week's class in your diary.'

---

20 A. Buck (2016) *Leadership Matters: How Leaders at all Levels can Create Good Schools*. Melton, Woodbridge: John Catt Educational Ltd.
21 A. Evans and M. Walters (2002) *From Absence to Attendance*. London: CIPD Publishing.
22 R. Chande, M. Luca, M. Sanders et al. (2017) *Increasing Attendance and Attainment Among Adult Students in the UK: Evidence from a Field Experiment*. Working paper. London: Behavioural Insights Team.

- 'You are making progress and can succeed [Name]. Well done, you've reached the mid-term break! Take time to practise what you've learned and stay connected: [link to online group].'
- 'This week you will be studying [topic] – why not get a head start by looking at these resources: [sample online revision]?'

The research noted an initial 4 per cent increase in average attendance with a 7 per cent increase over a full academic year. It also increased the chances of exam achievement by 8 per cent.

With most college software packages containing auto-text message systems, this can be quickly and easily set up. If cost is an issue, as above, target specific groups and monitor the impact.

As successful as this approach can be, there are opportunities to modify it. If a student has lessons on a Friday, a Monday text is unlikely to motivate them, so send out texts midweek. Also, confirm that students are happy to receive these texts at the start of the year (I was once accused of stalking a student due to these texts as she felt they were coming directly from me).

Using a similar system and utilizing peer support can also be enormously useful. Using online tools such as Microsoft Teams, Moodle or Zoom, setting up student peer support groups and encouraging motivational dialogue can be done with immediate impact (obviously, with all students confirming consent). We are much more likely to do what our peers do[23], and so harnessing the power of peer groups can be enormously effective.

Breakfast Clubs

A simple, yet effective tool which is used in the majority of colleges, but are we using it to its fullest extent? Students arrive for a funded breakfast – we have a captive audience: offer English and maths support groups during this time. As discussed in a previous chapter, make English and maths relevant by hosting workshops to support students with the challenges they face outside of college (bills, job applications, CVs, personal statements etc.).

Promoting this early attendance in college for breakfast and workshops will likely become a habit[24], become embedded and lead to better attendance.

It's Good to Talk and Build Relationships

The data has been analysed, the meetings have been held and non-attending students have been identified. We know that building positive relationships improves engagement[25], but how do we build these relationships if students don't attend? Well, initiate the relationship.

---

23 Behavioural Insight Team (2014) *EAST: Four Simple Ways to Apply Behavioural Insights.* London: Behavioural Insight Team.
24 J. Dean (2013) *Making Habits, Breaking Habits: How to make Changes that Stick.* London: Oneworld Publications.
25 S. Ellis and J. Tod (2018) *Behaviour for Learning: Promoting Positive Relationships in the Classroom.* Abingdon: Routledge.

Pair a student with a staff mentor – this does not have to be someone teaching on the student's course (it's better if they are not attached to this course or English and maths). Next, invite the student in for an informal meeting and introduce them to their mentor – explain that the mentor will be supporting their attendance and checking they have everything they need to be successful.

From this point, the mentor will contact the student on each day they have English and/or maths to confirm they are prepared for lessons and see if they require any support, while also reminding the student of times and locations of lessons. This contact can take a range of forms (all within safeguarding parameters, of course) – email, phone call, text or distance learning tool (Teams etc.) – and staff should look to be supportive and not threaten or discuss sanctions.

This contact may not fix the problem, but it can lead to positive change[26].

Talk to Students

What about next steps? What if the strategies here don't show an improvement in attendance? If these strategies prove ineffective, it's time for a dialogue. Setting up regular panels to discuss underlying problems with students can prove enormously effective. Held weekly or fortnightly, panels are attended by a senior leader, two or three middle leaders, the student and a parent or carer[27]. Panels are the last step before serious disciplinary action is taken (suspension, withdrawal) and act as an opportunity for students to discuss any support they need, but have not declared.

Though leaders and teachers can require some persuasion to attend these panels (it represents additional workload, after all), I have seen first-hand the positive impact they can have. The most striking thing about them was seeing the number of safeguarding and SEND issues which were raised almost immediately. When students enter an environment that they know to be safe, with college leaders and a parent/carer present, they are able to open up. In one panel, a student admitted he could barely read, and his non-attendance and behaviour had been to mask this. Relevant support was put in place and his attendance and engagement improved.

This will not be the case for all learners – there are those who don't attend simply because they don't want to – but it makes a difference to some, and that is why we do what we do.

It is important that staff attendance at panels is organised via rota and also that there are set guidelines (as well as a chair to the panel), but other than that, the meeting acts as an opportunity to include parents/carers and also get a more rounded picture around why a student doesn't attend.

---

26 B. Luke (2015) What is missing? Rethinking student absences, *Accounting Education*, 24(6): 569–72.

27 P. Martinez (2000) *Raising Achievement: A Guide to Successful Strategies*. London: Further Education Development Agency.

Pastoral Care and Flexibility

Though timetabling and flexibility rarely go hand in hand, we must try and make exceptions for students wherever we can. Students can face many challenges inside and outside of college – part-time jobs, childcare issues and travel issues, to name just a few.

To support students, sometimes we need to move them to sessions outside of intended lesson times, or sanction missed lessons where appropriate (while providing additional materials to catch up). Moving students to slots that start later in the day (due to childcare or travel issues) can show a trust that students will want to repay.

To complement this flexibility, using pastoral teams to make sure students have all the support they need is vital. Allocating members of the pastoral team to concentrate solely on attendance can be enormously effective, as they quickly develop relationships with students who need additional support. To be fully effective, however, there must be the time and resources available for pastoral attendance staff to build these relationships and also work as part of a broader team including administrative teams, academic staff, leaders and vocational tutors.

Conclusion

There are many strategies aimed at improving attendance and developing effective timetabling that are either ineffective or simply not right for the context they are applied in. The strategies and practices mentioned above are not to be taken as gospel, but rather adapted and innovated upon to find the best fit for whatever college they are trialled in. To be fully effective, use these strategies as a basis for research and identify individual issues and challenges. As far back as 1999, researchers and politicians suggested that further research should be done in Further Education[28] and it is obvious that there is still a paucity of research available into FE challenges[29] – we must conduct our own and attendance is a prime topic.

For attendance, as in many other areas of FE, accountability is vital. Expectations, responsibilities and accountabilities must be identified, communicated and monitored on a regular basis to develop a truly effective culture around attendance. The expectation is that students will attend 100 per cent of sessions and we will support them to do this. There will of course be those who don't achieve this – we must support them as best we can.

Providing childcare facilities (if possible), bursary payments, pairing students with mentors, using rewards and sanctions and motivating staff can all

---

28 M. Wicks (1999) Opening address to Further Education Development Agency Research Conference, Cambridge, 9 December.

29 D. Greatbatch and S. Tate (2018) *Teaching, Leadership and Governance in Further Education*. London: DfE.

play a part in improving attendance, but this must all take place college-wide and as part of a collaborative culture.

With Covid-19 meaning more remote and distance learning is taking place, relationships are more vital than ever in ensuring student engagement. Gaining student feedback is key to excellent engagement, and this should also play a role in student attendance.

The key here is to identify potential issues as soon as possible and work with everyone, including students and parents/carers, to develop curriculum-led timetabling and to support and guide students to attend so that they can reach their potential.

Summary

- Curriculum-led timetabling starts with English and maths and then becomes a collaborative endeavour.
- Wrap-around timetabling is key to supporting outstanding attendance.
- English and maths attendance is a whole-college responsibility – make sure everyone knows what part they play, and monitor this.
- Use the data – accurate data capture and analysis is the foundation of improving attendance.
- Before we start attendance sanctions, ask *why* there is non-attendance.
- Do your research – where are the problems? What can you do to offer support? Who is accountable? What resources do they need?

Reflection

- How do you check that timetabling models best serve students?
- What additional evidence can you use to support timetable creation?
- What can you put in place for students who do not 'fit' into existing time-tabling models?
- How do you support students with low attendance?
- How are practitioners communicating with students about attendance? Is it effective? What do students think/feel about this?

8 Assessment, Tracking and Feedback

'Another test? It doesn't matter what I get because I won't try. I'll just revise for the real one and pass.'

17-year-old engineering student (2018)

Despite this student's protests, assessment is crucial. However, with accountability used as a tool to improve standards and achievement (in schools and in colleges), there is the constant worry that students are over-tested, and disengaged as a result[1].

So, what can we do? Well, first we need to look at the assessment cycle.

The Stages of Assessment

Though there are many variations on the length, style and types of assessment teachers use, the majority of traditional assessment takes place using the main components of this cycle[2, 3]:

1 **Assess and evaluate**

   In FE, students complete a skills-based initial assessment (which is usually completed via computer) to identify a suitable course level. Once students have enrolled on a course at a relevant level, they then complete a course/unit assessment to evaluate their subject-specific strengths and weaknesses. For example, Michael wants to study construction. He first completes an initial assessment which shows a Level 2 course to be the most suitable. Then, having enrolled on a Level 2 construction course, he completes a subject-specific diagnostic assessment to identify his strengths and weaknesses in construction.

---

1   F.J. Brill, L. Grayson, L. Kuhn and S. O'Donnell (2018) *What Impact Does Accountability Have on Curriculum, Standards and Engagement in Education? A Literature Review.* Slough: NFER.
2   C. Flynn, D. Gilchrist and L. Olson (2004) Using the assessment cycle as a tool for collaboration, *Resource Sharing & Information Networks*, 17(1–2): 187–203.
3   D. Reinholz (2016) The assessment cycle: a model for learning through peer assessment, *Assessment and Evaluation in Higher Education*, 41(2): 301–15.

Figure 8.1

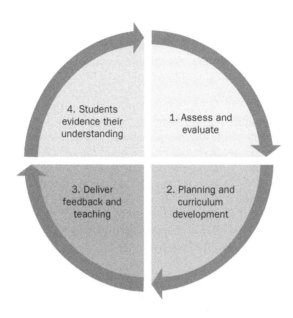

2 **Planning and curriculum development**

The result of this in-class assessment (or evaluation[4]) is then used to adapt or modify schemes of work, the focus of curriculum coverage and future lessons. Some topics and tasks will be covered in more detail, some in less, depending on the outcome of individual and whole-class assessments. In other words, we give less time to what they know and more time to what they don't know.

3 **Deliver feedback and teaching**

Having assessed and evaluated students' knowledge and understanding, and potentially adapting schemes of work, teachers then teach suitable content to develop students' skills, knowledge and understanding. Simply put, we teach them what they don't know, can't do or have misconceptions about.

4 **Students evidence their understanding**

Finally, students complete tasks to evidence their knowledge, skills and understanding of what has been taught. Taking many forms, this includes anything from an oral presentation to a final, standardised exam. Essentially, students' work will show us what they've understood. When this final stage is complete, the cycle will start again.

---

4   M. Scriven (1967) The methodology of evaluation, in R.W. Tyler, R.M. Gagné and M. Scriven (eds) *Perspectives of Curriculum Evaluation*. Chicago: Rand McNally, vol. I, pp. 39–83.

How we Assess

The stages of this cycle are not fixed and they can exchange places or happen at the same time – i.e. students can receive feedback as they evidence understanding; the lesson focus can change mid-task because of formative assessment responses.

Formative assessment (or assessment for learning[5]) is loosely defined as assessing students while learning happens, i.e. during lessons[6]. Occurring continuously, it helps adapt and modify teaching by identifying knowledge gaps through recap quizzes, peer/self-assessment and questioning. This lets teachers know what is 'going in' and what they need to revisit or review.

Summative assessment is the assessment completed at the end of units, topics or sequences of learning, and it takes the form of testing (e.g. GCSE exams) or coursework. In FE, this is generally a traditional assessment such as mock exams or lengthy exam-style tasks.

Each plays an important role and so it is vital that we assess effectively.

Effective Assessment

So, what does effective assessment look like? Firstly, it should be effective for both teachers *and* students. With teacher accountability[7] and student mental health suffering as a result of high-stakes exams[8] (particularly low achievers[9]), it's time for a rethink.

Evidence suggests student mental health suffers as a result of what high-stakes assessment represents[10, 11]. 'Failing' can represent future career failure, low earnings and low social status or self-esteem; we need to start with the perception of assessment.

A potential solution? Low-stakes assessment.

---

5   P. Black and D. Wiliam (1998) Inside the black box: raising standards through classroom assessment, *Phi Delta Kappan*, 80(2): 139–48.

6   D. Wiliam (2006) Formative assessment: getting the focus right, *Educational Assessment*, 11(3–4): 283–9.

7   W.C. Smith (2014) The global transformation toward testing for accountability, *Education Policy Analysis Archives*, 22(116), doi: 10.14507/epaa.v22.1571.

8   D.W. Putwain (2008) Examination stress and test anxiety, *Psychologist*, 21(12): 1026–9.

9   H. Goldstein (2004) Education for all: the globalization of learning targets, *Comparative Education*, 40(1): 7–14.

10 M. Denscombe (2000) Social conditions for stress: young people's experience of doing GCSEs, *British Educational Research Journal*, 26(3): 259–374.

11 D.W. Putwain (2009) Assessment and examination stress in KS4, *British Educational Research Journal*, 35(3): 391–411.

Low-stakes Assessment

As Craig Barton expertly details in his book *How I Wish I'd Taught Maths*[12], the use of low-stakes assessments in lessons to recap topics[13] and assess understanding can have a lasting positive impact. The 'testing effect'[14], which suggests that regular, active retrieval of knowledge improves retention, suggests that short, regular tests help students remember information.

Barton also states that the tests don't have to fit the style or format of an exam[15] and are just as effective in the form of multiple-choice questions or questions requiring brief answers. They effectively highlight gaps in knowledge (as they are done frequently) and can be a more accurate way to track student progress as well as helping student engagement.

What does this Look Like in the Classroom?

Barton's research shows that testing a variety of previously taught topics is best, so quizzes should assess a range of different content.

Having worked with a range of practitioners and leaders in a number of colleges to trial and develop these quizzes, it was found that best results are achieved by following these guidelines:

- Using 'quiz' or 'recap' instead of 'assessment' or 'test' was positively received by students.
- They were more beneficial when completed at the start of lessons for 10–15 minutes.
- Quizzes were completed either each lesson or weekly.
- A grid format was used for maths and listed questions for English (examples below).
- Use of self- and peer assessment was effective and cut teacher workload.
- Students' engagement improved when they could track their scores.

---

12 C. Barton (2018) *How I Wish I'd Taught Maths: Lessons Learned from Research, Conversations with Experts, and 12 Years of Mistakes.* Melton, Woodbridge: John Catt Educational Ltd.

13 R.A. Bjork and A.S. Benjamin (2011) On the symbiosis of remembering, forgetting, and learning, in A.S. Benjamin (ed.) *Successful Remembering and Successful Forgetting: A Festschrift in Honor of Robert A. Bjork.* New York: Taylor & Francis, pp. 1–22.

14 H.L. Roediger III, P.K. Agarwal, M.A. McDaniel et al. (2011) Test-enhanced learning in the classroom: long-term improvements from quizzing, *National Library of Medicines: Applied*, 17(4): 382–95.

15 K.B. McDermott, P.K. Agarwal, L. D'Antonio, H.L. Roediger III and M. McDaniel (2014) Both multiple-choice and short-answer quizzes enhance later exam performance in middle and high school classes, *Journal of Experimental Psychology: Applied*, 20(1): 3–21.

Figure 8.2

Number – Grid 1 (Non-calculator)		
Work out: $-6 + 8 \times 2 =$ $(2 + 6) \times 3^2 =$	Convert to decimals: $\dfrac{3}{5} =$ $\dfrac{1}{8} =$	Multiply: $6 \times 17 =$ $35 \times 28 =$
Percentages: 10% of £65 = 15% of £80 =	Number Machine Input ⊢ × 5 ⊢ -2 ⊢ Output Input = 3 Output = 3 Input = Output = 28	What is the **lowest common multiple** of 9 and 6?
Dividing by 10 & 100: $25 \div 10 =$ $720 \div 100 =$	List all of the **factors** of 30.	Answer: $8^2 =$ $\sqrt{100} =$

Created by Richard Walsh

Quizzes can take several forms, but a nine-question grid format for maths, distributed on A4 paper, like the one in Figure 8.2, was particularly effective.

If any student were to complete the quiz before time (or can't complete remaining questions), text books or extension activities are available. The teacher would then take students through the answers and they mark their own (or a friend's) work. It's also important to remember that teachers need to circulate to check that self- and peer marking is being done correctly, and this is also an excellent opportunity to quickly assess student understanding through checking answers in real time.

Students should keep the quizzes and either store them in class (in a folder) or take them home for revision. If kept in class, they can also be given out near exam time for revision.

For English, a grid format, as above, can easily be used; however, a list format is also beneficial with quizzes distributed on A4 paper. Again, students self- and peer assess to cut teacher workload. The GCSE English language example in Figure 8.3 includes images to further stimulate students.

As long as these overall key guidelines are followed, compromises can be made in how quizzes are applied. Though we know they should be used regularly to be effective, they can become progressively more difficult.

The number of questions is negotiable (though obviously 9 to 15 questions is optimal) and the time students are given to complete the quizzes can be adapted (though 10–15 minutes is best).

Figure 8.3

1. What is an adjective used for? (1)
2. Write one sentence to describe how this passage makes you feel:
   'I panicked as I grabbed the water desperate for something to clutch on to. There was nothing. No boat. Just inky cold water.' (1)
3. What is the focus in these sentences: 'Michael was driving. A thin, angular man, with a long, starved faced, he seemed to occupy almost all the seat, sprawling awkwardly.' (1)
4. Use a semi-colon in a sentence. (1)
5. Give an example of a metaphor. (1)
6. P2Q2: Summarise the difference between these two images: (2)

6a.  6b.

7. Give an example of a simile. (1)
8. Compare your viewpoints and feelings of school and college. (3)
9. *Every 16-year-old should be entitled to Jobseeker's Allowance* – name 3 points you would talk about in response to this statement. (3)
10. Give an example of a structural feature. (1)

6a. Image sourced from: www.flickr.com/photos/rlwilsonphotography/13773362623, available under a CCBY 2.0 license, credit Ricky Wilson via Flickr

6b. Image sourced from: www.flickr.com/photos/rhythmstrip/9634023394/, available under a CCBY 2.0 license, credit Edwin Martinez via Flickr

Although a move away from high-stakes testing (and accountability) is welcomed by most, there must be some motivation to achieve and do well. As a result, there must be something at stake or students may disengage[16].

Tracking Low-stakes Quizzes

Throughout teacher training, we are told that boys respond well to competitions and competitive tasks. Many of us have held quizzes and gleefully announced 'winners' (those coming in the top two or three) and marvelled at our own excellent practice as previously bored or apathetic students started to engage. The issue with this is that when announcing these scores, we don't focus on those who come last or nearer the bottom, and we definitely don't think about the impact this has on their self-esteem or confidence. As Matt Pinkett and

16 D. Didau and N. Rose (2016) *What Every Teacher Needs to Know About … Psychology*. Melton, Woodbridge: John Catt Educational Ltd.

Table 8.1

Week	Score	Area to improve
1	6/10	Sentence types
2	8/10	Language features
3	3/10	Punctuation
4	5/10	Punctuation
5	7/10	Structural features
6		
7		

Mark Roberts discuss in their excellent book *Boys Don't Try? Rethinking Masculinity in Schools*[17], the lasting impact of this can be profound.

As a result, it is vital to create a culture where students are only in competition with themselves. To do this, simple and bespoke tracking should be used to allow students to quickly check their progress.

Printing, cutting and sticking may be something more associated with Primary Education, but putting a template like Table 8.1 into a student's book means they are regularly able to check their own progress. Adding the third column, which asks students to identify an area of weakness from the quiz, also gives teachers a quick and effective method of checking what needs to be reviewed in future.

In this example, punctuation is identified as an area of development twice in the same half term; as a result, additional intervention or teaching around punctuation can then be the focus of future lessons. This can be further analysed by asking students to write *which* example of punctuation, language feature or mathematical operation they find challenging.

Whether glued into a book or placed in a folder, it is important that every effort is taken to stop students sharing scores as this negatively impacts students who receive lower marks.

These quizzes can also inject students with much needed enthusiasm and motivation for assessment as they try and improve upon previous scores. If students don't perform well, they will also have opportunities to improve within a relatively short period of time, unlike longer, traditional assessment methods where students may wait five to six weeks before another assessment or mock exam.

Like everything in education, consistency is key. To effectively use low-stakes quizzes and make sure they are used consistently, it is important to collaborate and create the quizzes with a group of colleagues or, ideally, as a

---

17 M. Pinkett and M. Roberts (2019) *Boys Don't Try? Rethinking Masculinity in Schools*. Abingdon and New York: Routledge.

department. Not only does this ensure that quizzes are similar in format, length and challenge, it also cuts workload[18].

The Role of Summative Assessment

So, what about 'traditional' summative assessment? Well, clearly, it still has a place.

Low-stakes quizzes are highly effective; however, summative assessment is just as important. Traditionally completed in two stages, summative assessment is first done via diagnostic assessment at the beginning of a unit and completed with a second (final) assessment at the end of a unit. The effectiveness of teaching is easily defined by achievement in the second assessment, with progress defined through analysing the improvement made between the first and final assessment.

Traditional Summative Assessment Timetable

Table 8.2 Traditional summative assessment timetable

Term 1, half term 1 (September – October)

Week 1	Week 2	Week 3	Week 4	Week 5	Week 6	Week 7
Diagnostic assessment	Normal teaching with low-stakes quiz	Normal teaching with low-stakes quiz	Normal teaching with low-stakes quiz	Normal teaching with low-stakes quiz	Normal teaching with low-stakes quiz	Final summative assessment

Table 8.3 Traditional summative assessment timetable

Term 1, half term 2 (November – December)

Week 1	Week 2	Week 3	Week 4	Week 5	Week 6	Week 7
Diagnostic assessment	Normal teaching with low-stakes quiz	Normal teaching with low-stakes quiz	Normal teaching with low-stakes quiz	Normal teaching with low-stakes quiz	Normal teaching with low-stakes quiz	Final summative assessment

---

18 L. Card (2016) Designing a sustainable curriculum and assessment system, in N. Ellis (ed.) *Managing Teacher Workload: A Whole-School Approach to Finding the Balance.* Melton, Woodbridge: John Catt Educational Ltd, pp. 34–44.

Though this does have its uses, there are problems with this approach in FE.

Firstly, when students know assessment dates, they may not attend due to previous negative assessment experiences. Additionally, repeating lengthy and immediate in-class assessments (a hallmark of school experience) is unlikely to reassure them that lessons will be anything different to school. Students have done lots of these assessments in school, and we know they are less motivated when completing repeat assessments[19], so we may not get a true reflection of their knowledge and understanding.

Instead, it is better to start with low-stakes quizzes for the initial few weeks and layer these assessments in the build-up to summative assessment. As discussed by Tom Sherrington in his analysis of *Rosenshine's Principles in Action*, this allows time to make knowledge and understanding more secure before we assess it.

An effective way to do this is to continue with two key assessments for each unit (or half term), and then space them out further (aiding retrieval practice[20]).

So, instead of testing at the beginning of a unit, where you know the score will be low, just *teach*. This helps build relationships with students and builds their confidence. Then, the first summative assessment takes place three to four weeks into each half term when students have actually experienced teaching. The assessment should take the form of a 'normal' lesson – i.e. students shouldn't spend a series of lessons preparing. Students will then be given a mark or score and relevant feedback (more on this later).

The second summative assessment is now replaced by a mock exam. This is a more effective way to assess overall knowledge and therefore better informs planning.

In short, there are now ***three*** summative assessments instead of ***four***:

- Don't complete a diagnostic assessment immediately – teach Unit 1 in the first half term.
- In week 3 or 4, students complete a diagnostic summative assessment on Unit 1.
- There is no final summative assessment for Unit 1 in that half term (give students time to learn!)
- Then, don't complete a diagnostic assessment immediately – teach Unit 2 in the second half term.
- In week 3 or 4, students complete a diagnostic summative assessment on Unit 2.
- In the last weeks of the second half term, students complete a mock exam which is the final summative assessment for Unit 1 and Unit 2.

This model is also repeated in the second term (see Table 8.4 and Table 8.5).

19 N. Anderson and S. Peart (2016) Back on track: exploring how a Further Education college re-motivates learners to re-sit previously failed qualifications at GCSE, *Research in Post-Compulsory Education*, 21(3): 196–213.

20 T. Sherrington (2019) *Rosenshine's Principles in Action.* Melton, Woodbridge: John Catt Educational Ltd.

Table 8.4 English and maths assessment timetable

Term 1, half term 1 (September – October)

Week 1	Week 2	Week 3	Week 4	Week 5	Week 6	Week 7
Normal teaching with low-stakes quiz	Normal teaching with low-stakes quiz	Normal teaching with low-stakes quiz	Summative assessment 1 (for Unit 1)	Normal teaching with low-stakes quiz	Normal teaching with low-stakes quiz	Normal teaching with low-stakes quiz

Table 8.5 English and maths assessment timetable

Term 1, half term 2 (November – December)

Week 1	Week 2	Week 3	Week 4	Week 5	Week 6	Week 7
Normal teaching with low-stakes quiz	Normal teaching with low-stakes quiz	Summative assessment point 1 for Unit 2	Normal teaching with low-stakes quiz	Normal teaching with low-stakes quiz	Mock exams: summative assessment 2 (for Unit 1 and Unit 2)	Normal teaching with low-stakes quiz

Mocks as a Second Progress Point

Useful for a number of reasons, mocks can quickly lose their impact if completed too often. Students are adept at motivating themselves if conditions are right, but quickly become disinterested if not properly challenged. If regularly experiencing high challenge, but receiving 'low' rewards, motivation evaporates.

This is why it is important to keep mock exams to a minimum. For Functional Skills, this means students should complete an in-class mock exam when close to assessment. For GCSE, two mock exam papers (or one series of exams) is enough. Because each one is completed near the end of term (i.e. December and March), students have a good indication of their knowledge and understanding while also minimizing staff workload. Steps should also be taken to ensure accuracy and fairness in marking:

- Standardise and moderate: to ensure accurate marking, take three to five exam papers which have already been given a definitive mark by exam boards. Removing marks and annotations, teachers then mark them and the marks are collected and compared by the head of department for English and maths (or equivalent). If within a 10–15 per cent tolerance, marking can begin. If not, teachers should be given feedback and support where they have been too generous or cautious.

- Redistribute exam papers: don't mark your own students' mock exam papers – it can lead to subconscious bias and inaccurate marking. Mix the papers up and mark an equal number of papers from other teachers' classes.
- Communication: let students know about mocks – regularly. Tell them in class, send letters, tell tutors, send texts, display dates and times around the building and phone home – if need be. Offer sanctions and rewards for attendance at mocks, because if they don't attend they will be less prepared for the real thing.
- For GCSE maths, with most exam boards offering three exam papers, teachers should collaborate to decide which paper will be used for each mock or create a hybrid paper using the existing three papers.

Tracking

When tracking results (for summative assessments or mocks), consistency is king and it is important to remember that every added level of sophistication makes consistency more difficult. This is why tracking progress and achievement should be as streamlined as possible.

No matter who is scrutinizing a tracking document (English and maths teachers, senior leaders etc.), all staff should be able to analyse assessment results without needing a degree in English or maths or a PhD in spreadsheets.

With this in mind, tracking should take place in two ways:

- In student books (primarily for students)
- Electronically (for all staff to access)

Tracking in Student Books

In student books, this either takes the form of a simple grid (Table 8.6) or it can include additional information on units and components (Table 8.7). Both formats should show summative assessment and mock exam results, and they should sit alongside low-stakes quiz tracking. The examples in Tables 8.6 and 8.7 show GCSE English language tracking.

Again, this is best utilised when in student exercise books and, much like the low-stakes quizzes, it is best used when students don't compare, and compete only with themselves. This way, they quickly identify their strengths and weaknesses and the progress they have made.

Electronic Tracking

Electronic tracking takes many forms, but it is usually seen in only two: software or spreadsheet. Either way, it should comply with the following principles:

Table 8.6 Tracking in simple grid

	Summative assessment score	Mock exam score
Question 1	2	3
Question 2	3	6
Question 3	5	4
Question 4	8	
Question 5 (AO5)	11	
Question 5 (AO6)	7	
TOTAL		

Table 8.7 Tracking with additional information

			Assessment score	Mock score
Section A **Reading**	Q1 4 marks	Can you select the appropriate information? AO1 – List 4 things …	2	3
	Q2 8 marks	Language analysis of a selected paragraph of the text. AO2 – How does the writer use language to …	3	6
	Q3 8 marks	Analysis of structural features. AO2 – How has the writer structured the text to interest you as a reader?	5	4
	Q4 20 marks	Evaluate a text and respond to an opinion. Use evidence to evaluate language and structure. AO4 – to what extent do you agree?	7	
Section B **Writing**	Q5 40 marks	Produce a piece of narrative or descriptive writing. 24 marks (AO5) and 16 marks (AO6)	AO5: 11 AO6: 7	AO5: AO6:
	TOTAL			

- Accessibility – electronic tracking should be accessible at all times to all staff
- Information – it contains all relevant student information
- Analysis – it contains tools and filters to analyse sub-trends and subgroups, and identifies areas of strength and improvement

In short, it communicates everything we need to know.
Basic tracking should include:

- Student name
- Student number
- Vocational area
- Vocational tutor
- English and/or maths teacher
- SEND information
- Summative assessment data
- Mock exam data

This can also be supplemented with previous GCSE/Functional Skills result(s) and attendance data.

Supporting Vocational Teachers to Support English and Maths

It is vital that vocational teams access and use this document – many are held accountable for English and maths achievement in their areas, and we need to support their understanding of English and maths assessments. To do this, add a simple explanation or summary for each element that is being assessed. The easiest way to do this is to create an A4 information sheet which complements tracking and shows what is being assessed and how vocational teams can support (Table 8.8).

Trends and Subgroups

Once consistent tracking is in place, teachers and leaders should look continuously for trends, groups and subgroups. For example, Teacher A (a maths

Table 8.8

	Task	What is being assessed	How to support
Paper 1 Question 5	Narrative or descriptive writing	Students need to use a range of sentence types, vocabulary, punctuation and language devices.	Check student work for spelling, punctuation and grammar and use resources provided by the English team to recap sophisticated punctuation in assignments.

teacher) might find that sports students are consistently achieving low scores in algebra, while Teacher B (a colleague) achieves better results. Having identified this, Teacher A can collaborate with Teacher B to see what Teacher B is doing differently. If an entire cohort struggle with a topic (e.g. construction students with descriptive writing), English and maths resources can be embedded in the relevant vocational area. This could be through sharing quizzes or starter activities or even giving training to vocational staff teachers to better embed English and maths into vocational lessons.

Feedback

As in everything else we do, simplicity and consistency are key. With this in mind, feedback is no different and should follow simple and specific guidelines[21,22]:

- **Less is more:** with attention spans declining due to social media and the internet[23], and fewer UK students reading for pleasure[24], if teachers want students to take notice of feedback, it needs to be short, specific and clear. Tell them what they did well and what they need to do next time, and get to the point.
- **We want it now:** students need to have feedback as quickly as possible following a task. If teachers take too long to give this feedback, students are less motivated by it. If you cook your partner a meal tomorrow, you want to know what it tastes like as they are eating it, not in three weeks' time.
- **Keep it positive:** feedback should always be positive, but not too positive. If too positive, students can develop false confidence and feel they don't need to improve. If there is no positivity, students won't engage with feedback.
- **Keep it focused:** keep feedback focused on the task and let students know specifically what they can do to develop their work. As above, get to the point – what specific action do they need to complete to improve?
- **Even less is more:** over time, too much feedback can make students dependent on teachers. To make sure this doesn't happen, begin to decrease the amount of feedback students receive throughout the year. Gradually, this will make them more reflective and more independent[25].

21 Card, Designing a sustainable curriculum.
22 Didau and Rose, *What Every Teacher Needs to Know.*
23 J. Firth, J. Torous, B. Stubbs et al. (2019) The 'online brain': how the internet may be changing our cognition, *World Psychiatry*, 18(2): 119–29.
24 C. Clark (2019) *Children and Young People's Reading in 2017/18: Findings from our Annual Literacy Survey*. London: National Literacy Trust.
25 Card, Designing a sustainable curriculum.

Cutting Workload, Maintaining Consistency

With UK teachers working some of the longest hours in world education[26], marking and feedback are often the cause. To cut workload, and remain effective, this section gives a range of techniques teachers can use to maintain high-quality feedback without the long evenings and weekends writing page after page of feedback.

Smart Marking (a.k.a. Coded Marking)

This simple but effective technique cuts teacher workload by creating a simple shorthand and asking students to share the workload.

The format in Table 8.9 is for basic errors or misconceptions.

Table 8.9   English smart marking

Code	Meaning	Code	Meaning
∧	Missing word	T	Tense
Sp	Spelling error	?	Meaning unclear
P	Punctuation needed	©	Capital letter
GR	Grammatical error	//	New paragraph
V	Add more detail	!	Not needed

Table 8.10   Maths smart marking

Code	Meaning	Code	Meaning
≠	Correct method, wrong answer	S!	Simplify
ċ	Correct answer, wrong method	M	Incorrect method
±?	Sign confusion	U	No unit given
!?	No working	U̇	Incorrect unit given

Created by Richard Walsh and reproduced here with permission.

This method can quickly be implemented college-wide and used as a tool for embedding English and maths in vocational and academic areas.

The second method asks students to share the workload as they write the majority of the feedback. Teachers split the relevant assessment criteria into a set of skills and then assign each skill a letter or symbol (Table 8.11).

---

26 www.tes.com/news/uk-teachers-work-some-longest-hours-world (accessed 11 January 2021).

Table 8.11

A	You use a great quote
B	Use speech marks ('quotes') around your quote
C	Make sure you say what language feature is in your quote (e.g. simile, metaphor, alliteration)
D	Pick a specific word or phrase and say what it means and why it has been used
E	Identify a key word and what type of word it is (e.g. verb, noun, adverb, adjective etc.)
F	Say what the quote makes the reader think and why
G	Say what the quote makes the reader feel and why
H	Explain why the writer chose the technique/word
I	Explain what you think will happen next
J	Explain what else the writer could be trying to tell the reader

Having read a student's work, teachers identify strengths and weaknesses and leave only the relevant symbols or letters. For example, traditional feedback could look like this:

> *Well done Jazmin. You have used language features in your quote and shown a good understanding of the text.*
>
> *Next time, explain why the writer chooses this technique.*

Using smart marking, the feedback now looks like this:

> *Well done – C:*
>
> *Next time – H:*

At the start of the following lesson, display the codes and explanations, and students then copy out their feedback. Alternatively, print coded marking on A3 paper or give students codes and explanations in September.

Highlighting

Before giving feedback, identify what a student needs to include to complete a task successfully. Having identified the skills required for each question, topic or task, add each one to a blank template[27]. Table 8.12 shows a GCSE English example.

Having read through the student's work, the teacher then uses green and red highlighters to identify how successful the student has been in each component

---

27 J. Webb (2019) *How to Teach English Literature: Overcoming Cultural Poverty.* Melton, Woodbridge: John Catt Educational Ltd.

Table 8.12

Paper 1 Question 2 – Language analysis
To be successful, you should …
✓ Say what the writer is trying to do and why
✓ Find a language feature and say why it was used
✓ Use an interesting quote from the text
✓ Say what the reader thinks/feels and say why
✓ Discuss if this message is the same/different elsewhere

Figure 8.4

P1Q2 Language Analysis - Success Criteria	
✓ Said what the writer is trying to do and why	
✓ Found a language feature and said why it was used	
✓ Use a 'juicy quote from the extract	
✓ What does the reader think/feel? Why?	
✓ Link - is the message the same/different throughout?	

by highlighting a rough percentage (Figure 8.4). In Figure 8.4, it is clear the student has been successful in discussing what the reader thinks or feels, but they need to develop their ability to find language features and say why they have been used. There is some workload when creating templates, but once completed, a class set of exercise books can be marked very efficiently.

Highlighting v2.0

Simpler than the above, read student work and highlight strengths in green and weaknesses in red. Then ask students to reread their work and identify what specifically they have done well and what they need to develop, using the highlighted sections as references. This also improves students' understanding of what is being assessed and their strengths and weaknesses.

Spot Marking

Completed during lessons, teachers circulate classrooms with a green and red biro, giving a green 'spot' where students have been successful, and a red 'spot' where students should add detail or have made a mistake. This either leads to immediate verbal feedback or questioning around *why* 'green spot' sections are successful and what they need to do to develop 'red spot' sections. Students can also be left to independently deduce their strengths and weaknesses, which helps to develop metacognition.

Peer and Self-assessment

By regularly modelling examples, training students to give themselves and peers effective feedback takes very little time. Throughout lessons, regularly signpost what students need to include to be successful and, at the end of lessons (or tasks), ask students to recap what they should have included. Write these elements on a whiteboard, including anything students have missed, and students then look for what is included or missing from this list in their own or a peer's work.

Failing this, show lots of examples of feedback on PowerPoint slides or the board and students then copy relevant feedback into their exercise books, providing instant, quality feedback. It is important that teachers still circulate and check feedback to avoid 'really nice handwriting' or 'u shud hav written mor' as feedback.

Whole-class Feedback

Firstly, create a blank class feedback template. This should include strengths, areas of development, common misconceptions and potentially a space for SPaG (spelling, punctuation and grammar) or errors in working (Table 8.13).

Then, read through student work and add any common mistakes or strengths to the whole-class feedback sheet (Table 8.14).

In the next lesson, give students their work back and share the overall class feedback (either via PowerPoint, A4 sheet or visualiser). Ask students to reread their work and identify which of the points in the feedback sheet refers to their work!

Table 8.13

Strengths	To develop
•	•
•	•
•	•
SPaG / Errors in working	**Misconceptions**
•	•
•	•
•	•

Table 8.14

Strengths	To develop
• Good use of language features • Discussed relevant quotes and attempted to explain their meaning • Used relevant terminology in analysis	• Must discuss what quotes make the reader feel • Need to give more detail when saying *why* the reader feels a certain way • Not enough detail when discussing why structural features are used
SPaG/Errors in working	**Misconceptions**
• Misuse of semicolons for majority of class • Capital letters at the start of some quotations	• The main character is happy that his friend has left the town • There need to be quotes for every single point

Figure 8.5 Example feedback and extension labels

> Next time, explain what the quote makes the reader think and why.

> Without a calculator, find the value of:
>
> $(6 \times 3 - 6) \times (13 \div 3)$

Yellow Box

Having read a student's work, identify a section that could be further improved by using a yellow highlighter to highlight or draw a box around it. Students can then either identify the errors in this section or even rewrite using whole-class, self- or peer-assessed feedback.

Labels

Though we can't predict weaknesses, we know areas students will find more difficult. With this in mind, preparing feedback and extension tasks can save enormous amounts of time. By printing commonly occurring feedback or extension tasks onto standard adhesive address labels, feedback can be given immediately and with little workload. With students completing work, teachers then identify the relevant feedback label (in class or afterwards) and stick this into the exercise books. Feedback takes seconds, and, if a teacher sets an extension label, students complete this in their next lesson (aiding retrieval practice).

Remote Learning Feedback

With minimal student training, each of these feedback options can be used in remote learning, but why not use self-marking multiple-choice quizzes as well?

The option to set these up is already included in Microsoft Teams and Google Classroom (plus others) and working collaboratively means many quizzes can be quickly created. Students receive instant feedback and will repeat quizzes for higher marks.

Timetable Feedback

To continue to cut workload, try to timetable the feedback type. An effective model? Teachers feedback in week 1, students self-assess in week 2 and peer assess in week 3. After that, restart the rota.

Challenges and Solutions in Assessment, Tracking and Feedback

The main challenges associated with the methods described in this chapter will likely come from a lack of engagement or a lack of consistency (from students and teachers). Included in other chapters are a range of methods to combat these inconsistencies, but the answer here is very simple: persevere with training students to use particular methods or find what method is best for you, your team and your students.

If self- or peer assessment is regularly unsuccessful in your classroom, give students additional training or try another feedback method. This also goes for all other methods of feedback – if it isn't working, try and find out why, or experiment with other types of feedback.

With mock exams and assessment (whether tracking or completing assessments), poor attendance may provide a barrier to effective assessment. For issues with this, look at the importance of rewards and sanctions in this book and Chapter 7 on timetabling and attendance.

Holding mock exams can be difficult in larger centres (with some centres having upwards of 3500 resit students in each subject[28]), but this doesn't mean they can't take place. If an exam hall is out of the question, complete mocks during normal lesson times and ask teachers to swap rooms and invigilate each other's students. Students are familiar enough with the teachers that they will model positive behaviours, but have not yet built up a relationship where they may be tempted to ask for concessions (i.e. 'Can we go early?' etc.). For issues with lesson length (i.e. some lessons are 1.5 hours long, and each mock paper is near or over 2 hours in length), collaborate with vocational leaders and ask that lessons can run over to accommodate exams (as a one-off) because they are done so infrequently, but they are so important.

---

28 www.tes.com/news/how-hold-gcse-exam-3700-students (accessed 11 January 2021).

Summary

- Use low-stakes assessments to cut workload and gain more effective (and efficient) feedback on what has 'gone in'.
- Keep tracking as streamlined as possible and open to all staff.
- Communicate assessment outcomes to vocational areas (and let them know what they need to do to support).
- There is no fixed model for feedback – if students know their strengths and areas for development, then feedback is good.
- Feedback should be delivered to students as promptly as possible to keep it relevant.
- Use a series of tools to give feedback – this cuts workload, helps students to understand what is expected and will deliver feedback more efficiently.

Reflection

- How do you track that students see and use the feedback they receive?
- Are assessment results and summaries available to all who need them?
- How can I better balance assessment workload against the impact it has on students and their learning?
- What can I do to make assessment more efficient and effective?
- How can students be more aware of their assessment results?

9 Achieving Consistency

'I'm trying my best, but it's difficult to be perfect all of the time'
16-year-old hairdressing student (2017)

Well isn't that just the truth. There will come a time for all departments when standards and expectations need to be raised. This can be a difficult process, and take longer than anticipated[1], but individuals and teams get there because they set themselves (or are set) long- and short-term goals.

Once these goals have been achieved, teams are then able to focus on the progress that has been made and can hopefully motivate themselves using this progress. A potential issue here, however, is the law of diminishing returns in hitting these goals[2].

When reaching or exceeding new standards, targets or expectations for the first time there is a general sense of euphoria and achievement within a team. This can be related to receiving improved attendance figures, exam results or outcomes and this sense of achievement can even be felt several times after this.

The potential issue is that teachers and teams are being asked to consistently replicate inputs and outcomes for the same reward, no matter if the level of challenge or workload changes. Yes, we can try strategies and techniques to continually motivate staff, but how do we achieve consistency once we have reached or exceeded the desired standard or expectation?

As consistency is evidenced in different ways to different people, we must first define what consistency is and is not. After all, refusing to complete any registers shows consistency. It is consistently poor practice, but it is still consistent. No, the consistency we wish to see in English and maths departments (and in the wider FE community) is something altogether different.

In their 2011 research report titled *To the Next Level: Good Schools becoming Outstanding*[3], the Education Development Trust repeatedly state the importance of consistency in the move from Ofsted graded Good to Outstanding. Mentioned in the context of school or college improvement, good practice is evidenced by average and above levels of achievement, progress, attendance and outcomes, and this is then deemed outstanding practice when these results are seen regularly and reliably.

---

1   K. Thompson (2016) *A Systematic Guide to Change Management*. Great Britain: CreateSpace Publishing.
2   K.E. Case and R.C. Fair (1999) *Principles of Economics*, 5th edn. Upper Saddle River, NJ: Prentice-Hall.
3   P. Dougill, M. Raleigh, R. Blatchford, L. Fryer, C.A. Robinson and J. Richmond (2011) *To the Next Level: Good Schools becoming Outstanding*. Reading: CfBT Education Trust.

Described as an 'integration of variety into unity'[4], simply put, consistency is all staff adhering to strategies, processes and policies with the same ethos to provide stability.

Having covered this, then the issue becomes identifying what is needed for consistency to occur. In the excellent *Leadership Matters 3.0*[5], Andy Buck identifies several core principles to achieving consistency. These core principles, Buck explains, must be present throughout a school for consistency to become fully embedded.

However, as I have regularly been told since first entering FE, colleges are not schools. Though this is quite literally true, having worked in both there are many similarities. Nevertheless there does still need to be adaptation when applying these principles to FE. As such, consistency for English and maths teachers, leaders and teams is achieved through a mixture of the following:

- *Obtaining buy-in and effective communication*

  Achieving buy-in from anyone with a stake in college-wide English and maths is absolutely vital to achieving consistency. This buy-in must include everyone: students, teachers, leaders, vocational teams, administrative teams, parents/carers and employers. If there is a single break in this chain, inconsistency can spread. A key part of this consistency is communicating clearly and effectively with all of the above.

- *Using external to support consistency*

  In Buck's core principles, support was required only from parents. However, in the ever changing world of FE, English and maths teams need college-wide support as a minimum, as well as support from home and any third party (employers etc.). When hearing 'college-wide', it is rare that we actually include the full college. Those on reception, library staff, in student services, classroom support and everyone in between should know English and maths expectations and how they support the process.

- *Student collaboration*

  Potentially the most challenging to secure, student collaboration is key to consistency in English and maths. From consistent behaviour, effort, attendance and work to communication with teachers and leaders, consistency in English and maths cannot be achieved without student collaboration. If there is inconsistency in any other area, this is likely to be the first principle to fall[6].

- *Keep it simple*

  A very effective way to make sure you are keeping things as simple as possible comes from an unlikely source. Having targeted a gold medal in rowing at the 2000 Olympic Games, Ben Hunt-Davis prefaced any and all

---

4   A. Critto (2000. *Consistency: Being Coherent.* Lanham, MD: University Press of America.

5   A. Buck (2016) *Leadership Matters: How Leaders at all Levels can Create Good Schools.* Melton, Woodbridge: John Catt Educational Ltd.

6   K. Lanning (2012) *Consistency, Scalability, and Personality Measurement.* New York: Springer Science & Business Media.

decisions with one question: 'Will it make the boat go faster?'[7] If the answer was 'yes', a change or adaptation was made. If the answer was 'no', the change was not made. Simply put, in whatever you are doing, does it make the boat go faster? Whatever process is being contemplated, will it improve effectiveness or efficiency? Viewing all decisions through this prism can save time, as well as workload[8].

* *Responding to non-compliance*

Responding to non-compliance (or even defiance) is one of the most challenging aspects of teaching or leading in Further Education. Challenging as it may be, though, it is a vital part of consistency because if any non-compliance or drop in standards is tolerated (or even perceived to be tolerated), it is likely there will be a further drop in standards[9].

* *A foundation of creativity and innovation*

This can be especially difficult to establish as creativity and innovation can only begin on top of a foundation of failure[10]. To truly develop and nurture an innovative culture, leaders must let teachers experiment and ultimately fail so that adaptations and revisions can be made for success. This can also take some time, but a department (and even college) culture can quickly change during the process of experimentation[11].

* *Building momentum*

This too can seem challenging at first. However, think of consistency as the boulder in Indiana Jones – at first, it will be heavy and slow, however once it builds momentum, it becomes almost unstoppable. The departments we work in are much like this – through patience and timing[12] momentum will slowly be built, and once expectations, standards and practices are fully embedded, consistency is easily achieved.

If we are to fully support and guide our students, consistency is absolutely key, but how can we nurture consistency when all staff are different?[13] Though we must hold all staff inputs to account, we must also make sure there are reasonable adjustments. Without this, we cannot fully embed consistency, and without consistency students (and teachers) can feel vulnerable[14].

---

7   B. Hunt-Davis and H. Beveridge (2012) *Will it Make the Boat Go Faster?* Leicester: Troubador.

8   S. Hartley (2015) *Stronger Together: How Great Teams Work*. London: Hachette UK.

9   L.A. Malandro (2009) *Fearless Leadership*. New York: McGraw-Hill.

10   S. Sinek (2009) *Start with Why: How Great Leaders Inspire Everyone to Take Action*. London and New York: Penguin.

11   Thompson, *A Systematic Guide to Change Management*.

12   J.C. Larréché (2008) *The Momentum Effect: How to Ignite Exceptional Growth*. New Jersey: Pearson Education.

13   D. Didau and N. Rose (2016) *What Every Teacher Needs to Know About … Psychology*. Melton, Woodbridge: John Catt Educational Ltd.

14   A. Pollard, K. Black-Hawkins, G. Cliff-Hodges, P. Dudley and M. James (2014) *Reflective Teaching in Schools: Evidence-Informed Professional Practice*. London: Bloomsbury Publishing.

There is of course the argument that consistency becomes near impossible if a department or college culture isn't 'right' (with many further arguments for the definition of the 'right' culture). Simply put, a department culture is a shared set of ideals, beliefs and goals, though a simpler definition comes from former Southwest Airline CEO Herb Kelleher: 'Culture is what people do when no one is looking'[15]. The 'right' culture, then, is one that is focused on helping students to succeed and which promotes continual development of practice. Consistency cannot exist without this culture.

Without consistency and the right culture, staff lose trust and we all face added challenges in reaching expected standards[16]. So, what does this look like?

Well, consistency can be different for teachers in comparison to leaders, and making this distinction is vital. As a result, the following strategies give a general overview, as well as role-specific information and guidance where appropriate.

Non-negotiables

For consistency to occur in any setting, non-negotiables must exist and be clearly communicated. If these non-negotiables are not followed, issues can develop not only with accountability, but also with trust[17].

These non-negotiables can be formed in many ways – through collaboration, consultation, debate, one-to-one discussion or decided solely by a leader (though there are also issues of trust with this approach). As with Buck's principles[18], these non-negotiable philosophies should be as simple and clear as possible to ensure all staff understand their roles within them.

It is also important to demonstrate what best practice looks like for each of these philosophies and also give an indication of what might be an acceptable exemption to any rule. Much like the guidelines for student behaviour, it is vital to create these philosophies within a framework so that they can be as tight and as flexible as they need to be. A good example of this can be found when outlining the non-negotiables around exercise book feedback:

Exercise Book Feedback

All students should receive weekly feedback on any work which is completed in their exercise book

15 C.A. Trower (2012) *The Practitioner's Guide to Governance as Leadership: Building High-performing Nonprofit Boards.* San Francisco, CA: John Wiley & Sons.

16 Thompson, *A Systematic Guide to Change Management.*

17 A.W. Stanfield (2009) *Defining Effective Leadership: Lead in Whatever you Do.* Mustang, OK: Tate Publishing.

18 Buck, *Leadership Matters.*

The basic non-negotiable is that students should receive feedback weekly (the 'tight' element). However, there is no explicit mention of teachers giving this feedback, meaning it can be delivered by students themselves or their peers (the 'flexible' element).

Outlining non-negotiables should be done as soon as possible and with training having already taken place (or at least scheduled). For teachers, non-negotiables should be communicated with students as soon as possible and take the form of outlining expectations at the start of the year, modelling how to complete tasks and overall expectations. For leaders, this follows a similar pattern, but there must be highly specific differentiation in training, where it is needed, and future support for those not unable or unwilling to meet standards.

Clear Evidence

It is also important to remember that consistency is not simply about the inputs, but the outcomes too. This isn't to say we ignore any of the obvious inputs, or focus purely on outcomes, but use a delicate measure of both.

The inputs are defined as anything we do to support and guide students – from planning and teaching lessons, to giving feedback, to completing administration and collaborating with vocational staff, all of these acts can be considered as inputs. The outcomes, then, become student achievement and results. Though there must be accountability in English and maths (more on that in Chapter 10), it isn't as easy to hold staff accountable for English and maths outcomes as there are so many other variables.

That being said, there is evidence we can analyse and scrutinise, identifying trends and sub-trends where possible (as detailed in Chapter 8). For leaders, this can manifest as scrutiny of student workbooks, analysis of data, regular lesson drop-ins, discussion with students or collaboration with vocational leaders. To develop this, watching teaching over time is an extremely valuable tool, looking for evidence of consistency. You can gain invaluable insight into teachers' 'normal' practice by spending 10–15 minutes in each teacher's lesson each week. Also, simple questioning of students can give starting points for scrutiny:

- What are you learning?
- Why are you learning it?
- Is it always like this? Do you normally do this?

Answers to the last question in particular can give leaders a range of information on which to act.

For teachers, evidence of consistency will mainly come from students – are they meeting expectations and standards? Are they doing as requested? Evidence here will come in the form of attendance reports, engagement with teacher feedback and performance in assessments (though it is obviously not limited to these factors).

Guided Independence

Rightly receiving much attention, Tom Sherrington's excellent Rosenshine's Principles in Action[19] details Barak Rosenshine's ten research-based principles of instruction and how they can be implemented in classrooms to support student achievement.

Engaging and a must-read for anyone in education, these principles provide a superb foundation for facilitating outstanding practice. However, more often than not, the principles are viewed only with school or college students in mind. When extended beyond this, into teacher training, CPD and leadership, they remain enormously effective.

Though all of the principles can apply to teacher training and teacher development, principles 8–10 are particularly effective for maintaining consistently excellent practice[20]:

8. Provide scaffolds for difficult tasks

Using Vygotsky's theory of scaffolding[21], Rosenshine states that giving students a framework (i.e. giving some elements of a successful response) to work within means tasks are more accessible and students are more likely to achieve. Scaffolds are then progressively taken away, leaving students able to fully complete tasks successfully. In terms of supporting and guiding teacher improvement, this strategy can be just as effective, although there are caveats and adaptations needed.

Firstly, this method requires discretion – self-esteem plays a huge role in teaching[22] and so it is always important that any support a teacher receives is completed confidentially. However, supporting staff explicitly by modelling outstanding practice and working collaboratively, or 'macro-scaffolding'[23], means that it is possible to offer support, CPD and guidance without a member of staff feeling targeted or as if they are 'failing'.

9. Independent practice

Having completed a range of scaffolded tasks (joint marking or planning, triangulated observation etc.), teachers can then practise and complete tasks independently. Again, this may sound difficult to facilitate without

19 T. Sherrington (2019) *Rosenshine's Principles in Action*. Melton, Woodbridge: John Catt Educational Ltd.

20 B. Rosenshine (2012) Principles of instruction: research-based strategies that all teachers should know, *American Educator*, 36(1): 12–19.

21 L.E. Berk and A. Winsler (1995) *Scaffolding Children's Learning: Vygotsky and Early Childhood Education*. NAEYC Research into Practice Series, Volume 7. Washington, DC: National Association for the Education of Young Children.

22 M. Ferkany (2008) The educational importance of self-esteem, *Journal of Philosophy of Education*, 42(1): 119–32.

23 M. Engin (2014) Macro-scaffolding: contextual support for teacher learning, *Australian Journal of Teacher Education*, 39(5), doi: 10.14221/ajte.2014v39n5.6.

harming self-esteem, but it can easily take the form of a new project (a research or action project) or initiative.

As a result of this continued practice, teachers (and learners) become more familiar with the elements which make up outstanding practice and develop practice more effectively – what Rosenshine calls 'overlearning'[24].

10. Regular reviews

Regular review and monitoring of practice is just as important as the CPD and training which informs it. This does not have to be an onerous task, or cause anxiety to teachers – observations do not mean spending an hour a week scrutinizing all elements of practice, and a scrutiny of exercise books does not mean spending hours looking for holes in student learning. This can, and should, be effectively completed to support teachers. More on this later.

Through applying these three principles to teacher development, teachers and leaders are effectively supported by using a solid foundation of trust[25] which can also develop relationships within English and maths teams.

Gradual Consistency

As much as we would like to develop consistency as quickly as possible, speed of change does not guarantee quality. If anything, the opposite can be true[26]. Changing policy or processes too quickly can result in teachers and leaders being left behind, and creating a fractured department where some succeed and others do not, simply based on their pre-existing skill set. As discussed above, the challenge in creating a consistently excellent department is taking everyone with you.

Unfortunately, I learned this the hard way. In my first role in Further Education, I attempted to quickly make sweeping changes to department and college-wide English and maths policy. Though there was some initial success, this negatively impacted the team and caused issues later on in the academic year.

The lesson I learned from this was to begin by measuring consistency only in focused areas (student feedback, assessment tracking etc.) and not in *all* areas. Start by monitoring the 'quick wins' of consistency – areas which can be improved effectively and efficiently. This is different in every educational setting, but after a thorough evaluation of a department, they should be apparent.

24 B. Rosenshine and R. Stevens (1986) Teaching functions, in M.C. Wittrock (ed.) *Handbook of Research on Teaching*, 3rd edn. New York: Macmillan, pp. 376–91.

25 M. Bottery (2004) Trust: its importance for educators, *Management in Education*, 18(5): 6–10.

26 M. Franklin (2014) *Agile Change Management: A Practical Framework for Successful Change Planning and Implementation*. London: Kogan Page Publishers.

To help with this gradual consistency, it is vital that there is an agreed time-line of key events, and that all staff with a stake in English and maths are aware of this timeline and these key events. Requirements for each event should also be communicated to all relevant staff. Key elements in this timeline should include events and deadlines only, with a separate communication around accountabilities (more on this in Chapter 10). To ensure this is created accu-rately, and communicated clearly, create and distribute this in collaboration with all English and maths practitioners, the head of department for English and maths, and senior leaders – as we are all teachers of English and maths, we must all know the key events. An example could look something like the time-line in Table 9.1.

Though clearly this timeline is missing events, it gives a broad indication of what can be included. Again, the additional detail would be distributed to rele-vant staff, with training to support any needs where appropriate.

Managing change is vital to leaders, but it is also key for teachers – teachers cannot monitor and evaluate all areas of their practice at once. This workload is unsustainable and, though initial success is buoying, it can lead to burnout[27]. A great way to develop gradual improvement in teaching practice is to set up and run a research project[28, 29], as discussed in Chapter 5.

Clear Feedback, Concrete Actions

Key to consistency, high-quality, clear feedback must be evident at all levels. Whether this is from teachers to students, middle leaders to teachers, or senior leaders to all staff, clarity is always preferable to brevity[30]. Simply put, every-one must know what is going well and what needs focused improvement, and the priority should never be how long it takes to communicate that message.

Whoever it comes from, and whoever it is delivered to, feedback should always be regularly given, clearly communicated and include concrete actions for improvement to ensure consistency. Keep following actions short and give additional information for clarity – When do these actions need to be com-pleted? What resources will be needed? What support is available?

For leaders, it is vital teachers are given the tools they need to succeed, whether this be a portion of the budget, an opportunity to collaborate, addi-tional time or just some understanding. It is also vital that leaders follow up – if

---

27 S. Bubb and P. Earley (2004) *Managing Teacher Workload: Work–life Balance and Wellbeing*. London: Sage.

28 J. McNiff (2016) *You and Your Action Research Project*. Abingdon and New York: Routledge.

29 D. Hopkins (2008) *A Teacher's Guide to Classroom Research*. Maidenhead: McGraw-Hill Open University Press.

30 L. Johnson (2017) *Cultivating Communication in the Classroom: Future-Ready Skills for Secondary Students*. Thousand Oaks, CA: Corwin Press.

Table 9.1 Academic year timeline

Aug	Results published. Enrolment and IA of all English and maths students.	*Sept*	Continued initial and diagnostic assessment delivered with advice and support to facilitate student placement on the appropriate qualification and level in English and maths. Teaching starts with delivery of non-negotiables in English and maths.
Oct	Monitoring of non-negotiables in English and maths with commencement of learning walks. Tutor liaison begins to identify student support need, intervention and exam concessions.	*Nov*	Continued liaison to support students who require support. Final preparations for Mock Exam 1. Data input and analysis for assessments completed in first half term.
Dec	Mock examinations held and progress updates for first term completed. First round of Functional Skills testing to be completed. Paperwork for exam entries submitted by teachers.	*Jan*	Data input and analysis of mock results completed. First round of student progress reports completed. Intervention occurs where appropriate. Completion of access arrangement paperwork. Term 1 tracking and predictions shared with Head of Department and Senior Leaders.
Feb	Completion of GCSE entry paperwork. Continuation of intervention and additional support where needed.	*March*	Second round of Functional Skills tests begin. S&L deadline for FS. Final preparations for and completion of Mock Exam 2. Data input and analysis for assessments completed. Second round of student progress reports completed.
April	Term 2 tracking and predictions shared with Head of Department and Senior Leaders. Analysis of assessment results to target final interventions.	*May*	Preparation for final exams, with final interventions put in place (including over half-term break). Final progress report given to tutors and vocational leaders.
June	GCSE exams. Remaining classes completed for GCSE students.	*July*	Functional Skills teaching formally ends and final exams are completed.

we make a promise, we must keep that promise. Trust and autonomy[31] are everything when extolling the virtues of consistency.

To complement this, feedback should be dialogic in nature – we cannot expect consistency with communication going only one way. There should be negotiation in next steps for consistency to become embedded[32]. For example, do teachers know when they will receive feedback? Do they know the form this will take? Has it been adapted for individual staff? Is there opportunity for follow-up? Do they know the parameters for giving their own feedback?

This can take time, but once these principles of feedback are in place, consistency is more simply achieved, and more fully embedded.

Monitoring and Evaluation

If a list was compiled of vocabulary which could provoke anxiety and stress in the hearts of teachers in all sectors of education, monitoring and evaluation would be somewhere near the top (no doubt quickly followed by 'Ofsted' and 'observation'). However, monitoring and evaluation do not need to be the burdensome, stressful processes that some have experienced.

There should also not be one method for monitoring and evaluation, but several. In the interests of effective monitoring, and workload, triangulation can be enormously effective. This takes the form of monitoring and evaluating three elements of practice (which all remain flexible):

1 Observation
2 Data analysis
3 Student talk

These elements are open to leaders, managers, colleagues, peers and stakeholders, but should always be viewed together and never individually. Also, no element is more important than any other and they should be viewed holistically as one whole.

Observation

There is conflicting research on observations. Some suggests observations are a highly effective tool[33], capable of developing both student and teacher. However, there is also research to suggest observations provide little impact to

---

31 D.H. Pink (2011) *Drive: The Surprising Truth about what Motivates us.* New York: Penguin.

32 D. Little (1995) Learning as dialogue: the dependence of learner autonomy on teacher autonomy, *System,* 23(2): 175–81.

33 Ofsted (2018) *Six Models of Lesson Observation: An International Perspective.* Manchester: Ofsted.

student outcomes or achievement[34]. But what is our alternative? It remains the most effective method to see teaching in action as well as to learn (and question) teaching practice.

To this end, how do we proceed with lesson observations? Primarily, as with student assessment, high-stakes, high-pressure accountability needs to be eradicated from the process. Long form, one-off observations can give very little indication of what regularly occurs in classrooms. Firstly, these observations are easier to prepare for unless they occur randomly (which in turn can cause teacher anxiety).

As a result, shorter, much more regular observations are preferable. Between 5 and 15 minutes per week (if possible) gives a much clearer indication of classroom reality than one annual hour-long observation. In addition, for effective observation to occur, leaders must identify a clear focus for observation. Entering a classroom with the intention of observing *everything* that is happening dilutes the effectiveness of any feedback, as well as creating excessive workload.

Identifying anything to focus on from questioning, classroom management, differentiation, engagement or lesson structure provides a range of elements to discuss and give feedback on. Communicating this focus to those who are being observed is also key. Having chosen and communicated a focus, make notes on what is seen in lessons and give feedback on the same day – this can be difficult, but, as with the feedback we give to students, the sooner it is delivered, the more impact it can have[35].

As practitioners, it is important to become used to regular, informal observation, as the regular feedback that comes from this can provide high-quality support to developing the quality of teaching. Try persuading managers and leaders to follow this pattern of informal observation, as it significantly cuts their workload, and provides high-quality impact when feedback is given in a timely manner.

Data Analysis

Covered in more detail in Chapter 8, this does not simply mean assessment data. This can include attendance or punctuality data, analysis of behaviour incidents and even comparison of performance in vocational lessons. If we think of data as the results of measuring elements of teaching, then we can analyse nearly everything students and teachers do.

With this in mind, we must caveat some data with 'why?'[36] Data should always be interrogated to its fullest before taking any additional steps to clarify or

---

34 J. Worth, J. Sizmur, M. Walker, S. Bradshaw and B. Styles (2017) *Teacher Observation: Evaluation Report and Executive Summary*. London: Education Endowment Foundation.

35 B. Opitz, N.K. Ferdinand and A. Mecklinger (2011) Timing matters: the impact of immediate and delayed feedback on artificial language learning, *Frontiers in Human Neuroscience*, 5: 8, doi: 10.3389/fnhum.2011.00008.

36 Sinek, *Start with Why*.

question outcomes, achievements and results. Can some data explain trends in other data? Do we need to further interrogate lessons, students, teachers, processes, practices?

We should also include all stakeholders in the analysis of this data – communicate results and responses to data with teachers, with leaders, with students – they provide insight and we must use it.

Analysis of data should occur roughly once per half term (with mock exams taking up 2/5 of the half terms). This information should be collated, summarised and shared with all staff, with an attached summary and opportunities for all staff to discuss in relevant forums.

As helpful as this can be, we can also be left with more questions than answers: Is Student A achieving poorly in English because of their attendance, or are they attending infrequently because of their lack of achievement? This is when we use the final part of triangulation – student talk – to obtain a more rounded picture when monitoring and evaluating.

Student Talk

Gaining feedback from students on all matters can be enormously effective, as well as fulfilling. Seen by some as a tool for college development[37], it can take many forms and deliver feedback of varying dependability.

With the right students, in the right context, it can deliver a valuable perspective on the college experience and the elements which should receive further focus. However, there is always the possibility that it will return stale, or even inaccurate feedback ('it's boring – lessons should only be 20 minutes long and we should be allowed our phones').

The key here is to hold these discussions in small groups (pairs or individually) with someone the student(s) does not know, but who has been endorsed by someone the student trusts (a teacher, tutor or leader). This will lead to honest feedback, while also ensuring that a range of topics can be discussed.

This can also take the form of a survey or questionnaire, but these responses should be monitored for safeguarding and authenticity.

It is likely that the responsibility to complete student voice will reside with middle and senior leaders, but this does not mean practitioners can't hold their own forums in lessons. Providing a safe and secure environment and asking students to give honest feedback (with a view to enhancing their experience) can have interesting results which help to shape future practice.

With triangulation in place, and various elements of practice analysed, accurate feedback is essential. Feedback should be as specific as possible[38] as

37 G. Czerniawski and W. Kidd, eds (2011) *Student Voice Handbook: Bridging the Academic/Practitioner Divide*. Bingley: Emerald Group Publishing.

38 J. Hattie and H. Timperley (2007) The power of feedback, *Review of Educational Research*, 77(1): 81–112.

teacher self-esteem is easily damaged when they feel 'everything' is an issue[39]. Evaluation and monitoring is one of the most challenging elements of teaching, leadership and education. Whether completing this reflectively, or observing through the lens of accountability, we must be fair, honest and transparent. With triangulation, this becomes much more simple.

Streamlining Scrutiny

A key component of monitoring and evaluating practice, which can easily fit into any and all of the triangulation elements, scrutiny of student work is also a vital part of remaining consistent.

Again, this need not take up entire mornings or afternoons of scrutiny and checklists or endless debate. To effectively monitor the quality of feedback being given, an entire department's worth of books can be scrutinised in a couple of hours or less with the right feedback policy.

As with any policy, this policy should retain as much flexibility as possible, while also communicating desired outcomes and how they can be achieved. Difficult, right? Well, not so much. Here is an example of a highly effective feedback policy[40]:

> **An effective feedback policy:**
>
> Effective feedback can take a variety of forms, but our priority should always be supporting student progression and achievement. To evidence this, students should be able to suitably answer two questions:
>
> - **What am I doing well in English and/or maths?**
> - **What do I need to do to improve my work in English and/or maths?**
>
> If students are able to reliably answer these questions, using subject-specific terminology, they are receiving high-quality feedback.

No mention of green, red, blue or purple pens or highlighters, no mention of dialogic marking or timelines for feedback, but teachers are still able to use these approaches if they feel they will be effective. The key here is to make a range of feedback tools available (as in Chapter 8) and let teachers identify the methods that will work for them and their students.

However, it is not always possible to discuss feedback and the impact it has with students, and the majority of time monitoring student work will be done in a static environment. This can be laborious and often tedious

---

39 K.R. Wentzel and D.B. Miele, eds (2009) *Handbook of Motivation at School*. New York and Abingdon: Routledge.

40 https://teaching.blog.gov.uk/2017/09/28/mark-however-you-think-best-a-year-in-the-life-of-a-meaningful-manageable-and-motivating-marking-policy-change/ (accessed 11 January 2021).

(looking at the same tasks completed by many students), and so we must find an alternative method to monitor and evaluate student work and the effectiveness of feedback.

A solution to this? Complete this activity with members of the team. Not only does this help to embed standards, it also allows for sharing of good practice to occur regularly, with debate and discussion about how and why techniques and strategies have been used. Collecting a set of books from each member of the English or maths team, identifying a focus and scrutinizing books with a colleague is enormously beneficial for consistency, overall standards and for individual development.

If a Head of Department has a teaching timetable, it is also important that the Head of Department for English and maths also present their books – Heads of Department are not above department standards and expectations. Feedback from this sharing good practice experience can be shared in any number of ways (as discussed above), but again, it must be clear and include concrete actions.

The Staff We Grow and Recruitment

As detailed in Chapter 5, 'growing your own'[41] can be an excellent method to develop motivated and innovative staff. It is also an excellent method to ensure consistency. Much like the most successful football teams[42], English and maths teams work in cycles. These cycles begin with development, training and experimentation, which then lead to success and culminate in change. This change can be brought about by any number of events, but is usually seen when a 'player' is 'transferred' or retires (in other words, a member of the team is promoted or moves to another role (for a number of reasons)). If the process outlined in Chapter 5 is followed, there should be a 'ready-made' member of staff to step into the breach.

This can ensure high standards and also maintain consistency throughout the team, but how do we identify these potential teachers? The consistency which must occur here is one of recruitment. There must be consistency in recruiting potential English and maths staff and 'growing our own' – this can come from the attributes we see in classrooms, or qualifications, but it is necessary for consistency.

When recruiting externally to replace a teacher, we have set parameters and these can remain, but for replacing a teacher internally, through the 'grow your own' model, there are adjustments to be made. The minimum expectation could be along these lines:

41 W.C. Byham, A.B. Smith and M.J. Paese (2002) *Grow your own Leaders: How to Identify, Develop, and Retain Leadership Talent.* Upper Saddle River, NJ: FT Press.
42 J. Wilson (2013) *Inverting the Pyramid: The History of Soccer Tactics.* New York: Bold Type Books.

Essential

- A Level 2 qualification in English and maths
- Degree-level qualification or considerable experience in Further Education
- Previous experience of supporting or teaching English and maths
- Willing to complete English and maths specific training
- Previously supported or taught in a vocational area
- Strong desire to support student achievement

Desirable

- A teaching or postgraduate qualification
- Primary or Secondary education experience
- Willingness to complete a teaching or postgraduate qualification

With external candidates, essential and desirable qualities are generally fixed – with internal recruitment, less so. We are able to see the above elements on a sliding scale – if a candidate is highly engaged with external English and maths training, the fact they may not have taught in a vocational area becomes less important.

Either way, 'growing your own' is an excellent method to maintain consistency through staff turnover. Again, this can take a certain level of management seniority to implement, but persuading leaders that this is a more efficient way of developing an outstanding practitioner (as well as much more resource- and cost-effective) will help to lay the groundwork to achieve this method of recruitment.

A Consistent Environment

Of course, it is not just students, teachers and leaders which are needed for consistency – the workplace itself (the classrooms, offices, buildings) must provide consistency. Not only this, but consistency in processes, interactions, expectations and standards is needed. Reasonable adjustments will be made, of course, because they are always necessary[43], but on the whole, these factors should change only minimally and incrementally.

Secure classrooms as soon as possible, and don't change them; keep an English and maths base in whatever office you can and change any process collaboratively, giving ownership to staff.

Above all, remain positive and praise those around you – a positive environment is enormously beneficial when striving for consistency. To facilitate this,

---

43 E. Kell (2018) *How to Survive in Teaching: Without Imploding, Exploding or Walking Away*. London: Bloomsbury Publishing.

collaboration should be welcomed and supported and this will help to drive a culture of consistent excellence.

Conclusion – and Too Much Consistency

As much as this chapter, and book, supports consistency and consistent practice, there can be such a thing as too much consistency. Continually checking, monitoring and evaluating can halt genuine innovation and damage a culture – staff become more concerned about perception, 'passing the test' and appearance, and less concerned about delivering true quality.

As Mary Myatt brilliantly says, 'done is better than perfect'[44].

I do and will continue to repeat that trusting staff is absolutely vital. We never want to get to a situation in which monitoring and evaluation suggest we do not trust teachers and leaders. Monitoring and evaluation are things that happen *with* staff, not only to them.

This will require training, patience and potentially minimal funding, but in the end, expectations and standards will be clear and an outstanding team of teachers will each know their role, and their importance.

Remember – don't do what you can't continue to deliver.

Summary

- Collaborate when monitoring and evaluating.
- Keep it simple (and by 'it' I mean 'everything').
- Clear communication is key to consistency – outline expectations and remember: clarity, not brevity.
- A consistent environment breeds consistent teams and students.
- When embedding consistency, are your actions 'making the boat go faster'?
- There can be 'too much' consistency – streamline where you can and collaborate where you can't.
- Don't do what you can't continue to deliver.

Reflection

- What does consistency look like in the classroom, department, college?
- What are the barriers to consistency in your environment? How can you change this?
- What benefits are there to the monitoring and evaluation of teaching?
- How can scrutiny be streamlined in your department or college?
- What are your non-negotiables? Do these match up with those of your peers?

---

44 M. Myatt (2016) *High Challenge, Low Threat: Finding the Balance*. Melton, Woodbridge: John Catt Educational Ltd.

10 Accountability

'We can do it this way and I'll be accountable, or you can do it totally differently, and you will be accountable.'

A senior leader (2017)

I first heard the above statement as a young(ish) middle leader in my first role in Further Education. To this day, it is some of the best advice I have ever received. Why? Because it highlights that, though opinions may differ on strategy, policy or process, we are all accountable for student achievement. It is easy to argue that accountability has become a dirty word in education[1]. Even the mention of it will conjure images of teachers being dragged into little offices to explain why little Billy didn't achieve a grade 4 when he had been predicted one; why a class didn't make the progress that was expected; why task X hasn't been completed or why results weren't achieved.

But, as Fahey and Köster point out in *Means, Ends and Meaning in Accountability for Strategic Education Governance*, 'accountability in itself is an essentially neutral concept'[2]. More often than not, it is people or accountability processes[3] which add an emotional bias to accountability.

Take the case of the statement at the start of the chapter. This statement is not delivered in a condescending or inflammatory manner, yet it is easy to interpret the words as being delivered that way (or even during an angry exchange). Again though, if construed in this way, it is more than likely due to the reader's previous negative experiences (as covered in Chapter 11, students are not the only ones to have these).

The statement is simply a reminder that we are all accountable for supporting students (with middle and senior leaders holding ultimate accountability) as, left unchecked, there is the real possibility students may not be supported effectively[4]. It is also a reminder that practitioners are free to deviate from college, department and subject policy and processes, but they must take the accountability that comes with that freedom.

---

1   G. Fahey and F. Köster (2019) *Means, Ends and Meaning in Accountability for Strategic Education Governance*. OECD Working Papers, No. 204. Paris: OECD.
2   Fahey and Köster, *Means, Ends and Meaning*.
3   R. Behn (2001) *Rethinking Democratic Accountability*. Washington, DC: Brookings Institute Press.
4   J.A. Anderson and International Institute for Educational Planning (2005) *Accountability in Education*. Paris: International Institute for Educational Planning.

With this in mind, what is, and what do we mean by, accountability (a potentially ambiguous concept in itself[5])?

In *Accountability in Education: A Philosophical Inquiry*[6], Robert Wagner links accountability to 'obligation, responsibility and entitlement' and discusses an 'accountability relationship'. An excellent start, but it can be argued that this raises more questions than it answers – Who is obligated or responsible? Who demands the obligation or responsibility? Are teachers entitled to accountability as well?

Using Wagner's quote as a starting point, an accountability definition should be split into two groups: an abstract, ambiguous and emotional element, and the practical, measurable element – with even these subgroups of accountability easily split in many ways in different contexts.

The abstract, more ambiguous model of accountability tends to use vocabulary such as culture, ethos or philosophy. Depending on context, circumstance and even morale, these descriptors can be anything from a series of motivational frameworks to something more like a punchline. In this sense, accountability can draw a much more emotional response from teachers and leaders – this level of accountability makes us feel connected to or disconnected from an organization (with an organization meaning college, department, team or even a small group of staff[7]). We are emotionally connected to our workplace, our students and each other; therefore, we are accountable. The issue here, however, is that emotional accountability can lead to burnout[8] – we care deeply for students and do not want to let them down. As a result, we don't always know when to switch off.

Though we are all familiar with the impact of this side of accountability, we tend to think more towards the measurable and practical elements of accountability. By this I mean the analysis of data, the focus on achievement and results, and the general use and evaluation of systems and processes associated with accountability – quantifiable accountability.

Accountability as a quantifiable tool represents something completely different to all teachers and leaders, and it is more heavily linked to achievement and outcomes. As Jo Anne Anderson states in *Accountability In Education*, 'Accountability systems are based on the expectation that students can and will achieve the goals of schooling'[9].

---

5   M.J. Dubnick and H.G. Frederickson, eds (2014) *Accountable Governance: Problems and Promises*. Abingdon and New York: Routledge.

6   R.B. Wagner (2013) *Accountability in Education: A Philosophical Inquiry*. New York: Routledge.

7   M.A.P. Bovens, W. Ford and M. Bovens (1998) *The Quest for Responsibility: Accountability and Citizenship in Complex Organisations*. Cambridge: Cambridge University Press.

8   J. Berryhill, J.A. Linney, and J. Fromewick (2009) The effects of education accountability on teachers: are policies too-stress provoking for their own good?, *International Journal of Education Policy and Leadership*, 4(5): 1–14.

9   Anderson and International Institute for Educational Planning, *Accountability in Education*.

Though Anderson is correct, there is also ample research to show that no one accountability system is prevalent[10], and so (like teaching, learning and assessment) each college's model must be slightly different. Having said this, every college should include some form of accountability at all levels for English and maths – we are all teachers of English and maths and so we are all accountable.

As a result, this chapter looks to deal with how consistency is a key driver of accountability and will also detail who is responsible for each element of English and maths in an accountability system which focuses on whole-college responsibility. It is also important to remember that accountability (a key driver for outstanding practice) must be as consistent as possible, and so this will be discussed and linked to Chapter 9.

I do feel as though there should be additional caveats about what this chapter will and will not cover simply because of how loaded the word 'accountability' has become. Particularly in schools over the last 10–15 years[11], accountability has become a byword for over-scrutiny, increased (and ineffective) workload, and in some cases even bullying and harassment. It has even coined new terminology to describe the continued evaluation: hyper-accountability[12].

This chapter is not about *that* type (genre?) of accountability but more about how we support students by making sure college-wide staff (from receptionist to Principal) are meeting their responsibilities to our students. It is not a guide for catching people out, or forcing people out of a college; there is enough anecdotal evidence in every staffroom, website and forum on that.

This chapter seeks to discuss how we can support staff to meet their responsibilities to students and how we can develop achievement through consistently meeting continually high standards. Simply put, this chapter focuses on how we monitor others, our response to being monitored and the processes which this monitoring starts.

Aims and Accountabilities

Deciding accountabilities is an enormously sophisticated task that takes in all staff, at all levels, and also incorporates students and external stakeholders. Even though the majority of accountabilities will be decided by a range of factors (senior leaders, contractual obligation, additional responsibility etc.), regularly communicating these accountabilities is vital. It is important to remember

---

10 P. Slattery (2013) *Curriculum Development in the Postmodern Era: Teaching and Learning in an Age of Accountability.* New York: Routledge.

11 R.M. McGill (2015) *Teacher Toolkit: Helping you Survive your First Five Years.* London: Bloomsbury Publishing.

12 W. Mansell (2011) Improving exam results, but to what end? The limitations of New Labour's control mechanism for schools: assessment-based accountability, *Journal of Educational Administration and History*, 43(4): 291–308.

that high-quality, explicit communication with all staff provides the foundation of outstanding accountability – collaboration is our priority, not judgement[13].

In English and maths, with constant changes to qualifications, policy and funding, it is also vital that these accountabilities are refreshed and communicated on a regular basis. An effective method for efficiently completing this process is to collaborate with all relevant staff.

In the majority of colleges, so many staff play a role in delivering English and maths that high-quality communication can be difficult to execute[14]. Think about the college you currently work in (and previous colleges for that matter); with teaching and support assistants, administrative staff, pastoral staff and senior leaders involved (before including English and maths teachers themselves, or vocational areas), can you guarantee that everyone in the building knows their English and maths accountabilities?

Furthermore, can you guarantee that everyone who is aware of their accountabilities is meeting them? How do you check? How do you feed back this information? Who to?

If you are unsure of any of the answers to those questions, it may be the case that students are not receiving the level of support they could be in English and maths. High-performing schools and colleges need and have excellent accountability[15] – this is not a coincidence.

So, how do we resolve this? The first step is to define the aims and objectives of the English and maths team and then consult all relevant staff[16] against these aims. The aims are not necessarily data- or achievement-driven (i.e. we should look to achieve X per cent grade 4+) but centred more around inputs. As English and maths is nearly 100 per cent assessed via exams, it can be that all staff are doing everything 'right', but achievement doesn't mirror this. As a result, measuring inputs, as a first step, is important. What aims or objectives should we measure then?

As with all of the suggestions in this book, aims or objectives should be as concise as possible, while communicating as much as possible (clarity is always better than brevity[17]). As such, our aims could adhere to the following guidelines:

1   Deliver outstanding, objective guidance to students for appropriate placement on English and maths qualifications at relevant levels.
2   Develop a consistent approach to the delivery of English and maths.
3   Provide high-quality support to specialist English and maths teams through thorough training, monitoring and evaluation.

13 B. Rogers, ed. (2002) *Teacher Leadership and Behaviour Management*. London: Sage.
14 D. Greatbatch and S. Tate (2018) *Teaching, Leadership and Governance in Further Education*. London: DfE.
15 A. Buck (2016) *Leadership Matters: How Leaders at all Levels can Create Good Schools*. Melton, Woodbridge: John Catt Educational Ltd.
16 A. Pollard and J. Collins (2005) *Reflective Teaching*. London: A&C Black.
17 L. Johnson (2017) *Cultivating Communication in the Classroom: Future-Ready Skills for Secondary Students*. Thousand Oaks, CA: Corwin Press.

4 Focus on developing high-quality teaching, learning and assessment in English and maths.

5 Consistently promote and embed English and maths through bespoke and consistent intervention and provide students with progression routes (where needed).

6 Encourage and provide guidance to students to overcome challenges in English and maths.

Though these aims are by no means exhaustive, they provide a solid foundation to lay out key expectations and are enough to set standards by. They are simply communicated but also leave room for development – should this be needed in future.

To complete a truly accountable culture, everyone should play a role in signing off responsibilities and actions. The first stage here is to either draft a new set of accountabilities (giving staff responsibilities to the students, the English and maths team, colleagues and the college) or existing accountabilities can be used.

Having done this, distribute this document to all relevant staff – if their role is mentioned, they need to read it.

Following this, informal, one-to-one meetings (or 'catch-ups') are held with the Head of English and maths (or equivalent role). This can also take the form of a 'two-to-one' – with a senior leader in attendance for balance or to discuss issues which might impact whole-college policy. These meetings should also be used to discuss any and all areas of English and maths, and changes staff would like to see made (as well as the identification of effective elements). This is also a good way of promoting collaboration[18] because, like it or not, staff will discuss their meetings with each other.

Likely questions and topics in these meetings could include (but are obviously not limited to):

- Who is responsible for English and maths attendance and behaviour?[19]
- What steps would you like to see made to reward and sanction students?
- What English and maths challenges would you like further support with?
- What do we do well?
- Can you tell me about what support you would like from other areas or senior leaders?

Prior to working in Further Education, I'd heard and used the term 'stakeholder' in two very different contexts:

1 The private and commercial business world
2 For people who ate at meat restaurants without using knives and forks

---

18 UNESCO (2017) *Accountability in Education: Meeting our Commitments*. Global Education Monitoring Report. Paris: UNESCO Publishing.

19 Wagner, *Accountability in Education: A Philosophical Inquiry.*

As bad as that joke is, you get the idea. 'Stakeholder' was a term which was far removed from my experiences in the classroom (both as student and teacher) and in any communication I had while working in the secondary sector.

However, since joining FE, it has become a more and more relevant and important term. There are those who hate it, and I understand why (they feel it represents something else), but it is a useful term, and when I use it here, it is to summarise everyone who has a stake in English and maths: students, teachers, leaders, support workers, external organizations etc.

With this in mind, the one-to-one or two-to-one informal meetings should be held to seek feedback on the provisional accountabilities which are circulated prior to meetings. Much like in lessons, discussion and questioning in these meetings is vital, and they should be treated as a confidential forum as a result. Though professionalism is expected, no topic should be 'off limits' as the outcome of these meetings is to inform all stakeholders (that word again) of their responsibilities.

As discussed, these informal meetings will focus on accountabilities, but this should not be the only topic open to debate. All areas and processes can form part of the meeting – specifically the areas that staff would like to see changed, updated or removed.

The meetings should be roughly 30–45 minutes in length (though obviously they can be longer or shorter depending on the feedback) and all concerns or positive feedback should be noted. This cycle of meetings should be held with all stakeholders: English and maths teachers and leaders, vocational teams and leaders, senior leaders, SEND co-ordinator (SENDCo), admin staff, other relevant Heads of Department, pastoral staff, student services teams and any other relevant staff.

English and maths is a whole-college priority, so we must engage the whole college.

Having sought and received this feedback, a redraft of accountabilities will likely be needed, though many will probably already be in place by definition of the college structure or current standards.

So, what are the next steps? Who is accountable for what and how do we communicate this?

What are our Accountabilities?

If 'accountability means people can count on each other'[20], we need to know who we can and should count on. For this to occur, leaders need to identify all relevant processes and strategies for effective English and maths provision, and use the feedback from all meetings with all stakeholders to assign responsibilities accordingly.

---

20 M. Samuel and B. Novak (2001) *The Accountability Revolution: Achieve Breakthrough Results in Half the Time.* Blairsville, GA: Facts on Demand Press.

Though this document, and discussion, will be different in every college (for every context) a potential draft of accountabilities can be similar to a reward/sanction policy: it should be flexible enough for interpretation (when needed) and strict (or 'tight') enough that all stakeholders know their role.

Using the aims outlined in the last section, a potential layout could include key tasks or strategies and then the accountabilities for each group of staff – with staff split into leadership, teaching, support and administrative teams, and students. Teaching, support and administrative teams also incorporate support assistants, SENDCo, pastoral teams and administrative staff (Table 10.1).

Though it is again obvious that the creation, sanctioning and distribution of something along the lines of the example document will require a lot of consultation and consent from senior leaders, the results it can have are well worth it. Persuade leaders that this document is truly necessary by highlighting how it will help to support teachers in knowing their accountabilities, highlight those who perhaps are not meeting those accountabilities (for whatever reason) and also showcase those who are performing to an outstanding level. Even with the mention of highlighting those not currently meeting standards (or accountabilities), some of you may instantly be thinking of the punitive action that will follow – this is not the case. Identifying those who aren't meeting their responsibilities is, firstly, an opportunity to support any and all staff.

Clearly identifying the areas which lead to effective English and maths provision is the first step in creating a truly collaborative and supportive culture as it is nearly impossible to support students if we are unsure what role we play. Though the above process clearly illuminates accountabilities and responsibilities, it is equally important that bespoke CPD and support are provided to all stakeholders throughout this process[21] – if we don't support teams in embedding English and maths, they can't support students.

Having identified who is accountable, and what they are accountable for, how do we then hold teachers, leaders and students to account? With students held to account by robust reward and sanction policies (as outlined in Chapters 3 and 4), what about teachers and leaders?

Teacher Accountability

Accountability processes in any organization are generically similar in many ways – the triggers, actions and accountability timescales throughout education are broadly comparable whether centred around lesson observation, overall conduct or administrative tasks. If there is a failure to uphold or meet reasonable standards or expectations, an accountability process can be triggered (see Figure 10.1).

The issue here, however, is that once an official process of competency or support begins, it is difficult to exit this process. In other words, it is likely that

Table 10.1

Aims and objectives	Leaders	Teachers, support and administrative teams	Students
1. Deliver a clear strategy outlining responsibilities for all college stakeholders including relevant processes, procedures and associated communication.	Communicate all responsibilities and expectations to relevant stakeholders and ensure relevant training is available (where appropriate and necessary).	Identify responsibilities and expectations and implement in all areas of practice. Communicate expectations to students.	Uphold college standards and expectations and work to the best of their ability.
2. Develop strong relationships among vocational staff and the English and maths team to fully embed English and maths college-wide.	Facilitate strong relationships between vocational areas and English and maths teachers (including observation, sharing good practice events and other relevant opportunities).	Work collaboratively with college-wide teams to identify and develop outstanding teaching, learning and assessment in English and maths (whether embedding in vocational areas or in the English and maths team).	Identify links in English and maths use in English and maths and in vocational areas and appreciate the relevance of English and maths.
3. Effectively timetable to meet the needs of all students.	Facilitate curriculum-led timetabling which ensures effective timetabling of English and maths within vocational areas using data and other measures.	Ensure flexibility in giving feedback on timetable design and support learners by making student-centred choices in relation to timetabling.	Clearly communicate with teachers and leaders where timetabling is ineffective and ensure maximum attendance.

Table 10.1 (*Continued*)

Aims and objectives	Leaders	Teachers, support and administrative teams	Students
4. Embed consistent behavioural and classroom management standards with clarity in rewards and sanctions. Ask why behaviour happens and use suitable and relevant interventions to support students.	Ensure high-quality transition which is complemented by relevant training for teachers in classroom management. Create and embed relevant sanction and reward policies and facilitate teachers to effectively implement them. Continue to support teachers in the application of this process.	Provide safe and secure environments for students to develop their knowledge and understanding. Identify and effectively manage behavioural challenges and consistently follow up repeated issues.	Identify areas of strength and improvement and clearly communicate relevant issues. Uphold college standards and always give their best.
5. Identify whole-college CPD needs regarding English and maths and work to ensure all staff have the relevant knowledge, understanding and confidence to deliver high-quality English and maths support.	Facilitate teaching staff in identifying their own English and maths strengths and developmental areas. Provide occasion for training and CPD in English and maths and support staff throughout this process.	Evaluate and reflect on own practice to identify areas of strength and development. Clearly communicate these areas and complete relevant training/CPD.	N/A
6. Develop a clear process for identifying starting points and tracking assessment and progress.	Collate IA, marks and grades into a single depository for analysis (MIS) and profiling; use of ProM/ specialist spreadsheets for accurate target setting and action review.	Regular marking of student work, setting clear targets and reviewing milestones. Integrate non-negotiable approach to marking and exam preparation techniques.	Work towards the HARTS values and Student Charter – RESILIENCE, AMBITION and HARD WORK being key attributes.

Figure 10.1

Having identified a failure to meet set standards, in the first instance, a line manager will complete an informal discussion to outline expectations and investigate potential support.

The staff member is monitored, with a specific focus on the area which previously failed to meet expectations. Support or guidance is offered.

Following this, if expectations are still not met, a formal intervention will take place. Support is put in place along with improvement timescales (and relevant action plan). This is monitored, with additional support put in place if needed with a revised action plan.

Normal monitoring and evaluation of individual and team performance. Identification of individual failing to meet expected standard.

Further monitoring is completed – potentially with additional staff to add balance to the process. Depending on levels of improvement, this will then either lead to improvement and a return to previous levels of monitoring, or competency proceedings.

the practices and habits which have led to the need for additional support are fully embedded and therefore extremely difficult to change.

There are, however, obvious steps we can take before this stage. With strategies to support staff discussed at length in Chapters 5 and 6, and sanctions detailed above, what can leaders do to prevent sanctions?

First, we must be wary of the impact our monitoring can have. Though we may be aware of the 'Hawthorne Effect' (a change of an individual's behaviour brought about due to an awareness of being observed)[22], do leaders take this into account when observing? Or is there a greater likelihood they may pat themselves on the back for developing such outstanding staff?

Further to this, leaders spend even less time attempting to counterbalance the 'John Henry Effect' – the phenomenon in which individuals will attempt to outwork or outperform peers who have perceived advantages when both are observed[23]. In education, this can be represented by a teacher without a support assistant working harder than a teacher with a support assistant to bridge the perceived gap.

These two occurrences can be overcome by using the monitoring and evaluation methods described in Chapter 9 and by clearly communicating with teachers – let them know what you are monitoring, why you are evaluating and

22 R. McCarney, J. Warner, S. Iliffe, R. van Haselen, M. Griffin and P. Fisher (2007) The Hawthorne Effect: a randomised, controlled trial, *BMC Medical Research Methodology*, 7: 30, https://doi.org/10.1186/1471-2288-7-30 (accessed 11 January 2021).

23 G. Saretsky (1972) The OEO PC experiment and the John Henry effect, *The Phi Delta Kappan*, 53(9): 579–81.

how you can support development. If this proves ineffective, this may be the time to employ a 'difficult conversation'[24].

Difficult Conversations

A difficult conversation is one which involves the discussion of potentially emotionally charged subjects such as addressing poor performance, complaints or accusations, or other issues such as sharing difficult information (e.g. redundancy). These conversations usually take place on a one-to-one basis between a manager and a member of staff.

Difficult conversations represent one of the most challenging aspects of leadership[25] simply because of how uncomfortable and unpredictable the discussion can be. There is no guarantee that a member of staff will accept what is being said, and no issue can be resolved without this acceptance[26].

As challenging as these interactions can be, the following principles, adapted from Susan Scott's *Fierce Conversations*, will make the process as painless, and effective, as possible:

1 *Timing*

Though difficult conversations can be extremely stressful (for everyone concerned), putting them off or delaying them can also increase stress for all involved. Timing is absolutely key[27] – it may seem prudent to hold a difficult conversation towards the end of the week, but that may mean the person involved has all weekend to worry or become angry. We have a responsibility to uphold standards, yes, but we also have a responsibility to take care of staff. To avoid this problem, hold difficult conversations nearer the beginning of the week, and then follow up with another much more informal meeting later in the week. This informal meeting can diffuse any resentment or anger and give the member of staff an opportunity to ease any anxieties.

2 *Introduce the issue and detail a specific example*

It is important to outline the reason for the conversation and also give a specific example. If it refers to a specific incident (i.e. a missed deadline), give the main details around that incident – what, when, where, how etc. If it refers to a number of incidents, it is best to summarise these incidents into one coherent whole – spending an extended amount of time detailing and listing issues can be perceived as a personal attack[28], and a response will likely worsen the situation. It is important to give at least one example which

24 McGill, *Teacher Toolkit*.
25 McGill, *Teacher Toolkit*.
26 S. Scott (2004) *Fierce Conversations: Achieving Success at Work and in Life, One Conversation at a Time*. New York: Penguin.
27 J. Abrams (2009) *Having Hard Conversations*. Thousand Oaks, CA: Corwin Press.
28 Buck, *Leadership Matters*.

can be agreed upon – this allows both parties to discuss motivations for the event (or events) which have sparked the conversation.

3 *Give your feelings on the issue*

Though it may feel like the least relevant topic, a leader's feelings and emotions on the issue are very important. This allows teams to see the leader's motivations and their perspective – something which is not always readily available. Done properly, this can support high-quality relationships between leaders and teachers, as long as leaders explain why they feel the way they do.

4 *Clearly explain the stakes and why they are important*

A very important step in moving forward, explaining the stakes lets staff know why it is important that expectations are met, and subtly lets them know about the potential impact their actions can have on students. This is also an opportunity to discuss what staff need to do to meet expectations in future, and is an opportunity for leaders to outline their own expectations. This is an excellent opportunity to link accountabilities and department/college aims to events and actions within the department and make strategy and vision something much more real than an internal document.

5 *Discuss your involvement in the problem*

Whether we like it or not, leaders are fundamentally accountable and responsible for the actions of their team in some way. Whether this is a failure to offer relevant training, to evaluate or monitor, or simply to communicate expectations, leaders must take responsibility for the actions of those in their team. As a result, in difficult conversations, there must be some time put aside for a leader to discuss how they are involved. This does not have to be an enormous confession ('it's all *my* fault!'), but there does have to be an admittance that the leader is partly responsible.

6 *Indicate your wish to resolve the issue*

So, how do we fix the issue? After accepting what is being discussed, a teacher will immediately want to focus on this stage – What is going to be put in place? What are the next steps? How will the situation be improved? What support will be offered, or action taken? This is a leader's opportunity to show that the discussion has been held to support and guide – to offer assistance. Many teachers in this situation will immediately feel that all of their actions are now under deep scrutiny, and even that they are being forced out of their role. This is a chance to prioritise well-being during this process.

7 *Welcome any feedback*

Too often, difficult conversations can become too one-way, with little to no feedback being received from a teacher. Offer this opportunity – it is important to get feedback on what has been said, what will happen next and some of the events which have led to the conversation in the first place[29]. Without

---

29 Scott, *Fierce Conversations.*

this element, we are depriving staff of the opportunity to be heard, and potentially the opportunity to learn and develop. Remember – perceived autonomy as a motivational tool is extremely important.

8 *Have an agenda, make notes and follow up*

Making notes on the main points of discussion is enormously important for many reasons. Firstly, it will act as a record of what was said and by whom. Secondly, these notes can easily be shared to be endorsed by other parties. If the events are agreed on, both parties have a foundation of trust, and it is much easier to move to next steps. It is important to reassure all parties that these notes are to create a record – not as a way to punish, but just for accuracy[30]. It is not as vital to make notes in the informal, secondary meeting, though notes can be made here too if appropriate.

With solid aims, accountability and communication, effective standards and consistency can be developed and maintained at the heart of everything related to English and maths. Difficult conversations will become part of this journey, but they play an important role in motivating other staff and building relationships within teams. But what about leaders? When are our leaders accountable?

Accountable Leaders

The leaders we work with don't just signify a role or set of responsibilities, they can come to represent and define our values and beliefs. If this is the case, how do we hold them accountable?

Yes, every college has (or has the tools to create) an accountabilities framework, but the very nature of line management generally means that it is those above who evaluate and monitor those below. How can teachers hold leaders to account without circumventing the system or damaging relationships? It is easy to go to senior leaders to ask for leaders to be made accountable, but at what cost?

However, whether it is easy or not, accountability is for all and leaders are also accountable to staff and students.

To create a department culture, leaders must be responsible and accountable for preparing teams for their role and the challenges ahead (through CPD), for communicating effectively and for providing the resources needed to succeed. As a former line manager once told me, 'My job is to help you do yours.'

Firstly, communication here is vital – we have to remember its importance because accountability does have its limits[31]. Teams should be able to evaluate a manager's performance and there should be an open dialogue when teams feel

---

30 M. Myatt (2016) *High Challenge, Low Threat: Finding the Balance.* Melton, Woodbridge: John Catt Educational Ltd.

31 R. Mulgan (2003) *Holding Power to Account: Accountability in Modern Democracies.* New York: Springer.

they are being let down – or held to a different standard. This in itself can be extremely challenging – can teams have difficult conversations with leaders?

In a word, yes. This can initially be difficult to negotiate, but if handled with honesty and integrity, it can be transformational. As with difficult conversations, holding a one-to-one with a leader and outlining concerns, feelings and potential details around an example event opens a dialogue and asks leaders to be more reflective, which will ultimately lead to improved actions (though not immediately in all cases).

Will all leaders be open to this form of dialogue? They should be – being an openly accountable leader develops trust, honesty and professionalism[32], and so, whether we like it or not, being challenged as a leader (or challenging one) will develop high-quality relationships in the long term. It also highlights that teams work *with* leaders, not *for* them.

As beneficial as it would be to have a conclusive framework on holding teacher–leader accountability discussions or difficult conversations, it is not that simple – unfortunately. As all colleges, structures, leaders and departments are different, so are all perceived infractions that leaders need to be held to account for. As a result, use the above difficult conversation process as a starting point, and begin with a one-to-one meeting. A whole-team meeting can also be enormously useful and cement a perception of unity among the team. Either way, we are all accountable and should all have opportunities to improve.

Conclusion

Being accountable can be difficult, and holding others to account even more so, but it is still a massively important part of becoming an effective English and maths teacher, leader or team. As much as we would all like to be popular in classrooms, staffrooms and colleges, we mustn't be afraid to make unpopular decisions – sometimes there is no other option[33]. Having said this, there are always options and variations around communicating unpopular decisions and, as long as decisions are made with the latest and most up-to-date information, teachers and leaders will gain respect.

A by-product of solid monitoring, evaluation and accountability, respect, will ultimately further develop relationships and trust in a department, and this is vital. English and maths can be successful without teachers and leaders being liked by everyone all of the time, but success is impossible without respect. As long as all stakeholders know that decisions and actions are made with students' best interests at heart, collaboration and co-operation will

---

32 C.A. Mullen and R.J. Jones (2008) Teacher leadership capacity building: developing democratically accountable leaders in schools, *Teacher Development*, 12(4): 329–40.

33 E. Turner (2019) *Be More Toddler: A Leadership Education from our Little Learners.* Melton, Woodbridge: John Catt Educational Ltd.

flourish. As Myatt says, 'top leaders … don't set out to be popular, they set out to do the right thing'[34].

With this in mind, there will also be powerful opponents that we must be wary of[35]. As discussed in Chapter 5, there will be those who oppose the decisions we make, the way that we make them and the collaborations which enable them. The opponents come in two forms: those who oppose with compliance, and those who oppose without compliance. Compliant opponents can be an enormously refreshing element in any team and allow leaders to evaluate and reflect following their feedback. They don't agree, but they co-operate – this gives a new perspective to the majority of decisions.

Those who do not comply, however, are likely to become the first involved in the difficult conversations mentioned above. By using the steps outlined above, they can become key collaborative players, or further steps may need to be taken. This is a very challenging process, but all stakeholders must be held to account, and sometimes managing staff out is the only remaining step.

When accountability is easy – when staff are performing, and meeting and exceeding standards – departments thrive, students achieve and we create a fantastic culture. When accountability is difficult – when difficult conversations seem never-ending, and students bear the brunt – motivation can be hard to find. To stay motivated through challenging accountability all we need to do is reflect on three simple questions:

1 Would I be happy if my children were in that class?
2 Would I be happy if my children studied here?
3 Do I feel my children would be successful in these conditions?

If the answer is 'yes' to all three, accountability is good and all staff are meeting expectations. If the answer is 'no' to even one of these questions, there is work to be done on accountability, communication of that accountability and development of standards.

Summary

- Collaborate and use existing expertise to create, embed and maintain accountability frameworks and practices.
- Define aims and accountabilities collaboratively with all stakeholders.
- Communicate clearly and remember that clarity is paramount.
- Hold leaders to account when needed – we are all teachers of English and maths.
- Identify and collaborate with powerful opponents.
- Difficult conversations aren't easy, but they are necessary. Use them when needed and learn from them.

34 Myatt, *High Challenge, Low Threat.*
35 Thompson, *A Systematic Guide to Change Management.*

Reflection

- What am I accountable for?
- Do the people I rely on know their accountabilities?
- How can I support those who are not meeting their accountabilities?
- Who do I need to work with to be more accountable?
- What feedback and support is needed to support full accountability? How can this feedback be gathered?

11 Vocational Links, Support and Embedding English and Maths

'It's not my job to teach English or maths.'

Vocational lecturer (2017)

'We need to make sure it's properly embedded to help our students.'

Vocational leader (2017)

Above are two very different perspectives on English and maths from vocational staff – though neither is uncommon. With students attending between 1.5 to 3 hours of FE English and maths per week, and attendance in English and maths an area of national concern[1], FE is some way off providing the 4 to 5 hours per week attended in KS4 (which doesn't include any additional intervention, homework, revision, before/after-school booster sessions, extra sessions during holidays and even weekend lessons in school or through paid residentials).

As a result, it is easy to make the argument that students are often already at a disadvantage when resitting in FE as they receive significantly less support due to funding, and see exam grade boundaries continue to rise as exams are perceived to be more challenging[2]. Put simply, having had an enormous amount of support and additional guidance at school, students did not quite achieve their target, but they must now do so with a substantial amount of that support removed and while studying a full-time vocational programme. Many students also have responsibilities outside of college (part-time jobs etc.). In some cases, students need to markedly improve on their previous performance just to achieve the same grade.

Furthermore, the additional time spent in school classrooms can have the unintended consequence of making students more reliant on teacher support[3], and students can then struggle to work independently in English and maths in FE as a consequence. This is particularly evident in students who display lower

---

1   J. Higton, R. Archer, D. Dalby et al. (2017) *Effective Practice in the Delivery and Teaching of English and Mathematics to 16–18 year olds.* London: DfE.

2   www.bbc.co.uk/news/education-49441019 (accessed 11 January 2021).

3   A. Mazenod, B. Francis, L. Archer et al. (2019) Nurturing learning or encouraging dependency? Teacher constructions of students in lower attainment groups in English secondary schools, *Cambridge Journal of Education*, 49(1): 53–68.

academic ability, in part due to the potentially negative impact of ability group-ing or setting[4].

A 'whole-college approach' is often touted as being one solution. As much as utilizing this approach can be beneficial, there are challenges here too: a lack of specialists in English and maths departments has been an issue for a number of years, as has a lack of English and maths proficiency in vocational areas[5]. As the statements which introduced this chapter testify, a 'whole-college approach' can include much inconsistency.

So, how do we make up this additional time? How do we make sure that students receive a diverse and rich whole-college English and maths curricu-lum with less contact time, fewer resources and a shortage of specialist staff? To give students the best opportunities to achieve in English and maths, collab-oration with vocational teachers and leaders is absolutely key, and this should represent the beginning of our collaborations.

As well as working with vocational staff, fully engaging with/supporting SEND and support staff can uncover a wealth of knowledge and knowhow, and this can be used to better support all learners – specifically the most vulnerable or disadvantaged (who regularly fail to achieve in line with their peers)[6].

English and maths success cannot be achieved without the collaboration of all college staff, but first, there are some uncomfortable truths which must be confronted before we can start to successfully work on a whole-college basis.

Firstly, we must remember that many vocational teachers may have had very similar educational experiences to the students we currently teach, and could potentially identify more closely with students than with English and maths teachers. Some of them may even have experienced Susan Wallace's 'Four Big Demotivators'[7] and may have carried one or more of these over from school into industry and even into their teaching careers.

Of the 'Four Big Demotivators', the impact is more keenly felt from the fol-lowing two:

- **Fear**

  Much like many students, vocational teachers are fearful of being per-ceived as incompetent in English and maths by peers or managers[8]. There is the obvious embarrassment, but also the additional fear of potential

4   J. Boaler, D. Wiliam and M. Brown (2000) Students' experiences of ability grouping – disaffection, polarisation and the construction of failure, *British Educational Research Journal*, 26(5): 631–48.

5   D. Greatbatch and S. Tate (2018) *Teaching, Leadership and Governance in Further Education*. London: DfE.

6   S. Macleod, C. Sharp, D. Bernardinelli, A. Skipp and S. Higgins (2015) *Supporting the Attainment of Disadvantaged Pupils: Articulating Success and Good Practice*, Research brief, November 2015. London: DfE.

7   S. Wallace (2017) *Motivating Unwilling Learners in Further Education: The Key to Improving Behaviour*. London: Bloomsbury.

8   D. Allan (2017) *Teaching English and Maths in FE: What Works for Vocational Learners?* London: Learning Matters.

professional repercussions – for the majority of FE posts, English and maths competency at Level 2 is a job requirement and, though staff may possess the necessary qualifications, there is an expectation that this knowledge will be embedded on a day-to-day basis in lessons. Failure, or perceived failure, to do this brings a fear of additional scrutiny (lesson observations, student voice, work scrutiny etc.). With research suggesting that only around 22 per cent of UK adults have numeracy skills at Level 2 or above[9], and one in six adults are described as having 'very poor literacy skills'[10], it would be naive to think that a proportion of these adults don't work in FE.

- **Previous Negative Experience**
  A potential driver for failing to address these problems is that vocational staff may have suffered a range of previous negative experiences in English and maths. They can share similar experiences to students (struggling in school with English and maths, having to resit GCSEs or Functional Skills) or negative experiences can occur during their career. With vocational teachers more and more accountable for English and maths achievement in their areas, they can find embedding English and maths extremely challenging and find they are suddenly being evaluated on it (lesson observations, work scrutiny etc.). Put simply, if teachers aren't comfortable using English and maths, this can become a source of real anxiety when leaders begin to observe lessons looking for high-quality embedding of English and maths.

This is not to say these are the only two factors in limiting vocational impact in English and maths (lack of CPD or funding also plays a role[11]), but they are the most visible.

With this in mind, how do we tackle these issues and how can we also tackle staff apathy towards English and maths? The first step is to identify all staff who are engaged in teaching English and maths. This is very quickly and simply done because we are all teachers of English and maths. Every single teacher, lecturer, practitioner or staff member must use English and maths at all times and in all elements of their planning, teaching and assessment. Communicating this message throughout college is the first challenge, but also the first step to success.

This message must be effectively communicated at all levels – if only communicated using a 'top-down' model (i.e. by senior leaders, but not supported by middle leaders or teachers), the message can lose authenticity[12]. Therefore,

---

9   C. Harding, E. Romanou, J. Williams et al. (2012) *The 2011 Skills for Life Survey: A Survey of Literacy, Numeracy and ICT Levels in England.* London: BIS.

10 M. Kuczera, S. Field and H.C. Windisch (2016) *Building Skills for All: A Review of England: Policy Insights from the Survey of Adult Skills.* OECD Skills Studies. Paris: OECD. Available at: www.oecd.org/unitedkingdom/building-skills-for-all-reviewof-england.pdf (accessed 27 December 2020).

11 Greatbatch and Tate, *Teaching, Leadership and Governance.*

12 M. Myatt (2016) *High Challenge, Low Threat: Finding the Balance.* Melton, Woodbridge: John Catt Educational Ltd.

not only will there be a limited impact, but workload will be increased for senior leaders who have a range of priorities away from teaching and learning[13].

To effectively communicate this message at all levels, we must properly and fully collaborate with vocational teachers and leaders. But what does this look like?

Vocational Collaboration: Beginnings and Ownership

In too many colleges there's often a persistent stand-off between English and maths and vocational departments, with those in English and maths feeling that the vocational areas don't do enough to support them, and vocational areas occasionally begrudging the additional English and maths workload[14]. Honestly, I have never understood this. We serve and support the same students to reach the same goals, and working collaboratively is the most effective way to do this!

To start this collaboration, English and maths leaders must assess the English and maths needs of all involved. This should be done at department, sub-department/team, and individual level, and there is no room for generalization or estimation – hold open forums to discuss the challenges that are being faced, and use a range of methods to communicate what you want to achieve.

First, informally meet vocational teams in groups to get a rough idea of common challenges in embedding and teaching English and maths. This will immediately give some rough priorities. Having done this, meet with each vocational leader individually – ask them what their area needs (resources etc.), how they would like resources delivering, what challenges are likely with students and teachers in their area etc.

There are other ways of doing this – qualification audits of vocational teachers, some form of staff initial assessment – but the workload involved and scrutiny can lead to resentment and a lack of engagement from the very staff we are trying to engage and support. Simply put, if vocational teams are forced to engage, their engagement will be limited. Additionally, smaller, incremental changes are much more likely to become embedded and become habit[15], and this start supports that approach.

Some may feel this represents additional workload for the English and maths department. It doesn't. It's taking ownership of the college-wide quality of English and maths[16] and effectively supporting colleagues to support students.

13 Greatbatch and Tate, *Teaching, Leadership and Governance*.

14 H. Casey, O. Cara, J. Eldred et al. (2006) *'You Wouldn't Expect a Maths Teacher to Teach Plastering ...': Embedding Literacy, Language and Numeracy in Post-16 Vocational Programmes – the Impact on Learning and Achievement*. London: NRDC.

15 J. Dean (2013) *Making Habits, Breaking Habits: How to make Changes that Stick*. London: Oneworld Publications.

16 K. Thompson (2016) *A Systematic Guide to Change Management*. Great Britain: CreateSpace Publishing.

The areas highlighted by vocational leaders are likely to be familiar ones: unfamiliarity with modern teaching techniques for English and maths, lack of confidence with subject knowledge and the 'Four Big Demotivators'[17].

Creating Resources for Vocational Staff

Having discussed potential priorities and challenges with vocational leaders as a group and individually, the next step is to use this feedback to create resources for vocational teachers to implement in lessons. There are those who may complain that vocational teachers should create these resources themselves, but it is much more efficient for English and maths teams to modify resources they already have than it is for vocational teams to create resources from scratch. Also, consistency is assured if English and maths teachers are authoring college-wide resources – English and maths teams now know that algebra, sentence types, trigonometry and other topics are all being taught using consistent approaches, whether in English and maths or vocational classrooms. Even if it is only the shared classroom vocabulary which is adapted, this can make a difference[18].

It can be argued that English and maths teachers and vocational teachers should meet and collaborate before these resources are created, but without a structured dialogue, any collaboration can break down. By producing resources for vocational teams first, not only does giving feedback on these resources provide a basis for discussion, it also allows resources to be efficiently fine-tuned as a result. Simply put, if you put vocational and English and maths teachers in a room and ask them to collaborate, a starting point can prove elusive. Give vocational teachers resources and ask them to give feedback. This then becomes the starting point for discussion, and English and maths teams can quickly adapt and improve resources.

In his book *Black Box Thinking: Why Most People Never Learn from their Mistakes – But Some Do*[19], Matthew Syed discusses the cloud-based storage site Dropbox as an example of the success of this approach. Armed with a minimal budget in comparison to their competitors, leaders at Dropbox launched a basic initial version of their product and consistently adapted their site using customer feedback. As a result of this constant fine-tuning, they quickly established themselves as the market leader. Following this approach, English and maths resources can quickly be adapted and integrated, and become essential to vocational teaching. This also allows everyone to contribute and play a part in whole-college English and maths improvement and strategy, and vocational staff and leaders then become much more invested[20].

---

17 Wallace, *Motivating Unwilling Learners.*

18 A. Quigley (2018) *Closing the Vocabulary Gap.* Abingdon and New York: Routledge.

19 M. Syed (2015) *Black Box Thinking: Why Most People Never Learn from their Mistakes – But Some Do.* London: Penguin.

20 A. Buck (2016) *Leadership Matters: How Leaders at all Levels can Create Good Schools.* Melton, Woodbridge: John Catt Educational Ltd.

An additional positive: this approach also proves an ideal opportunity for bespoke, tailored CPD as English and maths teachers are able to identify and discuss vocational teachers' misconceptions in English and maths.

Embedding English and Maths Through Planning

Though using resources authored by English and maths teams in vocational lessons aids consistency and student knowledge retention and helps to change student perceptions[21], embedding should continue into all areas of practice. With the resources described above, English and maths becomes embedded in teaching and, with the simple whole-college English and maths assessment techniques described in Chapter 8, it becomes embedded in assessment over time. However, we still need to embed in planning.

To achieve this, further collaboration between English and maths teachers and vocational teams needs to take place. As with other areas of embedding, two criteria need to be satisfied:

1 Consistency
2 Natural occurrence of English and maths[22]

For consistency, this is achieved firstly through the vision and strategy outlined by the Head of English and maths (or relevant equivalent), communicated to teachers of English and maths and, as an extension of this, then communicated from English and maths teachers to vocational teachers. If everyone knows what the standard and expectation is, consistency will result.

Secondly, English and maths is best embedded when naturally occurring. This is to say, if English and maths are forced into lessons, the work becomes inauthentic[23] and this can lead to students doubting vocational staff's integrity (i.e. they are only teaching English and maths because they have to, not because it is relevant or useful).

To effectively and fully embed English and maths, collaborative vocational planning should occur. This should be completed at the end of each academic year, when planning the following year, and should take the form of an informal meeting between a vocational teacher and an English and/or maths teacher. With the vocational teacher giving details about the topic for each week, the English or maths teacher can give feedback about when English or maths will naturally occur. This then plants the seed for future collaboration – the vocational teacher can adapt the scheme of work to show when English and maths

21 Greatbatch and Tate, *Teaching, Leadership and Governance*.
22 J. Kay (2020) *Success, TES Awards and the power of consistency*, Association of Colleges website, 19 February. Available at: www.aoc-services.co.uk/thepowerof-consistency (accessed 24 July 2020).
23 Casey, Cara, Eldred et al., 'You wouldn't expect a maths teacher to teach plastering ...'.

naturally occur[24]; request resources or training from English and maths staff; discuss possible strategies and approaches for teaching English and maths topics and explore a host of other potential avenues to aid embedding of English and maths. This can also lead to opportunities for incremental coaching[25].

To make sure this planning is as effective as possible, it should also follow these guidelines:

- Both English and maths and vocational teachers should discuss the common English and maths strengths and weaknesses students usually exhibit.
- Collaboratively decide how these issues will be resolved throughout the scheme of work.
- Concentrate on finding solutions to these issues.
- English and maths and vocational teachers should review planning and embedded English and maths content after it is taught.

This can also be extended by discussing English and maths schemes of work with vocational staff, though this can be a much greater task as English and maths teachers invariably teach students from several vocational areas. There is also the option here for follow-up sessions as this type of planning generally takes longer than expected[26].

On that note, what can we do to make sure that the above workload is completed as efficiently as possible? Delegate.

Vocational Collaboration: Sharing the Load

In the above points, I have detailed how there should be regular collaboration between vocational staff and English and maths teachers. For a variety of reasons, this will improve embedding and provide more effective English and maths teaching, but how can this be achieved while maintaining a workload-neutral effect (i.e. the workload it causes is cancelled out by the time savings it brings)? An effective way to do this is to have an English and maths representative for each vocational department.

Ideally, this would mean assigning a maths teacher and an English teacher as an English and maths liaison to each vocational area (i.e. a maths teacher and an English teacher 'assigned' to construction, a maths teacher and an English teacher 'assigned' to travel and tourism etc.) and planning regular informal meetings for collaboration and to discuss general challenges.

---

24 M. Murray (2019) *Reframing Education: Radically Rethinking Perspectives on Education in the Light of Research.* Melton, Woodbridge: John Catt Educational Ltd.
25 Buck, *Leadership Matters.*
26 B. Busch and E. Watson (2019) *The Science of Learning: 77 Studies that Every Teacher Needs to Know.* Abingdon: Routledge.

English and maths teachers can then meet as a team and feed back the common English and maths challenges being faced throughout all vocational areas. The Head of English and maths (or equivalent) can then attempt to match this to what has been covered in the discussion with vocational leaders and see if there are any further CPD or embedding opportunities. Also, it is a good method to identify if vocational leaders are aware of the English and maths CPD requirements of their staff because, as has already been mentioned, teachers are not always forthcoming with their English and maths weaknesses (because of the 'Four Big Demotivators'[27]). This CPD can also take the form of maths and English enhancement programmes[28].

Alternatives and Next Steps for Embedding

Another potential method to facilitate collaboration between English and maths and vocational teachers, is to introduce drop-in sessions. Firstly, ensure this is always held in the same place (an office, a classroom or a support room) and timetable slots for vocational teachers to attend drop-ins to discuss embedding English and maths, or to seek support for any English and maths challenges they are having. This support timetable should be distributed fairly throughout the English and maths department, with no member of the English and maths team receiving more than 2 hours per week (1 hour is ideal).

This is for two reasons: firstly, there's minimal preparation and no assessment required, so giving any member of the English and maths team more time during drop-in slots will unfairly impact workload across the team[29]. Secondly, this prevents an over-reliance on any one member of staff – vocational teachers need to be able to approach *any* member of the English and maths team, not just a friend or favoured teacher.

The issue here is that drop-in sessions are voluntary and initial take-up can be disappointing. As a result, it can be better to start with compulsory collaboration sessions for planning and sharing of resources and then follow up with drop-in sessions.

A continuing issue in effectively embedding English and maths is that English and maths teachers lack relevant vocational knowledge[30]. To get around this, learning walks are another method which can be used to effectively develop embedding. With English and maths and vocational staff informally observing each other for short bursts (10–15 minutes in as few as one to three lessons) there are a range of opportunities to develop teaching, learning

27 Wallace, *Motivating Unwilling Learners.*

28 N. Porter (2015) *Crossing the Line: Improving Success Rates among Students Retaking English and Maths GCSEs.* A Policy Exchange Policy Bite. London: Policy Exchange.

29 N. Ellis, ed. (2016) *Managing Teacher Workload: A Whole-School Approach to Finding the Balance.* Melton, Woodbridge: John Catt Educational Ltd.

30 Commission on Adult Vocational Teaching and Learning (2013) *It's About Work …: Excellent Adult Vocational Teaching and Learning.* Coventry: Learning and Skills Improvement Service.

and assessment in English and maths. There can be initial problems with this (not least how teachers feel they are being perceived and potential delivery of feedback[31]), but this process can spark continued reflection and self-improvement in English and maths and vocational teachers[32].

English and Maths Training and CPD for Vocational Teachers

To complement these collaborations, additional training should be made available to any and all staff who feel they would benefit. This doesn't need to take the form of overly long CPD 'lectures' or require a heavy workload to organise – this can be 'micro'-teaches lasting no more than 10–20 minutes and delivered whenever convenient. The content can also be easily canvassed from English and maths team meetings in which all English and maths teachers report back the challenges they have discussed with vocational teachers[33].

Simply put, if a majority of vocational teams have highlighted issues with sentence structure with English staff, highlight this during the next English and maths meeting and arrange a micro-teach[34]. Run this session two or three times during a half term, email the relevant resources and share some potential teaching resources on the college shared area, and there is ample opportunity here for vocational teachers to engage with high-quality resources.

These sessions should also be made available college-wide – yes, we are all teachers of English and maths, but we are all also practitioners of English and maths, and so everyone from receptionist to Principal should have the opportunity to develop (though the CPD focus should be decided by senior leaders[35]).

The Collaboration Cycle

All of the stages detailed above should generally happen in quick succession and lead to evaluation, reflection and repetition (with relevant changes made to each stage). To simplify the stages (and chronology), adhering to the collaboration cycle in Figure 11.1 can be helpful.

This is not to say that this is the only way to successfully embed English and maths in vocational areas. There are many others:

- Webinars/external CPD opportunities
- Critical friendships with local, regional and national colleges

---

31 G.F. Kohut, C. Burnap and M.G. Yon (2007) Peer observation of teaching: perceptions of the observer and the observed, *College Teaching*, 55(1): 19–25.

32 A. Bell, and R. Mladenovic (2008) The benefits of peer observation of teaching for tutor development, *Higher Education*, 55(6): 735–52.

33 L. Darling-Hammond, M.E. Hyler and M. Gardner (2017) *Effective Teacher Professional Development*. Palo Alto, CA: Learning Policy Institute.

34 D.W. Allen (1967) *Micro-teaching: A Description*. Stanford, CA: Stanford University.

35 Department for Education (2016) *Standard for Teachers' Professional Development: Implementation Guidance for School Leaders, Teachers, and Organisations that offer Professional Development for Teachers*. London: DfE.

Figure 11.1

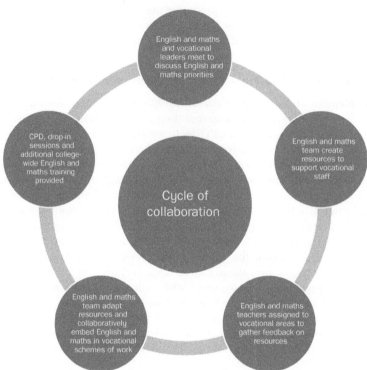

- Best practice exchanges with local, regional and national colleges
- Embedding through accountability-driven measures
- Different and individual approaches in each department

The issue here, however, is that each of these methods is open to interpretation, meaning near guaranteed variability in quality, delivery and consistency. In other words, if all vocational staff embed English and maths differently, there are likely to be very different outcomes.

It is also important to show vocational teams they are a significant part of the process and that they are valued[36]. As an extension of this, it is important that vocational staff have the final say on what would and would not work effectively for English and maths in a vocational classroom. They know their students best in a vocational context, and English and maths should not undermine this. Simply put, if vocational staff have better ideas, use them.

Again, due to previous negative experiences and fear towards English and maths, it may be that managers need to make some or all of these measures

---

36 M. Coalter (2018) *Talent Architects: How to Make Your School a Great Place to Work.* Melton, Woodbridge: John Catt Educational Ltd.

mandatory to begin with, but once these collaborations occur, and relationships are built, English and maths becomes more seamlessly ingrained throughout the college; these interactions will continue freely in the long term.

Support Staff in English and Maths

Just as college staff can prefer any title from teacher, practitioner, lecturer and a host of others, those who provide support in our classrooms can have similar preferences. For this section, I will refer to any member of staff who provides additional support in lessons as a support assistant. This phrase is meant to encompass all roles including teaching assistants, learning support assistants and any other title referring to support staff.

To properly and fully make sure that all of our learners are given relevant support, we must collaborate with support staff, SENDcos and all others who provide additional guidance and support in lessons.

Use of these invaluable staff can vary wildly in education, from best practice examples where staff almost take on the role of an additional teacher, to ineffective deployment of support assistants (for a number of reasons) as little more than 'Velcro-prodders'. For those who've never heard this term, the definition of a Velcro-prodder is two-part and generally occurs due to poor communication between support assistant and teacher:

Velcro – a member of staff is 'stuck' next to a student needing additional support (like Velcro).
Prodder – they occasionally poke or prod a student and ask them to do some work.

Firstly, it is absolutely vital that any support assistant giving additional support in English and maths has the relevant subject knowledge and skills to support students. If support assistants don't have Functional Skills Level 1 or 2 or GCSEs in English and/or maths, they may not be able to effectively support students at that level.

If this is the case, support assistants and any staff working in SEND departments should have relevant English and maths training and CPD made available to them all year round. To extend this, offering staff the opportunity to achieve GCSE and Functional Skills qualifications can be an invaluable motivational tool as well as an opportunity to develop their knowledge and skill in supporting students.

Where possible, it is also best to have a core group of support assistants who regularly support in English and maths. This group of staff then become familiar with the curriculum and core resources and materials, and so can better support students in these areas. This can also be an excellent model to develop future staff, or 'grow your own' as discussed in other areas of this book.

Become Embedded in Vocational Areas

One approach to effectively embedding English and maths into vocational areas is to base an English and/or maths teacher in a vocational area and have them teach English and maths only within that area. This has several positives: teachers quickly identify the challenges within that vocational area and can better resolve them; teachers can work more closely with vocational teachers and develop strategies to support English and maths; communication between vocational and English and maths teachers is excellent (as English and maths staff are generally based in the same office); and there is a greater sense of teamwork when working so closely.

However, challenges also arise. Firstly, staff morale suffers enormously when based in a vocational area with a majority of challenging students, in comparison to colleagues who have very few challenges. Also, as well as a lack of evidence to suggest this approach is more beneficial than any other, it can stop English and maths teachers effectively collaborating as they are not based together.

Where staff are based should not be the priority – the priority should be giving staff opportunities to collaborate, develop and implement good planning, teaching and assessment with vocational support.

Shared Activities

Though the above will help to develop outstanding embedding of English and maths, it is important that this is not seen as a one-off activity: any gains made will quickly be lost if there is not continued consistency. As part of this, it is important that English and maths and vocational teachers have opportunities to collaborate and share good practice at a range of events. Setting up whole-college sharing good practice events can be an excellent way of doing this. For example, a Dragon's Den-style event, round table or showcase events (in which teachers show examples of strategies that have worked in their classroom) can be excellent opportunities to discuss how English and maths can be further embedded.

Motivating Vocational Practitioners of English and maths

Just as important as effective whole-college embedding of English and maths, it is vital that those vocational teachers who teach English and maths are well supported and motivated. There are those in Further Education who are teaching English and maths simply because they have remaining hours on their timetable which must be filled. For example, a hairdressing teacher would ordinarily teach 24 hours of hairdressing; however, there were insufficient students so he/she has a timetable of 20 hours. As a result, the hairdresser is given 4 hours of Functional Skills English teaching time.

This can present a range of challenges to the English and maths department, students and the hairdressing teacher. A lack of subject specialism can produce anxiety and fear in the teacher, additional workload for English and maths teachers, loss of faith from students (who feel they would be better served by a subject specialist) and a lack of coherence in teaching[37]. An additional challenge is that if the hairdressing teacher is successful in English, they are likely to be given further hours the following year.

To resolve this, facilitating bespoke CPD, access to high-quality resources, a support link within English and maths, close and frequent communication with the English and maths team and regular collaboration are all ways to make sure the vocational staff member is motivated when teaching English and/or maths. It is easy to forget, also, that the unpredictability of Further Education means there can be changes to staffing (redundancies, changes to the size of a college, outsourcing, course offering changes etc.). The ability to teach English and/or maths is very much a strength and should be viewed as a future-proofing tool. It is another string to a teacher's bow and, coupled with the training opportunities detailed above, can lead to a range of strong extensions to the core English and maths team.

Vocational Support of English and Maths and Being Visible

To further develop whole-college embedding of English and maths, it is important that students are aware of how highly regarded English and maths is within the college – and, by extension, English and maths teachers. The most effective way to achieve this is through visibility – vocational teachers must be visible within English and maths. This takes many forms:

- Briefly visiting an English and maths classroom to see how students are performing (not to check behaviour, not to sanction students – simply out of interest).
- Supporting attendance and student conduct at mock and final exams.
- Communicating dates, times and locations of revision sessions, mocks and final exams and English and maths lessons.
- Including English and maths in all discussions about careers/future roles/ future study.

All of these strategies are low effort and high impact – they require very, very little preparation or workload, but they will help to quickly and effectively embed English and maths within the culture of a college.

---

37 P. Huddleston and L. Unwin (2013) *Teaching and Learning in Further Education: Diversity and Change*. Abingdon and New York: Routledge.

Conclusion

It is very tempting to simply list activities and tasks for embedding English and maths into vocational areas and incorporating vocational skills into English and maths lessons through contextualisation. However, the issue with this is that it has already been done far better than I can do it (and far more succinctly) and this can quickly fall down depending on college context, student profile, English and maths department structure and a host of other reasons. Simply put, there is no magic formula for embedding English and maths – it takes extended collaboration, an acceptance that failure will be part of the embedding process[38] and the motivation to consistently ask 'why' approaches are and are not successful[39].

One size does not fit all and it can be a difficult journey, but consistently embedding and revisiting topics, tasks and resources in all areas will help students to remember it[40] so we must persevere.

It is also important to remember that with embedding, much of the teacher preparation can be completed at the end of an academic year (when the majority of students have completed their course) and then implemented at the start of the following academic year (before students have enrolled or started programmes). As a result, any additional work should not occur during periods of high workload and, with collaboration key to success, this can be shared anyway.

It is also important that the accountabilities for English and maths are shared fairly. Vocational teams are accountable for English and maths and this must be accepted. This is not to say they are accountable for exam results, progress, achievement etc., but they must be accountable for inputs – they must be accountable for supporting English and maths, for collaborating on embedding and for developing their own practice in relation to English and maths. After all, we are all teachers of English and maths.

Summary

- Collaboration in planning, teaching and assessment is key to effective embedding of English and maths.
- Provide regular opportunities for English and maths CPD, resource sharing and planning to fully embed English and maths.
- This is an ongoing process and should be treated as such – set aside time to meet and discuss English and maths challenges and priorities with vocational teams.

---

38 Syed, *Black Box Thinking*.
39 S. Sinek (2009) *Start with Why: How Great Leaders Inspire Everyone to Take Action*. London and New York: Penguin.
40 C. Hendrick and R. Macpherson (2017) *What Does this Look Like in the Classroom?: Bridging the Gap Between Research and Practice*. Melton, Woodbridge: John Catt Educational Ltd.

- For a range of case studies and examples, check out Terry Sharrock's *Embedding English and Maths: Practical Strategies for FE and Post-16 Tutors* (2016) and the range of courses and resources at the Education and Training Foundation's website – www.et-foundation.co.uk.
- Consistency is key – make sure all staff know English and maths expectations.

Reflection

- What opportunities are there to collaborate with vocational staff?
- What support is available for vocational staff to support English and maths?
- How can we better understand the place of English and maths in specific vocational areas?
- Are regular English and maths links made in vocational sessions? Likewise, are vocational links regularly made in English and maths sessions?
- What support can vocational areas offer to English and maths practitioners?

Next Steps

'Honestly, I never thought I'd get my GCSE in English. Thank you to you and to everyone else in the team.'

A Further Education student (2019)

Developing a strong culture within any department or college can be a long and difficult task. It requires every policy, process or strategy to be aligned and for all staff to be aware of their accountabilities and responsibilities when enacting them. Individuals and teams must be as effective at working collaboratively as they are in isolation, and be fluid when moving between the two. There is no room for ego or arrogance – it is more about collectively making a system work for students by offering opportunities to staff[1].

These opportunities can be as simple as offering something which is not available in other colleges or settings. They can be cutting workload and providing a more well-being-centred environment for staff or creating a reflective environment[2].

Having said this, to disrupt or even destroy a culture is relatively easy. All that is needed is inaction at any level and additional workload can mount. Where this workload is left, a strong culture can crumble; where the workload is picked up by others, resentment can set in and the culture similarly crumbles from within. And all of this only requires inaction from one member of staff. A single toxic member of staff can spread negativity like a virus through a department and, ultimately, potentially spread this college-wide[3].

Therefore, when a strong, positive culture has been so hard fought for and effectively implemented, it is important that we plan to renew staffing cycles and continue to reflect[4]. For this to happen, leaders and managers should always aim some of their focus at replacing those who are likely to grow and look to continue this growth. This growth does not always have to be professional. Though, often, this does involve promotion in their current setting or elsewhere, this growth can also take the form of changing roles entirely, changing working patterns (for a greater work–life balance, or due to new or existing family commitments) or simply a desire to investigate different professional avenues.

1   A. Pollard, K. Black-Hawkins, G. Cliff-Hodges, P. Dudley and M. James (2014) *Reflective Teaching in Schools: Evidence-Informed Professional Practice*. London: Bloomsbury Publishing.
2   A. Bryman (2016) *Social Research Methods*. Oxford: Oxford University Press.
3   S. Gruenert and T. Whitaker (2019) *Committing to the Culture: How Leaders Can Create and Sustain Positive Schools*. Alexandria, VA: ASCD.
4   A. Pollard, ed. (2002) *Readings for Reflective Teaching*. London: A&C Black.

With this in mind, who will fill the void that can be left in a culture when an effective member of staff changes their circumstances? When the systems, strategies and processes which are detailed throughout this book are in place, who will be next to implement them and support student success?

The strength in the majority of these systems, strategies and approaches is that they are all easily adapted to a range of settings and, therefore, a range of staff rooms, teams and individuals. With effective staff in place, there is also potential for these strategies to adapt to individuals, and students will reap the benefits.

Using the skill sets of new staff to enhance the department, leaders can find their workload eases or changes to suit the strengths of their team[5]. Identifying attributes and skills in new members of staff is an exciting journey for leaders, as they are the first to see the benefits that will occur within the team, with students and potentially college-wide when facilitating new staff. As a result, it is vital that, as much as we reflect on yesterday, and enjoy the success of today, we are constantly looking at the challenges and solutions for tomorrow.

So, it is important to think about how we can continue this culture, even if staff change and potentially even if the systems we rely on change also. How can we do this? What are the challenges? How can we mitigate against these challenges and the risks which are inherent in making any changes?

This final chapter seeks to offer some guidance on this issue, and also discuss what is needed in the sector to truly help all students achieve their potential and develop into resilient, life-long learners.

Keeping the Culture

There are two strands to keeping an effective culture which (as discussed) has been so hard fought for. Firstly, there is the promise of department or college improvement and success. This promise can be intoxicating to some staff – they will be aligned with the success of the department and the college, and perceptions of their effectiveness will grow. The second is the promise of personal improvement and success. As discussed, this can mean a promotion, improved self-esteem[6], improved career opportunities or the quick and satisfying benefit of a higher salary.

To keep a successful culture, as well as keeping an eye on tomorrow for the department, leaders must also have an eye on the tomorrow of each member of the English and maths team – whether this be within the team or elsewhere.

It is not enough to appear to care. Leaders must actually care about their teams and build solid relationships on these foundations. Leaders and managers do not look to cut workload because Ofsted will be impressed, or to tick a

5   Coalter, M. (2018) *Talent Architects: How to Make Your School a Great Place to Work.* Melton, Woodbridge: John Catt Educational Ltd.

6   K.R. Wentzel and D.B. Miele, eds (2009) *Handbook of Motivation at School.* New York and Abingdon: Routledge.

well-being box. Leaders and managers cut workload to support staff – to give them more time to do the important things (again, whether this be inside or outside of college).

As a result, it is important to utilise tools such as enquiry-based research in colleges. Give staff the tools to investigate the methods which will benefit them[7]. Make teachers independent, and make them part of conversations around changing the way they work[8]. Using whatever means of communication are necessary – whether this be the collaborative approaches detailed in Chapters 5 and 6, or the difficult conversations detailed elsewhere.

Harbouring innovation and developing an environment where it is okay to fail is vital to finding that elusive culture. Staff and teams must feel it is okay to make mistakes, as long as they recognise and reflect on the steps which led to the eventual error[9]. Leaders and managers must give staff the tools to recognise and evaluate these mistakes and make sure processes are developed to mitigate similar mistakes in future.

Simply put, know you've made a mistake, recognise why, and don't make it again. Additionally, help others and make sure they don't make these same mistakes. Each one, teach one[10].

This starts by first identifying errors throughout departments and colleges – congregate staff and discuss what they feel the problems are. They are on the ground level, and will potentially have a greater knowledge of the day-to-day issues than a leader or manager. This insight allows leaders and managers to focus on starting points for change management[11].

Potentially, staff may not come forward with issues in a whole-team environment – provide opportunities to discuss in smaller groups, individually or through a confidential (or even anonymous) forum for sharing information.

Having done this, and identified issues which require additional focus, seek potential solutions from teams. It is vital here that leaders and managers do not unduly influence teams and individuals when feedback is being given. If possible, leaders and managers should wait to give their opinion or point of view after the rest of the team have given their input. Too often, teachers and English and maths staff will look to mirror or mimic the opinion of leaders – 'If my manager believes something, it must be the "right" way.' This potentially strips the team of original understanding of challenges, and (worse still) potential solutions.

With feedback from all staff, delegate enquiry-based research – as discussed in previous chapters, set the question that staff wish to answer and give them

7   D. Hopkins (2008) *A Teacher's Guide to Classroom Research*. Maidenhead: McGraw-Hill Open University Press.

8   M. Myatt (2018) *High Challenge, Low Threat: Finding the Balance*. Melton, Woodbridge: John Catt Educational Ltd.

9   M. Syed (2015) *Black Box Thinking: Why Most People Never Learn from their Mistakes – But Some Do*. London: Penguin.

10 R. Casanova (1996) *Each one Teach one: Up and out of Poverty: Memoirs of a Street Activist*. Willimantic, CT: Curbstone Press.

11 K. Thompson (2016) *A Systematic Guide to Change Management*. Great Britain: CreateSpace Publishing.

the parameters within which they will work. Though enquiry-based learning and research have been covered in this book in detail in previous chapters, it is potentially the single greatest tool leaders and managers have at their disposal – it benefits all stakeholders and builds a fantastic relationship between teachers and leaders, and also empowers teachers quickly and permanently[12].

When all of these steps have been taken, the only threat to a successful department is that of a breakdown in the processes which enable the culture. If this is even suspected, the initial step is to gather staff together and discuss previous successes, and what steps were taken to achieve these successes. A reminder of former glory can work well, initially, to ensure everyone is accountable and responsible (as discussed in Chapter 10).

If there is any additional threat of a breakdown in culture, identify the problem as quickly as possible and take the necessary action. If it is a process or strategy which is at fault, this is easily fixed – follow the steps of communication, feedback, adaptation and implementation which brought the successful strategy about in the first place. This can be more difficult if the problem is an individual, but the structures and support systems are there to train, guide and act accordingly. At all costs, an organization or departmental culture must be maintained. This allows for changes of personnel and flexibility – an over-reliance on good staff can be just as damaging as the wrong individuals in the right culture.

Regardless, it is important to enjoy an effective culture and have balance around priorities. We must always enjoy the success of today, as well as reflecting on yesterday and planning for tomorrow – it may not last forever, and good people can be difficult to source[13] – and spend time appreciating the hard work staff, leaders and managers have done (whichever category you fall into).

So, What Next?

With strategies and processes safely used and a culture safeguarded, what more can we do to give students the best possible opportunities to succeed? With staff workload a constant area of concern[14], and managers and leaders doing everything in their power to facilitate and support staff, students and all other stakeholders, what else is required in Further Education English and maths? Where can we find these resources?

The answer is as simple as it is overdue: to fully support and develop the quality of provision in English and maths in post-16 education, additional resources and funding are needed. As has been mentioned many times during

---

12 P.A. Danaher, K. Noble, K.M. Larkin et al. eds (2016) *Empowering Educators: Proven Principles and Successful Strategies*. London: Palgrave Macmillan.

13 D. Greatbatch and S. Tate (2018) *Teaching, Leadership and Governance in Further Education*. London: DfE.

14 L. Card (2016) Designing a sustainable curriculum and assessment system, in N. Ellis (ed.) *Managing Teacher Workload: A Whole-School Approach to Finding the Balance*. Melton, Woodbridge: John Catt Educational Ltd, pp. 34–44.

this book, there remain serious issues with the way Further Education as a whole is funded, let alone English and maths and the lack of specific, ring-fenced funding which is available for it.

However, this funding and the resources available do not reference finance alone, but also the most essential resource available – and the resource which teachers from across all sectors request in abundance – time. With the majority of students receiving 5 hours per week of English and maths when in key stage 4, they must then come to Further Education, having failed to achieve a grade they have been told is vital, and start a resit programme which only offers as much as 3 and possibly as little as 1.5 hours per week.

If Functional Skills is truly a viable alternative for GCSE, why then does it only necessitate 1.5 hours of teaching? It can be argued that learners on Entry Level and Level 1 Functional Skills courses require additional support, having failed to achieve the required level at KS4[15]. Giving these students additional time to develop and hone their English and maths skills around a more vocationally accessible qualification could be the difference between success at Level 2 or GCSE, and failure to achieve at all.

With this in mind, additional research is desperately needed in the field of post-16 English and maths. There is a paucity of specific research in this area[16] and what little research there is can offer a narrow focus (attendance being one example[17]). Longitudinal studies, trials of new innovation and research aimed at developing teacher effectiveness are long overdue in Further Education, and the impact of Covid-19 offers an opportunity to observe conditions in post-16 education and analyse what intervention would best impact and support students, teachers, leaders and colleges.

What is needed is the means to carry out these projects and research tasks – the initial expertise to support the planning and implementation of projects (which could easily come from within FE), the funding to capture and analyse the data, and the availability of the outstanding FE staff who make the entire sector work despite the many challenges outlined in this book and beyond.

With this in mind, high-quality, free CPD and training is necessary at all levels and for all staff to ensure that adaptation and innovation thrives in the most diverse and ever changing educational sector. If we are to strive for higher standards, we need higher quality, regular training and we need it on a consistent basis. Part of this is in setting up hubs for collaboration, but not simply limiting this to a gathering of like-minded Further Education professionals – open up Further Education to primary schools, secondary schools, sixth forms and all other providers.

It is the diversity of FE which makes it such a rich environment from which other providers can support, guide and benefit. Something as simple as the

---

15 B. Lenon (2018) *Other People's Children: What Happens to those in the Bottom 50% Academically?* Melton, Woodbridge: John Catt Educational Ltd.

16 Greatbatch and Tate, *Teaching, Leadership and Governance.*

17 Behavioural Insight Team (2014) *EAST: Four Simple Ways to Apply Behavioural Insights.* London: Behavioural Insight Team.

facilitation of placements or days shadowing colleagues in secondary, primary, sixth form and HE (who then shadow in FE) could provide a range of insights and learning opportunities for all concerned.

More rigorous (and free) qualifications and entry requirements for staff (with time and options to do this 'on the job' for those who don't have them) should also be made available, including the option to complete QTLS (Qualified Teacher Learning and Skills) for all staff.

We must also focus on the starting points and transitions between secondary and Further Education and investigate how we can make a student's journey as seamless as possible, while gathering all of the information and data we need to support them. If colleges had access to raw GCSE marks, course placement could be done much more efficiently and effectively. Gaining this data from schools is sometimes near impossible as students transfer to different colleges/ enter the world of work, or there is simply isn't a strong enough relationship between individual feeder schools and a central college.

Thousands of pounds are spent annually on maintaining and using IA software to give potentially inaccurate results – could we instead divert this money elsewhere to support students? Some exam boards have already started to offer services which allow colleges to track data over the school–college transition. If it is possible for exam boards, why can't the Department for Education create a national database of results, available to any college, which can provide evidence that a student has enrolled? Existing IA software providers could create and maintain databases holding all English and maths GCSE data – why not task them with liaising with and compiling this information from exam boards and ask colleges to pay a subscription/maintenance fee for this service?

Instant access to results would allow colleges to accurately place students at the correct level, on the correct course, and would be a universally consistent system used by all colleges. Surely this would hold some attraction to the armies of exam officers and administrators currently chasing paperwork? Diversity is part of the reason FE is so celebrated, but this can also mean inconsistency – this move could be a start to sector-wide consistency in enrolment and initial assessment.

Amplification and Simplification

Finally, if this book hopes to accomplish anything, it is actually hoping to achieve two things: amplification and simplification. For the strategies which are overwhelmingly effective and successful in Further Education, we need to identify the characteristics – the 'why'[18] – and amplify these characteristics: spread them into other areas, vocational and academic, and provide support to our colleagues so that they may also learn and amplify these characteristics.

---

18 S. Sinek (2009) *Start with Why: How Great Leaders Inspire Everyone to Take Action.* London and New York: Penguin.

What will hopefully remain are the strategies which are less successful – those which have become overcomplicated or lost the initial qualities which made them so attractive in the first place. Here, we first need a simplification – strip out anything that is ineffective; remove what we don't need. Simplify the process, the characteristics, and develop from there. When the process is effective, we begin to amplify once more, and continue to look for ways to simplify. This cycle will serve Further Education English and maths leaders, managers and teachers well, and is a potential starting point before applying any of the strategies detailed in this book.

The writing of this book has provided a timely reminder that the professionals, the practitioners and the people within Further Education do phenomenal work, throughout rural areas, towns and cities, and we would be lost as a society without the professionals they help to shape.

Very finally, if this book achieves anything, hopefully it will be a dialogue between professionals in English and maths and also between these professionals and the vocational staff who work so hard to support students and help them to achieve their goals, their dreams and provide happy futures.

Above all, we must remember that we are all teachers of English and maths.

Bibliography

Abrams, J. (2009) *Having Hard Conversations*. Thousand Oaks, CA: Corwin Press.

Adamou, B. (2018) *Games and Gamification in Market Research: Increasing Consumer Engagement in Research for Business Success*. London: Kogan Page.

Addison, R. and Brundrett, M. (2008) Motivation and demotivation of teachers in primary schools: the challenge of change, *Education 3–13*, 36(1): 79–94.

Allan, D. (2017) *Teaching English and Maths in FE: What Works for Vocational Learners?* London: Learning Matters.

Allan, T., Rodger, J., Dodd, M. and Cutmore, M. (2016) *Effective Practice in Supporting Entry/Level 1 Students in Post-16 Institutions (2015/27)*. London: DfE.

Allen, D.W. (1967) *Micro-teaching: A Description*. Stanford, CA: Stanford University.

Allison, S. (2014) *Perfect Teacher-led CPD*. Carmarthen: Crown House Publishing.

Amabile, T. and Kramer, S. (2011) *The Progress Principle: Using Small Wins to Ignite Joy, Engagement, and Creativity at Work*. Boston, MA: Harvard Business Press.

Anderson, J.A. and International Institute for Educational Planning (2005) *Accountability in Education*. Paris: International Institute for Educational Planning.

Anderson, N. and Peart, S. (2016) Back on track: exploring how a Further Education college re-motivates learners to re-sit previously failed qualifications at GCSE, *Research in Post-Compulsory Education*, 21(3): 196–213.

Association of Colleges (2020) *AoC English and Maths Survey January 2020*. Available at: www.aoc.co.uk/files/aoc-english-and-maths-survey-report-march-2020pdf (accessed 25 July 2020).

Audit Commission (2010) *Against the Odds: Re-engaging Young People in Education, Employment or Training*. London: Audit Commission.

Balwant, P.T. (2018) The meaning of student engagement and disengagement in the classroom context: lessons from organisational behaviour, *Journal of Further and Higher Education*, 42(3): 389–401.

Barton, C. (2018) *How I Wish I'd Taught Maths: Lessons Learned from Research, Conversations with Experts, and 12 Years of Mistakes*. Melton, Woodbridge: John Catt Educational Ltd.

Behavioural Insight Team (2014) *EAST: Four Simple Ways to Apply Behavioural Insights*. London: Behavioural Insight Team.

Behn, R. (2001) *Rethinking Democratic Accountability*. Washington, DC: Brookings Institute Press.

Bell, A. and Mladenovic, R. (2008) The benefits of peer observation of teaching for tutor development, *Higher Education*, 55(6): 735–52.

Bennett, T. (2010) *The Behaviour Guru: Behaviour Management Solutions for Teachers*. London: Continuum.

Bennett, T. (2017) *Creating a Culture: How School Leaders Can Optimise Behaviour*. London: DfE.

Bergin, C. and Bergin, D. (2009) Attachment in the classroom, *Educational Psychology Review*, 21(2): 141–70.

Berk, L.E. and Winsler, A. (1995) *Scaffolding Children's Learning: Vygotsky and Early Childhood Education*. NAEYC Research into Practice Series, Volume 7. Washington, DC: National Association for the Education of Young Children.

Berryhill, J., Linney, J.A. and Fromewick, J. (2009) The effects of education accountability on teachers: are policies too-stress provoking for their own good?, *International Journal of Education Policy and Leadership*, 4(5): 1–14.

Bjork, R.A. and Benjamin, A.S. (2011) On the symbiosis of remembering, forgetting, and learning, in A.S. Benjamin (ed.) *Successful Remembering and Successful Forgetting: A Festschrift in Honor of Robert A. Bjork*. New York: Taylor & Francis, pp. 1–22.

Black, P. and Wiliam, D. (1998) Inside the black box: raising standards through classroom assessment, *Phi Delta Kappan*, 80(2): 139–48.

Black, P.J. (1998) *Testing, Friend or Foe?: The Theory and Practice of Assessment and Testing*. Hove, East Sussex: Psychology Press.

Blandford, S. (2017) *Born to Fail?: Social Mobility: A Working Class View*. Melton, Woodbridge: John Catt Educational Ltd.

Boaler, J., Wiliam, D. and Brown, M. (2000) Students' experiences of ability grouping – disaffection, polarisation and the construction of failure, *British Educational Research Journal*, 26(5): 631–48.

Bottery, M. (2004) Trust: its importance for educators, *Management in Education*, 18(5): 6–10.

Bovens, M.A.P., Ford, W. and Bovens, M. (1998) *The Quest for Responsibility: Accountability and Citizenship in Complex Organisations*. Cambridge: Cambridge University Press.

Brill, F.J., Grayson, L., Kuhn, L. and O'Donnell, S. (2018) *What Impact Does Accountability Have on Curriculum, Standards and Engagement in Education? A Literature Review*. Slough: NFER.

Britton, J., Farquharson, C. and Sibieta, L. (2019) *2019 Annual Report on Education Spending in England*. London: Institute for Fiscal Studies.

Brooks, V. (2002) *Assessment in Secondary Schools: The New Teacher's Guide to Monitoring, Assessment, Recording, Reporting, and Accountability*. Buckingham: McGraw-Hill Education.

Brundrett, M. and Terrell, I. (eds) (2003) *Learning to Lead in the Secondary School: Becoming an Effective Head of Department*. Abingdon: Routledge.

Bryk, A.S. and Schneider, B. (2003) Trust in schools: a core resource for school reform, *Educational Leadership*, 60(6): 40–5.

Bryman, A. (2016) *Social Research Methods*. Oxford: Oxford University Press.

Bubb, S. and Earley, P. (2004) *Managing Teacher Workload: Work–life Balance and Wellbeing*. London: Sage.

Buck, A. (2016) *Leadership Matters: How Leaders at all Levels can Create Good Schools*. Melton, Woodbridge: John Catt Educational Ltd.

Burstow, B. (2017) *Effective Teacher Development: Theory and Practice in Professional Learning*. London: Bloomsbury Publishing.

Busch, B. and Watson, E. (2019) *The Science of Learning: 77 Studies that Every Teacher Needs to Know*. Abingdon: Routledge.

Byham, W.C., Smith, A.B. and Paese, M.J. (2002) *Grow your own Leaders: How to Identify, Develop, and Retain Leadership Talent*. Upper Saddle River, NJ: FT Press.

Card, L. (2016) Designing a sustainable curriculum and assessment system, in N. Ellis (ed.) *Managing Teacher Workload: A Whole-School Approach to Finding the Balance*. Melton, Woodbridge: John Catt Educational Ltd, pp. 34–44.

Casanova, R. (1996) *Each one Teach one: Up and out of Poverty: Memoirs of a Street Activist*. Willimantic, CT: Curbstone Press.

Case, K.E. and Fair, R.C. (1999) *Principles of Economics*, 5th edn. Upper Saddle River, NJ: Prentice-Hall.

Casey, H., Cara, O., Eldred, J. et al. (2006) '*You Wouldn't Expect a Maths Teacher to Teach Plastering …*': *Embedding Literacy, Language and Numeracy in Post-16 Vocational Programmes – the Impact on Learning and Achievement*. London: NRDC.

Chan, C., Chang, M.L., Westwood, P. and Yuen, M.T. (2002) Teaching adaptively: how easy is differentiation in practice?, *The Asia-Pacific Education Researcher*, 11(1): 27–58.

Chande, R., Luca, M., Sanders, M. et al. (2017) *Increasing Attendance and Attainment Among Adult Students in the UK: Evidence from a Field Experiment*. Working paper. London: Behavioural Insights Team.

Chatterjee, R. (2018) *The Stress Solution: The 4 Steps to a Calmer, Happier, Healthier You*. London: Penguin.

Clark, C. (2019) *Children and Young People's Reading in 2017/18: Findings from our Annual Literacy Survey*. London: National Literacy Trust.

Clay, B. and Weston, D. (2018) *Unleashing Great Teaching: The Secrets to the Most Effective Teacher Development*. Abingdon: Routledge.

Clough, L. and Foster, A. (2001) *Initial Assessment of Learning and Support Needs and Planning Learning to Meet Needs*. Sheffield: DfEE.

Coalter, M. (2018) *Talent Architects: How to Make Your School a Great Place to Work*. Melton, Woodbridge: John Catt Educational Ltd.

Cole, G.A. (2004) *Management Theory and Practice*. Andover: Cengage Learning EMEA.

Cole, R.W. (2008) *Educating Everybody's Children: Diverse Teaching Strategies for Diverse Learners*. Alexandria, VA: ASCD.

Commission on Adult Vocational Teaching and Learning (2013) *It's About Work …: Excellent Adult Vocational Teaching and Learning*. Coventry: Learning and Skills Improvement Service.

Cowan, A. (2013) *The Art of Writing Fiction*. Abingdon: Routledge.

Cowley, S. (2006) *Getting the Buggers to Behave*. London: A&C Black.

Crawford, C. and Cribb, J. (2015) *The Link between Childhood Reading Skills and Adult Outcomes: Analysis of a Cohort of British Children*. IFS Briefing Note BN169. London: Institute for Fiscal Studies.

Critto, A. (2000) *Consistency: Being Coherent*. Lanham, MD: University Press of America.

CV-Library (2019) The 10 Least and Most Trusted Professions in the UK. Available at: www.cv-library.co.uk/recruitment-insight/10-least-trusted-professions-uk/ (accessed January 2021).

Czerniawski, G. and Kidd, W. (eds) (2011) *Student Voice Handbook: Bridging the Academic/Practitioner Divide*. Bingley: Emerald Group Publishing.

Danaher, P.A., Noble, K., Larkin, K.M., Kawka, M., van Rensburg, H., Brodie, L. and Rensburg, H. (eds) (2016) *Empowering Educators: Proven Principles and Successful Strategies*. London: Palgrave Macmillan.

Darling-Hammond, L., Hyler, M.E. and Gardner, M. (2017) *Effective Teacher Professional Development*. Palo Alto, CA: Learning Policy Institute.

Davison, J. and Moss, J. (eds) (2002) *Issues in English Teaching*. Abingdon: Routledge.

Dean, J. (2013) *Making Habits, Breaking Habits: How to make Changes that Stick*. London: Oneworld Publications.

Deci, E.L. (1971) Effects of externally mediated rewards on intrinsic motivation, *Journal of Personality and Social Psychology*, 18(1): 105–15.

Denscombe, M. (2000) Social conditions for stress: young people's experience of doing GCSEs, *British Educational Research Journal*, 26(3): 259–374.

Department for Business, Innovation and Skills (2012) *The 2011 Skills for Life Survey: A Survey of Literacy, Numeracy and ICT Levels in England*. BIS Research paper number 81. London: BIS.

Department for Education (2016) *Standard for Teachers' Professional Development.* London: DfE.

Department for Education (2016) *Standard for Teachers' Professional Development: Implementation Guidance for School Leaders, Teachers, and Organisations that offer Professional Development for Teachers.* London: DfE.

Department for Education (2018) *Mental Health and Behaviour in Schools* [Departmental advice]. London: DfE.

Didau, D. and Rose, N. (2016) *What Every Teacher Needs to Know About … Psychology.* Melton, Woodbridge: John Catt Educational Ltd.

Dive, B. (2008) *The Accountable Leader: Developing Effective Leadership through Managerial Accountability.* London and Philadelphia: Kogan Page Publishers.

Dix, P. (2017) *When the Adults Change, Everything Changes: Seismic Shifts in School Behaviour.* Carmarthen: Crown House Publishing.

Dolton, P., Marcenaro, O., Vries, R.D. and She, P.W. (2018) *Global Teacher Status Index 2018.* London: Varkey Foundation.

Dougill, P., Raleigh, M., Blatchford, R., Fryer, L., Robinson, C.A. and Richmond, J. (2011) *To the Next Level: Good Schools becoming Outstanding.* Reading: CfBT Education Trust.

Dreon, O. and Polly, D. (eds) (2016) *Teacher Education for Ethical Professional Practice in the 21st Century.* Hershey, PA: IGI Global.

Dubnick, M.J. and Frederickson, H.G. (eds) (2014) *Accountable Governance: Problems and Promises.* Abingdon and New York: Routledge.

Duckworth, A.L., Peterson, C., Matthews, M.D. and Kelly, D.R. (2007) Grit: perseverance and passion for long-term goals, *Journal of Personality and Social Psychology,* 92(6): 1087–101.

Duckworth, A.L., Weir, D., Tsukayama, E. and Kwok, D. (2012) Who does well in life? Conscientious adults excel in both objective and subjective success, Frontiers in Psychology, 3: 356, doi: 10.3389/fpsyg.2012.00356.

Duhigg, C. (2016) *Smarter Faster Better: The Secrets of being Productive in Life and Business.* New York: Random House.

Dweck, C. (2015) Carol Dweck revisits the growth mindset, *Education Week,* 35(5): 20–4.

Education and Training Foundation (2014) *Professional Standards for Teachers and Trainers in Education and Training – England.* London: ETF.

Ellis, N. (ed.) (2016) *Managing Teacher Workload: A Whole-School Approach to Finding the Balance.* Melton, Woodbridge: John Catt Educational Ltd.

Ellis, S. and Tod, J. (2018) *Behaviour for Learning: Promoting Positive Relationships in the Classroom.* Abingdon: Routledge.

Engin, M. (2014) Macro-scaffolding: contextual support for teacher learning, *Australian Journal of Teacher Education,* 39(5), doi: 10.14221/ajte.2014v39n5.6.

Evans, A. and Walters, M. (2002) *From Absence to Attendance.* London: CIPD Publishing.

Evans, M. (2019) *Leaders With Substance: An Antidote to Leadership Genericism in Schools.* Melton, Woodbridge: John Catt Educational Ltd.

Fahey, G. and Köster, F. (2019) *Means, Ends and Meaning in Accountability for Strategic Education Governance.* OECD Working Papers, No. 204. Paris: OECD.

Ferguson, A. (2015) *Leading: Lessons in Leadership from the Legendary Manchester United Manager.* London: Hachette UK.

Ferkany, M. (2008) The educational importance of self-esteem, *Journal of Philosophy of Education,* 42(1): 119–32.

Fielding, M. (2006) Leadership, radical student engagement and the necessity of person-centred education, *International Journal of Leadership in Education,* 9(4): 299–313.

Firth J., Torous, J., Stubbs, B. et al. (2019) The 'online brain': how the internet may be changing our cognition, *World Psychiatry,* 18(2): 119–29.

Fletcher, D. and Sarkar, M. (2016) Mental fortitude training: an evidence-based approach to developing psychological resilience for sustained success, *Journal of Sport Psychology in Action*, 7(3): 135–57.

Flynn, C., Gilchrist, D. and Olson, L. (2004) Using the assessment cycle as a tool for collaboration, *Resource Sharing & Information Networks*, 17(1–2): 187–203.

Foster, D. (2015) Private journals versus public blogs: the impact of peer readership on low-stakes reflective writing, *Teaching Sociology*, 43(2): 104–14.

Franklin, M. (2014) *Agile Change Management: A Practical Framework for Successful Change Planning and Implementation*. London: Kogan Page Publishers.

Frattaroli, J., Thomas, M. and Lyubomirsky, S. (2011) Opening up in the classroom: effects of expressive writing on graduate school entrance exam performance, *Emotion*, 11(3): 691–6.

Fullan, M. and Hargreaves, A. (1991) *What's Worth Fighting For?: Working Together for your School*. Toronto: Ontario Public School Teachers' Federation.

Fuller, C. and Macfadyen, T. (2012) 'What with your grades?' Students' motivation for and experiences of vocational courses in Further Education, *Journal of Vocational Education & Training*, 64(1): 87–101.

Galambos, N.L. and Tilton-Weaver, L.C. (2000) Adolescents' psychosocial maturity, problem behavior, and subjective age: in search of the adultoid, *Applied Developmental Science*, 4(4): 178–92.

Gazzaley, A. and Rosen, L.D. (2016) *The Distracted Mind: Ancient Brains in a High-tech World*. Cambridge, MA: MIT Press.

Gilbert, I. (2007) *The Little Book of Thunks: 260 Questions to Make your Brain go Ouch!* Carmarthen: Crown House Publishing.

Gilbert, L., Teravainen, A., Clark, A. and Shaw, S. (2018) *Literacy and Life Expectancy: An Evidence Review Exploring the Link between Literacy and Life Expectancy in England through Health and Socioeconomic Factors*. London: National Literacy Trust.

Gill, S. (2002) *Successful Difficult Conversations in School: Improve your team's performance, Behaviour and Attitude with Kindness and Success*. Melton, Woodbridge: John Catt Educational Ltd.

Goffman, E. (2009) *Stigma: Notes on the Management of Spoiled Identity*. London: Simon & Schuster.

Gold, A. and Evans, J.M. (1998) *Reflecting on School Management*. Hove, East Sussex: Psychology Press.

Goldstein, H. (2004) Education for all: the globalization of learning targets, *Comparative Education*, 40(1): 7–14.

Greatbatch, D. and Tate, S. (2018) *Teaching, Leadership and Governance in Further Education*. London: DfE.

Greenberg, K.L. (1986) *Writing Assessment: Issues and Strategies*. Longman Series in College Composition and Communication. New York: Longman.

Gregory, A. and Ripski, M.B. (2008) Adolescent trust in teachers: implications for behavior in the high school classroom, *School Psychology Review*, 37(3): 337–53.

Gruenert, S. and Whitaker, T. (2019) *Committing to the Culture: How Leaders Can Create and Sustain Positive Schools*. Alexandria, VA: ASCD.

Gruwell, E. (2007) *The Freedom Writers Diary: How a Teacher and 150 Teens Used Writing to Change Themselves and the World Around Them*. New York: Broadway Books.

Hall, D.T. and Foster, L.W. (1977) A psychological success cycle and goal setting: goals, performance, and attitudes, *Academy of Management Journal*, 20(2): 282–90.

Hallam, S. and Rogers, L. (2008) *Improving Behaviour and Attendance at School*. Buckingham: McGraw-Hill Education.

Harding, C., Romanou, E., Williams, J. et al. (2012) *The 2011 Skills for Life Survey: A Survey of Literacy, Numeracy and ICT Levels in England.* London: BIS.

Harlen, W., Gipps, C., Broadfoot, P. and Nuttall, D. (1992) Assessment and the improvement of education, *The Curriculum Journal*, 3(3): 215–30.

Harreveld, B. and Singh, M. (2009) Contextualising learning at the education–training–work interface, *Education and Training*, 51(2): 92–107.

Hartley, S. (2015) *Stronger Together: How Great Teams Work.* London: Hachette UK.

Hattie, J. (2012) *Visible Learning for Teachers: Maximizing Impact on Learning.* Abingdon and New York: Routledge.

Hattie, J. and Timperley, H. (2007) The power of feedback, *Review of Educational Research*, 77(1): 81–112.

Health and Safety Executive (2018) *Work-related Stress, Anxiety or Depression Statistics in Great Britain.* London: HSE.

Heath, C. and Heath, D. (2008) *Made to Stick: Why Some Ideas Take Hold and Others Come Unstuck.* London: Random House.

Heath, C. and Heath, D. (2010) *Switch: How to Change Things When Change is Hard.* London: Random House.

Hendrick, C. and Macpherson, R. (2017) *What Does this Look Like in the Classroom?: Bridging the Gap Between Research and Practice.* Melton, Woodbridge: John Catt Educational Ltd.

Higton, J., Archer, R., Dalby, D. et al. (2017) *Effective Practice in the Delivery and Teaching of English and Mathematics to 16–18 year olds.* London: DfE.

Hochman, J.C. and Wexler, N. (2017) *The Writing Revolution: A Guide to Advancing Thinking through Writing in all Subjects and Grades.* San Francisco: John Wiley & Sons.

Hodges, J., McIntosh, J. and Gentry, M. (2017) The effect of an out-of-school enrichment program on the academic achievement of high-potential students from low-income families, *Journal of Advanced Academics*, 28(3): 204–24.

Hopkins, D. (2008) *A Teacher's Guide to Classroom Research.* Maidenhead: McGraw-Hill Open University Press.

Hornby, G. (2016) *Inclusive Special Education.* New York: Springer-Verlag.

Hubley, A.M. and Arım, R.G. (2012) Subjective age in early adolescence: relationships with chronological age, pubertal timing, desired age, and problem behaviors, *Journal of Adolescence*, 35(2): 357–66.

Huddleston, P. and Unwin, L. (2013) *Teaching and Learning in Further Education: Diversity and Change.* Abingdon and New York: Routledge.

Hume, S., O'Reilly, F., Groot, B. et al. (2018) *Improving Engagement and Attainment in Maths and English Courses: Insights from Behavioural Research.* London: DfE.

Hume, S., O'Reilly, F., Groot, B. et al. (2018) *Retention and Success in Maths and English: A Practitioner Guide to Applying Behavioural Insights.* London: DfE and Behavioural Insights Team.

Hunt-Davis, B. and Beveridge, H. (2012) *Will it Make the Boat Go Faster?* Leicester: Troubador.

Iacocca, L.A. and Novak, W. (1986) *Iacocca: An Autobiography.* New York: Bantam.

Jarvis, P. and Griffin, C. (eds) (2003) *Adult and Continuing Education, Volume V: Adult Education – Viewed from the Disciplines.* London and New York: Taylor & Francis.

Joe, J.N., Tocci, C.M., Holtzman, S.L. and Williams, J.C. (2013) *Foundations of Observation: Considerations for Developing a Classroom Observation System that Helps Districts Achieve Consistent and Accurate Scores.* MET Project, Policy and Practice Brief. Seattle: Bill & Melinda Gates Foundation.

Johnson, L. (2017) *Cultivating Communication in the Classroom: Future-Ready Skills for Secondary Students.* Thousand Oaks, CA: Corwin Press.

Kay, J. (2020) *Success, TES Awards and the power of consistency*, Association of Colleges website, 19 February. Available at: www.aoc-services.co.uk/thepowerofconsistency (accessed: 24 July 2020).

Kell, E. (2018) *How to Survive in Teaching: Without Imploding, Exploding or Walking Away*. London: Bloomsbury Publishing.

Kellerman, B. (2004) *Bad Leadership: What it Is, How it Happens, Why it Matters*. Boston, MA: Harvard Business Press.

Kettlewell, K., Southcott, C., Stevens, E. and McCrone, T. (2012) *Engaging the Disengaged*. Slough: National Foundation for Educational Research.

Kohut, G.F., Burnap, C. and Yon, M.G. (2007) Peer observation of teaching: perceptions of the observer and the observed, *College Teaching*, 55(1): 19–25.

Koretz, D. (2017) *The Testing Charade: Pretending to Make Schools Better*. Chicago: University of Chicago Press.

Kotter, J.P. (2008) *Force for Change: How Leadership Differs from Management*. New York: Simon & Schuster.

Krause, A.J., Simon, E.B., Mander, B.A. et al. (2017) The sleep-deprived human brain, *Nature Reviews Neuroscience*, 18(7): 404–18.

Kuczera, M., Field, S. and Windisch, H.C. (2016) *Building Skills for All: A Review of England: Policy Insights from the Survey of Adult Skills*. OECD Skills Studies. Paris: OECD. Available at: www.oecd.org/unitedkingdom/building-skills-for-all-reviewof-england.pdf (accessed 27 December 2020).

Lambert, S. (2013) Defining a tri-dimensional role for leadership in Further Education colleges, *Management in Education*, 27(1): 39–42.

Lanning, K. (2012) *Consistency, Scalability, and Personality Measurement*. New York: Springer Science & Business Media.

Larréché, J.C. (2008) *The Momentum Effect: How to Ignite Exceptional Growth*. New Jersey: Pearson Education.

Lemov, D., Woolway, E. and Yezzi, K. (2012) *Practice Perfect: 42 Rules for Getting Better at Getting Better*. San Francisco, CA: John Wiley & Sons.

Lenon, B. (2018) *Other People's Children: What Happens to those in the Bottom 50% Academically?* Melton, Woodbridge: John Catt Educational Ltd.

Lepper, M., Greene, D. and Nisbett, R. (1973) Undermining children's intrinsic interest with extrinsic reward, *Journal of Personality and Social Psychology*, 28(1): 129–37.

Little, D. (1995) Learning as dialogue: the dependence of learner autonomy on teacher autonomy, *System*, 23(2): 175–81.

Longhurst, R.J. (1999) Why aren't they here? Student absenteeism in a Further Education college, *Journal of Further and Higher Education*, 23(1): 61–80.

Lopez, I. (2017) *Keeping it Real and Relevant: Building Authentic Relationships in Your Diverse Classroom*. Alexandria, VA: ASCD.

Louis K.S. (2003) Trust and improvement in schools. Paper presented at BELMAS annual conference, Milton Keynes, October.

Luchinskaya, D. and Dickinson, P. (2019) *The Adult Skills Gap: Is Falling Investment in UK Adults Stalling Social Mobility?* London: Social Mobility Commission.

Luke, B. (2015) What is missing? Rethinking student absences, *Accounting Education*, 24(6): 569–72.

Macleod, S., Sharp, C., Bernardinelli, D., Skipp, A. and Higgins, S. (2015) *Supporting the Attainment of Disadvantaged Pupils: Articulating Success and Good Practice*, Research brief, November 2015. London: DfE.

Madsen, S. (2019) *The Power of Project Leadership: 7 Keys to help you Transform from Project Manager to Project Leader*. London: Kogan Page.

Malandro, L.A. (2009) *Fearless Leadership*. New York: McGraw-Hill.

Mansell, W. (2011) Improving exam results, but to what end? The limitations of New Labour's control mechanism for schools: assessment-based accountability, *Journal of Educational Administration and History*, 43(4): 291–308.

Martin, A. (2010) *Building Classroom Success: Eliminating Academic Fear and Failure.* London: A&C Black.

Martinez, P. (2000) *Raising Achievement: A Guide to Successful Strategies.* London: Further Education Development Agency.

Maslow, A.H. (1981) *Motivation and Personality.* New Delhi: Prabhat Prakashan.

Mazenod, A., Francis, B., Archer, L. et al. (2019) Nurturing learning or encouraging dependency? Teacher constructions of students in lower attainment groups in English secondary schools, *Cambridge Journal of Education*, 49(1): 53–68.

McCarney, R., Warner, J., Iliffe, S., van Haselen, R., Griffin, M. and Fisher, P. (2007) The Hawthorne Effect: a randomised, controlled trial, *BMC Medical Research Methodology*, 7: 30, https://doi.org/10.1186/1471-2288-7-30 (accessed 11 January 2021).

McDermott, K.B., Agarwal, P.K., D'Antonio, L., Roediger, H.L. III and McDaniel, M. (2014) Both multiple-choice and short-answer quizzes enhance later exam performance in middle and high school classes, *Journal of Experimental Psychology: Applied*, 20(1): 3–21.

McGill, R.M. (2015) *Teacher Toolkit: Helping you Survive your First Five Years.* London: Bloomsbury Publishing.

McNiff, J. (2016) *You and Your Action Research Project.* Abingdon and New York: Routledge.

McTavish, D. (2003) Aspects of public sector management: a case study of Further Education, ten years from the passage of the Further and Higher Education Act, *Educational Management and Administration*, 31(2): 175–87.

Milner, H.R. IV and Lomotey, K. (eds) (2013) *Handbook of Urban Education.* New York and Abingdon: Routledge.

Morehead, M.A. (1998) Professional behaviors for the beginning teacher, *American Secondary Education*, 26(4): 22–6.

Mulgan, R. (2003) *Holding Power to Account: Accountability in Modern Democracies.* New York: Springer.

Mullen, C.A. and Jones, R.J. (2008) Teacher leadership capacity-building: developing democratically accountable leaders in schools, *Teacher Development*, 12(4): 329–40.

Murray, M. (2019) *Reframing Education: Radically Rethinking Perspectives on Education in the Light of Research.* Melton, Woodbridge: John Catt Educational Ltd.

Myatt, M. (2018) *High Challenge, Low Threat: Finding the Balance.* Melton, Woodbridge: John Catt Educational Ltd.

National College for Teaching and Leadership (n.d.) *Managing meetings and communication* [online]. Available at: www.inspiringleaderstoday.com/ILTMaterials/LEVEL1_MSP-v4.0-2014_08_08-12_18_0/managing-systems-and-processes/msp-s7/msp-s7-t3.html (accessed 15 January 2021).

Niven, D. (2002) *The 100 Simple Secrets of Successful People: What Scientists have Learned and how you can Use it.* New York: Harper Collins.

Noyes, A., Dalby, D. and Lavis, Y. (2018) *A Survey of Teachers of Mathematics in England's Further Education Colleges: The Mathematics in Further Education Colleges Project: Interim Report.* Nottingham: University of Nottingham.

Ofsted (2013) *Improving Attendance and Punctuality: Strategies, Approaches and Lessons Learned from London Colleges: An AoC/Ofsted Action Learning Project.* Manchester: Ofsted. Available at: www.ofsted.gov.uk/resources/130212 (accessed 3 July 2020).

Ofsted (2018) *Six Models of Lesson Observation: An International Perspective.* Manchester: Ofsted.

Opitz, B., Ferdinand, N.K. and Mecklinger, A. (2011) Timing matters: the impact of immediate and delayed feedback on artificial language learning, *Frontiers in Human
Neuroscience*, 5: 8, doi: 10.3389/fnhum.2011.00008.

Orenstein, M. (2000) Picking up the clues: understanding undiagnosed learning disabili-
ties, shame, and imprisoned intelligence, *Journal of College Student Psychotherapy*,
15(2): 35–46.

Osborne, P. (2005) *Teaching English One to One*. London: Modern English Publishing.

Park, D., Ramirez, G. and Beilock, S.L. (2014) The role of expressive writing in math
anxiety, *Journal of Experimental Psychology: Applied*, 20(2): 103.

Parker, K.E., Pedersen, C.E., Gomez, A.M. et al. (2019) A paranigral VTA nociceptin circuit that constrains motivation for reward, *Cell*, 178(3): 653–71.

Parsonson, B.S. (2012) Evidence-based classroom management strategies, *Kairaranga*,
13(1): 16–23.

Pedder, D. and Opfer, V.D. (2011) Are we realising the full potential of teachers' professional learning in schools in England? Policy issues and recommendations from a
national study, *Professional Development in Education*, 37(5): 741–58.

Pennebaker, J.W., Kiecolt-Glaser, J.K. and Glaser, R. (1988) Disclosure of traumas and
immune function: health implications for psychotherapy, *Journal of Consulting and
Clinical Psychology*, 56(2): 239–45.

Persky, B. and Golubchick, L.H. (eds) (1991) *Early Childhood Education*. Lanham, MD:
University Press of America.

Pink, D.H. (2011) *Drive: The Surprising Truth about what Motivates us*. New York: Penguin.

Pinkett, M. and Roberts, M. (2019) *Boys Don't Try? Rethinking Masculinity in Schools*.
Abingdon and New York: Routledge.

Pollard, A. (ed.) (2002) *Readings for Reflective Teaching*. London: A&C Black.

Pollard, A., Black-Hawkins, K., Cliff-Hodges, G., Dudley, P. and James, M. (2014) *Reflective Teaching in Schools: Evidence-Informed Professional Practice*. London: Bloomsbury Publishing.

Pollard, A. and Collins, J. (2005) *Reflective Teaching*. London: A&C Black.

Porter, N. (2015) *Crossing the Line: Improving Success Rates among Students Retaking
English and Maths GCSEs*. A Policy Exchange Policy Bite. London: Policy Exchange.

Presson, P.K. and Benassi, V.A. (1996) Locus of control orientation and depressive symptomatology: a meta-analysis, *Journal of Social Behavior and Personality*, 11(1): 201–12.

Putwain, D.W. (2008) Examination stress and test anxiety, *Psychologist*, 21(12): 1026–9.

Putwain, D.W. (2009) Assessment and examination stress in KS4, *British Educational
Research Journal*, 35(3): 391–411.

Quigley, A. (2018) *Closing the Vocabulary Gap*. Abingdon and New York: Routledge.

Rankin, J.G. (2016) *First Aid for Teacher Burnout: How you can find Peace and Success*.
New York: Taylor & Francis.

Reid, K. (2013) *An Essential Guide to Improving Attendance in your School: Practical
Resources for all School Managers*. Abingdon: Routledge.

Reinholz, D. (2016) The assessment cycle: a model for learning through peer assessment,
Assessment and Evaluation in Higher Education, 41(2): 301–15.

Rigby, K. (2007) *Bullying in Schools: And What to Do About it*. Victoria: Australian Council for Educational Research.

Roberson, J. (2012) *The Discipline Coach*. Carmarthen: Independent Thinking Press.

Roberson, J. (2019) Strategies for engaging students. Paper presented at the mE+ Conference, Middlesbrough, February.

Robertson, B. (2020) *The Teaching Delusion: Why Teaching in Our Schools isn't Good
Enough (and How we can Make it Better)*. Melton, Woodbridge: John Catt Educational Ltd.

Roediger III, Henry L., Agarwal, P.K., McDaniel, M.A. et al. (2011) Test-enhanced learning in the classroom: long-term improvements from quizzing, *National Library of Medicines: Applied*, 17(4): 382–95.

Rogelberg, S.G. (2018) *The Surprising Science of Meetings: How you can Lead your Team to Peak Performance*. New York: Oxford University Press.

Rogers, B. (2002) *Classroom Behaviour*. London: Sage.

Rogers, B. (ed.) (2002) *Teacher Leadership and Behaviour Management*. London: Sage.

Roome, T. and Soan, C.A. (2019) GCSE exam stress: student perceptions of the effects on wellbeing and performance, *Pastoral Care in Education*, 37(4): 297–315.

Rosenshine, B. (2012) Principles of instruction: research-based strategies that all teachers should know, *American Educator*, 36(1): 12–19.

Rosenshine, B. and Stevens, R. (1986) Teaching functions, in M.C. Wittrock (ed.) *Handbook of Research on Teaching*, 3rd edn. New York: Macmillan, pp. 376–91.

Rosenthal, R. and Jacobson, L. (1992) *Pygmalion in the Classroom: Teacher Expectation and Pupils' Intellectual Development*, newly expanded edn. Carmarthen: Crown House Publishing.

Roth, K.J. (2006) *Teaching Science in Five Countries: Results from the TIMSS 1999 Video Study: Statistical Analysis Report*. Washington, DC: US Department of Education, National Center for Education Statistics.

Rouillard, L. (2003) *Goals and Goal Setting: Achieving Measured Objectives*. Boston, MA: Cengage Learning.

Rubie-Davies, C. (2014) *Becoming a High Expectation Teacher: Raising the Bar*. Abingdon and New York: Routledge.

Sagor, R. (2000) *Guiding School Improvement with Action Research: ASCD*. Alexandria, VA: ASCD.

Samuel, M. and Novak, B. (2001) *The Accountability Revolution: Achieve Breakthrough Results in Half the Time*. Blairsville, GA: Facts on Demand Press.

Saretsky, G. (1972) The OEO PC experiment and the John Henry effect, *The Phi Delta Kappan*, 53(9): 579–81.

Scott, S. (2004) *Fierce Conversations: Achieving Success at Work and in Life, One Conversation at a Time*. New York: Penguin.

Scriven, M. (1967) The methodology of evaluation, in R.W. Tyler, R.M. Gagné and M. Scriven (eds) *Perspectives of Curriculum Evaluation*. Chicago: Rand McNally, vol. I, pp. 39–83.

Scutt, C. and Harrison, S. (eds) (2019) *Teacher CPD: International Trends, Opportunities and Challenges*. London: Chartered College of Teaching.

Sharrock, T. (2016) *Embedding English and Maths: Practical Strategies for FE and Post-16 Tutors*. Northwich: Critical Publishing.

Sherrington, T. (2019) *Rosenshine's Principles in Action*. Melton, Woodbridge: John Catt Educational Ltd.

Sibieta, L. (2020) *Teacher Shortages in England: Analysis and Pay Options*. London: Education Policy Institute.

Simonsen, B., Fairbanks, S., Briesch, A., Myers, D. and Sugai, G. (2008) Evidence-based practices in classroom management: considerations for research to practice, *Education and Treatment of Children*, 31(3): 351–80.

Sinek, S. (2009) *Start with Why: How Great Leaders Inspire Everyone to Take Action*. London and New York: Penguin.

Skinner, B.F. (1965) *Science and Human Behavior*. New York: Simon and Schuster.

Slattery, P. (2013) *Curriculum Development in the Postmodern Era: Teaching and Learning in an Age of Accountability*. New York: Routledge.

Smith, P.K. (2016) Bullying: definition, types, causes, consequences and intervention, *Social and Personality Psychology Compass*, 10(9): 519–32.

Smith, W.C. (2014) The global transformation toward testing for accountability, *Education Policy Analysis Archives*, 22(116), doi: 10.14507/epaa.v22.1571.

Stanfield, A.W. (2009) *Defining Effective Leadership: Lead in Whatever you Do.* Mustang, OK: Tate Publishing.

Starkey, L. (2012) *Teaching and Learning in the Digital Age.* Abingdon: Routledge.

Strickland, S. (2020) *Education Exposed: Leading a School in a Time of Uncertainty.* Melton, Woodbridge: John Catt Educational Ltd.

Syed, M. (2015) *Black Box Thinking: Why Most People Never Learn from their Mistakes – But Some Do.* London: Penguin.

Taylor, C. (2012) *Improving Attendance at School.* London: DfE.

Thom, J. (2020) *A Quiet Education: Challenging the Extrovert Ideal in Schools.* Melton, Woodbridge: John Catt Educational Ltd.

Thompson, K. (2016) *A Systematic Guide to Change Management.* Great Britain: CreateSpace Publishing.

Tian, A.D., Schroeder, J., Häubl, G., Risen, J.L., Norton, M.I. and Gino, F. (2018) Enacting rituals to improve self-control, *Journal of Personality and Social Psychology*, 114(6): 851–76.

Torrance, H. and Pryor, J. (1998) *Investigating Formative Assessment: Teaching, Learning and Assessment in the Classroom.* Buckingham: McGraw-Hill Education.

Trower, C.A. (2012) *The Practitioner's Guide to Governance as Leadership: Building High-performing Nonprofit Boards.* San Francisco, CA: John Wiley & Sons.

Turner, E. (2019) *Be More Toddler: A Leadership Education from our Little Learners.* Melton, Woodbridge: John Catt Educational Ltd.

UNESCO (2017) *Accountability in Education: Meeting our Commitments.* Global Education Monitoring Report. Paris: UNESCO Publishing.

Wagner, R.B. (2013) *Accountability in Education: A Philosophical Inquiry.* New York: Routledge.

Walker, S. (2017) *The Captain Class: A New Theory of Leadership.* New York: Random House.

Walker, S. (2017) *The Captain Class: The Hidden Force that Creates the World's Greatest Teams.* New York: Random House.

Wallace, S. (2007) *Getting the Buggers Motivated in FE.* London and New York: A&C Black.

Wallace, S. (2017) *Motivating Unwilling Learners in Further Education: The Key to Improving Behaviour.* London: Bloomsbury.

Walton, M.S. (2004) *Generating Buy-in: Mastering the Language of Leadership.* New York: AMACOM.

Webb, J. (2019) *How to Teach English Literature: Overcoming Cultural Poverty.* Melton, Woodbridge: John Catt Educational Ltd.

Wentzel, K.R. and Miele, D.B. (eds) (2009) *Handbook of Motivation at School.* New York and Abingdon: Routledge.

Wheldall, K. and Merrett, F. (2017) *Positive Teaching: The Behavioural Approach.* Abingdon: Routledge.

Whitehouse, C. (2011) *Effective Continuing Professional Development for Teachers.* Manchester: Assessment and Qualifications Alliance.

Wicks, M. (1999) Opening address to Further Education Development Agency Research Conference, Cambridge, 9 December.

Wiliam, D. (2006) Formative assessment: getting the focus right, *Educational Assessment*, 11(3–4): 283–9.

Wiliam, D. (2013) Assessment: the bridge between teaching and learning, *Voices from the Middle*, 21(2): 15–20.

Williamson, A.M. and Feyer, A.M. (2000) Moderate sleep deprivation produces impairments in cognition and motor performance equivalent to legally prescribed levels of alcohol intoxication, *Occupational and Environmental Medicine*, 57(10): 649–55.

Willingham, D.T. (2009) *Why don't Students like School?: A Cognitive Scientist Answers Questions about How the Mind Works and What it Means for the Classroom*. San Francisco: Jossey-Bass.

Wilson, J. (2013) *Inverting the Pyramid: The History of Soccer Tactics*. New York: Bold Type Books.

Wilson, K. and Korn, J.H. (2007) Attention during lectures: beyond ten minutes, *Teaching of Psychology*, 34(2): 85–9.

Wolf, A. (2011) *Review of Vocational Education, 2011. The Wolf Report: Recommendations: Final Progress Report*. London: DfE.

Worth, J., Sizmur, J., Walker, M., Bradshaw, S. and Styles, B. (2017) *Teacher Observation: Evaluation Report and Executive Summary*. London: Education Endowment Foundation.

https://assets.publishing.service.gov.uk/government/uploads/system/uploads/attachment_data/file/840032/2019_KS4_Provisional_statistical_release.pdf

https://ffteducationdatalab.org.uk/2020/06/gcse-results-2020-a-look-at-the-grades-proposed-by-schools/

https://neu.org.uk/press-releases/reformed-gcses-are-damaging-mental-health-young-people-and-failing-accurately

https://teaching.blog.gov.uk/2017/09/28/mark-however-you-think-best-a-year-in-the-life-of-a-meaningful-manageable-and-motivating-marking-policy-change/

www.anti-bullyingalliance.org.uk/news-insight/news/ahead-anti-bullying-week-new-poll-shows-children-england-worry-about-being-seen-

www.aoc.co.uk/news/gcse-results-day-2019-aoc-comment

www.aoc-services.co.uk/events-and-training

www.aoc-services.co.uk/events-and-training/learningweek/

www.ascl.org.uk/Our-view/Campaigns/The-Forgotten-Third

www.bbc.co.uk/news/education-49441019

www.cambridgeassessment.org.uk/Images/476535-which-students-benefit-from-retaking-mathematics-and-english-gcses-post-16-.pdf

www.channel4.com/news/factcheck/do-graduates-earn-100000-more-than-non-graduates

www.et-foundation.co.uk/supporting/professional-development/maths-and-english/

www.gov.uk/government/news/every-pupil-in-england-to-see-another-rise-in-funding-in-2021

www.gov.uk/government/news/school-success-adds-140000-to-wages-research-reveals

www.gov.uk/government/publications/state-funded-schools-inspections-and-outcomes-as-at-31-december-2018/state-funded-schools-inspections-and-outcomes-as-at-31-december-2018

www.gov.uk/guidance/coronavirus-covid-19-catch-up-premium

www.mind.org.uk/information-support/types-of-mental-health-problems/stress/developing-resilience/

www.sundried.com/blogs/training/tagged/new-year

www.telegraph.co.uk/finance/personalfinance/9918813/Maths-skills-add-2100-to-your-salary.html

www.tes.com/news/how-hold-gcse-exam-3700-students

www.tes.com/news/teachers-work-more-unpaid-overtime-anyone-else

www.tes.com/news/uk-teachers-work-some-longest-hours-world

Index